Praise for *How to Lose Friends & Alienate People*:

'The thrill of this book is that the pariah taking on the world's most king-making city – if I can make it there, I'll make it anywhere! – is the most talented outsider since F. Scott Fitzgerald . . . Mr Young may never be one of the Great and the Good – but he is great and he is good, which is a far, far better thing' Julie Burchill, *Spectator*

'Wildly funny' *GQ*

'A masterpiece that made me laugh out loud. Young has made himself the anti-hero of the book, yet by the end the reader is hoping he will succeed, knowing he won't, and despising the criteria that New York sets for success anyhow' Andrew Roberts, *The Week*

'Hugely enjoyable' *Time Out*

'Though it hurts to admit it, I found this a fascinating memoir. Gossipy, funny, perceptive, self-mocking and even (considering the heartless and cynical pen from which it flows) rather moving' Lloyd Evans, *Daily Mail*

'Hysterical' *Tatler*

'On the surface this seems to be straightforward loser-lit. But this book is saved by its disarming honesty and Toby Young is – wait for it – an incredibly likeable narrator. More than just a memoir, this book is also an examination of the way in which work dominates in contemporary America and the utter shallowness of a media world obsessed with celebrity. It is funny, authentic and compelling' *Independent on Sunday*

'Graceful and authentic' *Guardian*

'This book has all the ingredients for a dire, self-serving and embarrassing memoir. Yet it's not: it's actually a highly entertaining rebuke to everyone who doubted Toby Young's abilities. It will not reopen any doors in America for him: but for those of us who like Schadenfreude and the spectacle of someone making an absolute ass of himself, it is delightful' Nicholas Lezard, *Evening Standard*

'An enjoyable, witty memoir' *Daily Express*

'The stories are just a little too good to be true . . . but that doesn't matter. It may all be an act, but it's a fine act' Andrew Anthony, *Observer*

'It'll make you feel a whole lot better about your own miserable career' *FHM*

'Don't be put off by Young's combination of naked ambition and ineptness. This book is just brilliant' *Independent*

'Toby Young is the most bumptious Englishman you are ever likely to meet, and any account of the five years he spent trying to make it as a magazine journalist in New York will be full of him vomiting drunkenly and offending people. His book should have been a bore, but it is surprisingly good' *Economist*

'A hilarious celebration of failure' *Hello!*

'Toby Young glories in his own loathsomeness. Throughout the book he relishes his small acts of crassness and thuggery. He sympathises with people who hate him. As a literary device for getting round new York, this works well . . . Toby Young provides a lively, enjoyable account of the ghastliness of the world of American high fashion' Amanda Mitchison, *Sunday Telegraph*

'As an exposé of the superficial world of fashionable magazines, *How To Lose Friends And Alienate People* is spot-on' Australian *Sun-Herald*

'A questionable excuse for failure, but it makes for good reading' *Time*

'Toby Young has managed to invent a whole new genre of writing: loser-lit. He's a whining, narcissistic git with the emotional depth of a hamster and the social skills of a land-mine. He plants himself in situations and then, often unwittingly, detonates. Why would you want to read about him? Because he is very, very funny' South African *Sunday Times*

'A bargain for anyone who wants a worm's-eye, outsider's view of what life is like at the top of the preening American media heap' *American Journalism Review*

'A thoroughly good read' *Big Issue*

'This wicked little memoir is like a shiv, lovingly sharpened during a long incarceration, which the author has been waiting to slip between the ribs of his jailers – in this case, the gate-keepers of Condé Nast in New York' *Hint Fashion Magazine*

'As a self-destruct manual it's hard to better; as a cheerfully desperate memoir, it's top notch' *Yorkshire Post*

'Given the title . . . one would expect a pithy tome exposing the ugly underbelly of the New York glitterati, replete with scandalous celebrity anecdotes and stories of hilarious cultural misunderstandings and humiliating social faux pas. That's exactly what Young delivers in a book that reads like a cross between *Bonfire of the Vanities* and an episode of *Seinfeld*' Australian *Courier-Mail*

'Young's irreverent and very funny book is worth a mountain of bland celebrity puffs' *The Times*

'Graydon's "Toby" Tale: The US version of Toby Young's *How To Lose Friends and Alienate People*, a memoir chronicling Young's disastrous stint as a *Vanity Fair* editor, will appear this summer, and word has leaked that a film version of the book about Young's experiences in downward mobility is also in development. But the man who figures most prominently in Young's memoirs, Graydon Carter, editor-in-chief of *Vanity Fair*, has been loath to comment on Young's book and "loser" rebranding campaign – until now. "Toby's a piece of gum that stuck to my shoe five years ago and that I still can't get off," Carter told *WWD*. "He had a worm's-eye view as it were, of what goes on at *Vanity Fair* – which explains the book, which has a little fact and a lot of fiction. He was on chemical substances most of the time, and no one ever let him near anything." Carter attributed Young's longevity at *Vanity Fair* to a casual bureaucratic oversight on his part. "Every day I make a list, and the last two years Toby was here there'd be an item on the list that read 'Fire Toby'. I guess I never got far enough down the list to do it, and I did have a soft spot for the guy. I basically forgot to fire Toby Young every day for two years.'" *Women's Wear Daily*

'We've been looking through our files, and we can't seem to find any record of a Toby Young ever having worked here' Beth Kseniak, Director of Public Relations, *Vanity Fair*

THE SOUND OF NO HANDS CLAPPING

A Memoir

TOBY YOUNG

ABACUS

First published in Great Britain as a paperback original
in 2006 by Abacus

The publisher is grateful for permission to reprint extracts from
'Street of Shame' by kind permission of *Private Eye*; 'Thousandth Man' by
Rudyard Kipling, courtesy of A. P. Watt on behalf of The National Trust for
Places of Historic Interest or Natural Beauty; 'Love' by Philip Larkin,
courtesy of Faber & Faber Ltd.

A CIP catalogue record for this book
is available from the British Library.

ISBN-13: 978-0-349-11851-2
ISBN-10: 0-349-11851-5

Typeset in Garamond by M Rules
Printed and bound in Great Britain by
Clays Ltd, St Ives plc

Abacus
An imprint of
Little, Brown Book Group
Brettenham House
Lancaster Place
London WC2E 7EN

A member of the Hachette Livre Group of Companies

www.littlebrown.co.uk

CONTENTS

PROLOGUE

9 October 2002

From the outside, the building I was in certainly didn't look like much. It was part of a cluster of prefabricated units that had been hastily erected in what was, to all intents and purposes, an industrial estate. The interior was scarcely any more impressive. The wall opposite me was decorated with a collection of posters advertising various long-forgotten Hollywood blockbusters and just in front of it there was a trestle table piled high with promotional bric-a-brac: pens, mugs, baseball caps. It could have been a distribution warehouse for a DVD mail-order company: buy one get one free.

In fact, it was the global headquarters of _____ _____, one of the most powerful producers in Hollywood. When I'd first met him earlier in the year he'd told me that, collectively, his films had made so much money that if you averaged it out each one had grossed over a hundred million dollars. The films advertised on the posters opposite, some of which had grossed three times that much, had all been produced by him. The prefabricated units might not look particularly fancy, but no other producer occupied such prime real estate, at least not on this lot. And it wasn't, strictly speaking, an industrial estate.

It was one of the eight major Hollywood studios.

The reason I was there is because three months earlier this producer had been sitting on a billionaire's yacht in the south of France when he happened to find a copy of *How to Lose Friends & Alienate People* under a throw cushion. (This was a book I'd written about trying – and failing – to take Manhattan.) By the time the yacht docked in Antibes, he'd made a couple of calls on his mobile phone and got my number.

I was in my Skoda heading to a wedding in Norfolk when I got the call.

'Is this Toby Young?'

'Hang on a minute,' I said, trying to wedge the phone between my ear and my shoulder. 'I'm just overtaking a lorry.'

After the usual cacophony of hooting and swearing – no one likes being overtaken by a Skoda – I was back on the line.

'Sorry about that. I've been stuck behind that fucker for the last twenty minutes.'

'Is this Toby Young?'

'Yes. Who's this?

'_____ _____.'

'Yeah, right. And I'm Hugh Grant.'

'No, really, it's me.'

'Langan? Is that you? It is, isn't it? You're going to have to work a lot harder on that American accent, my friend. You sound far too working class to be a Hollywood producer.'

'Listen, I don't have time for this. I'm going to give you the number of my production office in Los Angeles and I want you to call that number and ask to speak to Lauren – that's my second assistant – and she'll patch you through to my cell.'

Beat.

'Jesus Christ. I'm an idiot. Sorry about that. What can I do for you, Mr _____?'

'Where are you right now?'

I glanced out of the window.

'Somewhere between Colchester and Ipswich, I think.'

'No, I mean what country are you in?'

Duh!

'England. I'm in England.'

'Can you meet me in the lobby of the Hotel du Cap on Monday at noon? If you can't get a flight, I might be able to arrange for a private jet to pick you up.'

I let out an involuntary bark of laughter.

'A private jet? Are you *sure* this isn't a crank call?'

'Eight one eight, five four six—'

'Okay, okay, I believe you. What's this all about?'

'I want you to write a picture for me.'

Beat.

'I'm afraid you are going to have to give me that number after all. This is just too good to be true.'

After he'd hung up, I turned to my wife who was sitting beside me in the passenger seat.

'You'll never guess who that was.'

'Who?'

'_____ fucking _____.'

'What did *he* want?'

'He says he wants me to write a picture for him.'

'Are you sure it wasn't a crank call?'

This was the summons I'd been waiting for – if not all my life, certainly for the past two and a half years. Having failed as a glossy magazine editor in New York, I was determined to make it as a screenwriter. Since returning from America in 2000, I'd made numerous attempts to break into the movie business, but, unsurprisingly, none of these efforts had come to anything. Now, thanks to an extraordinary stroke of good fortune, I was being given a chance to play in the big leagues.

Perhaps I should have been more wary. After all, the annals of Hollywood are full of cautionary tales about young writers being lured to Los Angeles by the prospect of easy money, only to spend the next forty years doing nothing. Ernest Hemingway said that a writer should come no closer to Hollywood than the Nevada–California state line, should arrange to pick up his cheque at the border, and then turn round and head home. On the other hand, that cheque is nothing to sniff at. As one jaded screenwriter put it: 'They ruin your stories. They trample on your pride. They massacre your ideas. And what do you get for it? A fortune.'

It turned out the 'picture' _____ wanted me to write was a biopic about a notorious seventies record producer. He had acquired the rights to this man's unofficial biography back in 1994 and already hired several other writers to have a crack at adapting it. The reason none of them had succeeded, at least not to _____'s satisfaction, is because this particular individual, like most legendary record producers, was a spectacularly unpleasant human being. He ripped off all his artists, drove a famous singer to suicide and abandoned his only son. He had almost no redeeming qualities. On the face of it, it was simply impossible to tell his story in a way that wouldn't automatically alienate the audience.

'I'm the first to admit it – he's not a likeable guy,' said Mr Hollywood over lunch at the Hotel du Cap forty-eight hours after he'd first contacted me. 'But if I'm going to make a movie about this guy's life, I have to find a way to make him sympathetic. When I read your book, I thought, If anyone can do it, this guy can, because *you* did it. At the end of your book, I liked you. I don't know why I liked you, but I did. I mean, you do all this really dumb stuff, you fuck everything up, but when I got to the end I liked you. That's why you're the perfect guy to write this picture. I mean, if you were able to make yourself likeable, given all the horrible shit *you* pulled, you should be able to make this guy look like fucking Gandhi.'

When I got back to London, I immediately called Rob Long, the only person I know with any claims to being a Hollywood insider. I was introduced to him by William Cash, a fellow British journalist, on a trip to Los Angeles in 1992. Rob was only twenty-seven at the time, but he was already an executive producer of Cheers *and I persuaded him to write a column about the difficulties of sustaining such a meteoric career for a magazine I was then editing. The columns were subsequently collected into a cult book –* Conversations With My Agent *– that quickly became required reading for anyone seeking to understand 'the Business'. Since then, Rob has gone on to have a very successful career as a sitcom producer and, at one stage, served as an Adjunct Professor of Screenwriting at the UCLA School of Film, Theater and Television.*

Rob listened patiently while I offered my analysis of the situation. The problem was that no one had a clue about how to turn this misanthrope's life story into a commercial movie. _____ simply couldn't justify spending $64 million on it – the average cost of a Hollywood movie these days – when it so clearly wasn't going to be a hit. My job was to figure out a way to tell the story that, while remaining true to the source material, also rang bells at the box office.[1]

'Completely wrong,' said Rob. 'You let him worry about how to make it commercial. That's his job. He's the producer. He wants to make it commercial? Easy. He puts a star in the picture. You don't have to worry about the picture being made. You should be worrying about your career as a writer. You want to come out of this with a great writing sample, something that's going to get you hired on other movies. You want my opinion? Turn it into a comedy.'

After I hung up, I racked my brains, but the only way I could think of to make the story funny was to include myself as a character. As I envisaged it, The Schlockmeister *would be about this completely unknown writer who's summoned out of the blue by this big Hollywood producer and then saddled with this absurdly difficult*

1 $64 million was the average cost of making a movie in 2004, according to the Motion Picture Association of America. Of this, $34 million is the average cost of marketing a film domestically. Blockbusters can cost even more to market: as much as $60 million domestically and $125 million worldwide.

writing assignment. The story of the record producer could then be told as a film-within-a-film, focusing on one of the numerous episodes in which he plucked some completely unknown band from obscurity, promised them the earth, and then discarded them as soon as the next band came along, not even bothering to pay their travel expenses. The picture, which would switch back and forth between the A-story and the B-story, would begin with me receiving a phone call from _____ _____ as I was heading to a wedding in Norfolk.

'He doesn't want to make a film about you,*' said Rob when I told him this idea. 'In any case, it's been done. It's called* Adaptation. *Listen, you're thinking way too much about this. Writing for the movies is easy. There are only two rules: Make sure something interesting happens on every page and make sure the character changes. The character has to change. Don't worry about the three-act structure or any of that bullshit. And for God's sake don't read any of those goddamned screen-writing books. That's the kiss of death. The secret of success in this business is to not give people what they want. Over and over, you give these guys what they want, they don't like it. "It's hacky," they say. That's why he's interested in you. He's got twenty guys who can write com-mercial movies. He wants you to bring something new to the table.'*

Rob called me back five minutes later.

'One more thing. Don't call it The Schlockmeister. *That's the worst title I ever heard.'*

'Hi, are you waiting for _____?'

I snapped out of my reverie and looked up at one of the most beautiful faces I'd ever seen. *This must be Lauren, the famous second assistant,* I thought. Apparently, the man I'd flown over five thou-sand miles to see employed supermodels to fetch his dry-cleaning. This particular specimen didn't look a day over sixteen.

'Yes, I am, as a matter of fact,' I said. 'I don't suppose there's any chance of a coffee, is there?'

She gave me a quizzical expression.

'White, no sugar,' I added. 'Thanks.'

'I'm Stacey,' she said, extending her hand. 'I'm the Executive Vice-President of Production.'

'What were you expecting?' said Rob later. 'Rosa Klebb? They used to employ women like that back in the old days when the studios made fifty pictures a year. Now they employ women like Stacey. It's gotten to the point where I'm afraid to shake hands with a studio executive for fear of being picked up for child molestation.'

It turned out that Stacey wasn't the Executive Vice-President of Production for the entire studio, just the 'shingle' owned by _____ _____. But it was still a pretty impressive job title for a woman who looked like she should be on the cover of *Teen Vogue*. She took me through to her office, explaining that it might be some time before I could get in to see her boss.

'He's rapping,' she said, 'and when he starts rapping he loses all sense of time.'

'He's *rapping*?!? Wow. Is that, like, a hobby or something?'

She gave me a puzzled look.

'He's talking. *Talking*.'

Beat.

'Soooo,' she said. 'I read your book. I had to, actually.'

Apparently, she'd asked Mr Hollywood to tell her about this project and by way of response he'd given her a copy of my book.

'I couldn't really understand why you kept doing such dumb stuff,' she said. 'I mean, you just kept on doing it, over and over and over. What's with that? It's like you had Tourette's or something.'

'She's clearly irritated by the fact that she wasn't present when you guys first talked about this thing,' explained Rob. 'That's all these girls have. They don't actually do anything. They're just "in the loop".'

After several minutes had elapsed, another supermodel came in and told us the big guy was now off the phone. Stacey leapt out of her

chair and motioned for me to get up: *Come on, come on.* Clearly, the
boss didn't like to be kept waiting.

The first thing I noticed on entering his office were the Oscars –
four of them standing side by side in the fireplace. I had to fight the
urge to pick one up. I wanted to know what it felt like to hold one
in your hand.

'So, where are we with this?' asked Mr Hollywood. 'Is this a done
deal?'

'Yes,' I said confidently. 'I think it's pretty much a done deal.'

I regretted saying this as soon as the words came out of my
mouth. The studio's business affairs division had only just sent over
the 'Writer Employment Agreement' – a whopping, forty-eight-
page document – and my agent hadn't had a chance to read it yet.
What if she uncovered some appalling clause that she wanted to
dispute? 'Writer will indemnify Producer against any and all liabil-
ity, damages, costs and expenses, including attorney's fees, in
connection with . . . ' Presumably, _____ would simply say, 'But
Toby told me it was a done deal.'

His office was a large oblong, with an expensive water feature at
one end and a huge plasma screen at the other. On my right as I
walked in was a large desk and, in front of that, a seating area with
two leather sofas opposite each other. There were two phones in the
room, one on his desk and one on a little side table to the left of the
sofa facing the plasma. This was clearly his spot. As I later discovered,
he never liked to be more than an arm's reach from a telephone.

After we were all seated – Stacey was evidently going to be present at *this* meeting – he asked me how I was getting on. Had I had
any brainwaves yet?

I began by reciting the long list of the record producer's shortcomings. Even by the standards of Tin Pan Alley, he was a nasty
piece of work. Why would anyone want to watch a movie about
him? As I saw it, there were only two ways round this.

The first was to model the picture on *Wall Street* and tell the story
from the point of view of a fresh-faced ingénue. The film would

then become the story of this innocent's relationship with the seventies legend: hero-worship followed by gradual disillusionment and, eventually, disgust.

The second was to tell it like a gangster picture. Why not model it on *Scarface*? Depict him as this feral, predatory man, an ambitious sociopath who manages to conquer the music business by being more cunning and ruthless than any of his competitors. We know he's a terrible man but there's something compelling about him nevertheless . . .

'Well, obviously, I like the second one better,' said _____. 'Listen, the thing you have to remember about this guy is that he invented the cult of celebrity. He *invented* it. He created this world we live in. He knew about the importance of publicity, of generating buzz, and he turned this business into the celebrity-driven thing it is today. Okay, so he was no boy scout, but so what? With artists, we're prepared to forgive all these terrible things they do because, you know, they're artists. They're so *talented.* But where does it say producers can't be artists? How come artists can get away with all this crap, but producers are held to account for every tiny little goddamned thing?'

He became so impassioned in the course of this speech that, by the end of it, both Stacey and I were staring at him.

'I know, I know,' he laughed. 'People have said I identify with this guy. But I don't, I really don't. I just think he's a fascinating man.'

Towards the end of the meeting, _____ outlined his professional credo.

'I like to distinguish between action and activity. Activity is when you come into the office, you make thirty phone calls, and you go home. You come in the next day, you make another thirty phone calls, and you go home. Action is when you actually walk over to the fucking sound stage and you make a fucking movie. I was on the sound stage till two o'clock in the morning last night dubbing my latest picture. This is a motion picture production company. We make four to five motion pictures a year. I don't hire writers and then stick them in development hell. That's not what I do. If you write a movie that's even part of the way there, I will make the fucking movie. I promise you that.'

'That's the stump speech he gives to all the new writers,' explained Rob. 'In fact, activity is precisely what he does. That's what these producers do. They keep all these plates spinning in the air. And how does he do it? By making calls. That's all he does: talk, talk, talk, all day.'

As _____ was showing me out he asked if there was anything else he could do for me.

'Well, there is one thing. D'you mind if I pick up one of your Oscars?'

'Sure, be my guest. They're just techie Oscars – the only kind *I'm* ever gonna win.'

I bent down and picked one up: it was an Oscar for Best Sound. How come he had it? Had the sound engineer given it to him as a way of ensuring future employment? It's embarrassing to admit, but for a second I thought, If *The Schlockmeister* wins an Oscar for Best Original Screenplay, do I have to give the statuette to him?

'You could kill someone with one of these,' I said, weighing it in my hand.

I looked up to catch Mr Hollywood shooting Stacey a look, as if to say, 'Can you believe this rube?'

'Don't worry about it,' said Rob. 'People go out of their way in this town to appear innocent and unworldly. It makes them attractive to predators. Out here, you get paid a lot for being eaten alive.'

By now it was 7 p.m. and _____ said that since he was finished for the day he'd walk me out.

'So, when are you gonna move to LA?' he asked, as we strolled towards the car park.

'I'm not sure that's such a good idea. I mean, look what happened to me in New York.'

'Ah, you'll love it out here. That's the beauty of America. If you don't make it one city, you just move to another.'

'Well, I'll certainly give it some serious thought.'

'Well, if you do move out here, let me know. If you want an office to work out of, I can give you an office here.'

Not for the first time that afternoon, I pinched myself. Had I really just been offered an office on the back lot of one of the major Hollywood studios? Visions of having lunch in the commissary with a group of fellow writers danced before my eyes.

'So,' I said, turning to Stacey. 'I imagine you'll want to remove yourself as the go-between on this project as quickly as possible.'

Instead of answering, she made a movement with her eyes as if to say, 'Look behind you.' Again, there was that sense of urgency: *Quick, quick.*

I turned round to see Mr Hollywood waiting for me, his hand extended. How long had he been standing there like that? I grabbed his hand and shook it as heartily as I could, telling him how grateful I was for this fantastic opportunity.

'Well, just try not to fuck it up,' he said.

With that, he climbed into what I initially took for some sort of spaceship but was, in fact, a Cadillac Escalade. It was the biggest car I'd ever seen. As soon as the rear passenger door clunked shut, it glided off, the studio gates parting to speed him on his way.

When I got back to my hotel, my first inclination was to call my wife Caroline to tell her about everything that had happened – but I hesitated. The truth was, I passionately wanted to move to LA, but Caroline didn't. She'd been born and brought up in London – it was where all her family and friends lived – and she didn't want to live anywhere else. She wasn't the sort of wife who'd simply up sticks and follow her husband halfway across the world just because he thought it would be good for his career.

On the other hand, opportunities of this magnitude only came along once in a lifetime. *My own fucking office in a Hollywood studio!* There'd be no starting in the mailroom for me. With _____ acting as my mentor, the whole town would be open to me. I was being given a shot at the big time and if I didn't take it I knew I'd regret it for the rest of my life. I'd end up like Marlon Brando in *On The Waterfront*: *I coulda been a contender . . .*

So what should I do? Tell Caroline I was moving to LA and she could either come with me or stay in London, it was up to her? Or should I give up this dream as just another one of those 'childish things' I'd had to put away since merging my life with Caroline's?

What should I put first? My marriage or my career?

PART ONE

BONDED

1

BETTER WED THAN DEAD

Caroline agreed to marry me on 28 April 2000, which was rather miraculous considering my prospects at the time. I'd just returned to London, having spent the previous five years trying to make a name for myself as a journalist in Manhattan. I'd been sacked as the *Evening Standard*'s New York columnist, sacked as a contributing editor to *Vanity Fair*, sacked as the *Independent*'s New York columnist, sacked as a staff writer at *Gear* . . . Indeed, the only thing I'd learnt was what not to say when I'd just been sacked. Whenever I used some pathetic euphemism like 'it didn't work out' or 'I felt it was time to move on', the person I was talking to always gave me a pitying look, as if getting the sack had been such a devastating blow to my self-esteem that, in addition to being unemployed, I was now too insecure to admit I'd just been sacked. After five years of this at least I knew what to say if I was ever sacked again: 'I've been sacked.' Unfortunately, my latest gig showed every sign of being permanent – a column for the *Spectator* called 'No Life'. As Caroline pointed out, no one could accuse her of marrying me for my money.

The earliest date she was prepared to set for the wedding was 21 July of the following year, giving her plenty of time to change her mind. At the beginning of 2000, Caroline had agreed to live with me for three months on a 'trial basis' and when she finally accepted my proposal I took that as a sign that I'd 'passed'. But it soon dawned on me that, far from being over, the probationary period had simply been extended by fifteen months. Not for her the old-fashioned approach whereby marriage is a leap of faith. She wanted to road-test the merchandise before committing to a purchase. Consequently, by the time I carried her across the threshold of my Shepherd's Bush bedsit we'd been engaged for fifteen months.

Like all married people I became a self-styled 'expert' on the subject as soon as I tied the knot – and one of the many pieces of advice I now give to young people who are thinking of doing the same is to keep the engagement short. There are numerous problems with long engagements. For one thing, it gives you far too much time to quarrel about the arrangements. Scarcely a week went by without a heated argument breaking out about the flowers or the caterers or the marquee – and that was just between Caroline and her mother. The two of us were worse. They say that if you can survive the first year of marriage you have a pretty good chance of staying together for the rest of your life. But to my mind surviving a long engagement is a far more difficult test.

The fact that I have the diplomatic skills of Idi Amin didn't help. When Caroline and I finally agreed on the guest list, after six months of torturous negotiation, I ran my eye over the 130 names and said, 'So, d'you want to know how many of the women on this list I've shagged?'

We had to start again from scratch.

Perhaps more importantly, a long engagement gives both parties too much time to think about whether they actually want to get married in the first place. During my three-year courtship of Caroline I had my eye so firmly on the prize I never stopped to ask whether marrying her was something I really wanted to do. I'd proposed to her so often that when she finally agreed to become my wife she caught me off guard. It had never occurred to me that she might actually say yes.

I felt like someone who, as a schoolboy, had fantasised about playing for England, only to find himself being unexpectedly selected for the national squad at the advanced age of thirty-seven.

Should I have been more careful about what I wished for? I wasn't in any doubt that I loved Caroline. But why get married? Couldn't we just carry on living together indefinitely? After all, plenty of people manage it. At the time of writing, there are two million cohabiting couples in the UK and the number is expected to rise to 3.8 million by 2031.

I quickly discovered there are some very sound arguments for not getting married. According to the Institute of Social and Economic Research, men's disposable income falls by an average of 15 per cent when they tie the knot, while women's goes up by 28 per cent. For a man, getting married is like entering a new tax bracket without any corresponding increase in income; it's like moving to Denmark.

I consulted my accountant who confirmed that there was no tax benefit in getting married, at least not since the Government had abolished the married couple's allowance. The only advantage he could think of would be if I transferred some of my income-earning assets into Caroline's name in order to equalise our incomes, thereby reducing our joint tax burden. However, he quickly pointed out that I didn't have any income-earning assets and, even if I did, there'd be no guarantee that Caroline would give them back if we ever got divorced.

My only asset was my flat in Shepherd's Bush and, following a landmark decision by the law lords, that wouldn't be safe either if things went pear-shaped. It's a common misconception that under British law wives have always been able to lay claim to half their husbands' assets when, until recently, that was only true of Scotland, not of England and Wales. However, in 2000 the law lords decided that judges should regard a fifty-fifty split as a 'yardstick' when dividing a couple's assets. This meant that Caroline would almost certainly be entitled to half of everything I owned if we ended up getting divorced.

Then there was the cost of the wedding itself. I'd done the sums and even after our guest list had been pruned of the women I'd slept with (all three of them), I couldn't see us getting away with less than £20,000. It used to be the case that this cost was borne by the father of the bride, but not any more. That convention, along with all the other things that used to make marriage so attractive to men – like coming home to a nice hot meal and getting your socks darned – is now regarded as laughably out of date.

From a purely financial point of view, getting married is about as sensible as investing your life savings in an Internet start up – which might explain why the number of British citizens getting hitched declined by approximately 25 per cent between 1988 and 1998. Indeed, according to government statisticians, the institution of marriage is in terminal decline. They predict that by 2031 the number of unmarried men in the 45–54 age group will rise from 14 per cent to 40 per cent.

Of course, few men engage in this kind of calculation when deciding whether to get married. For most of us, the real stumbling block is having to be faithful to just one person for the rest of our lives. The issue doesn't turn on how attractive the woman in question is. She could be Marilyn Monroe and it wouldn't make any difference. Rather, it's the thought of never being able to have sex with anyone else that's so difficult to bear.

Is it possible to enjoy marriage without monogamy? Well, yes, provided you're prepared to cheat on your wife. In my case, though, that wasn't really an option because (a) I'm a terrible liar; and (b) the consequences of being caught were too horrendous to contemplate. I remember watching *Waiting to Exhale* with Caroline and telling her I thought Angela Bassett's reaction to her husband's infidelity – she sets fire to his suits – was a bit over the top. She looked at me calmly and said, 'If you're ever unfaithful to me, I'll Bobbitt you.'

She meant it, too.

Another alternative is to have a European-style marriage,

whereby wives tolerate their husbands' little peccadilloes provided they're discreet about it. Admittedly, it's not exactly ideal from the women's point of view, but at least they're likely to stay married, with all the attendant social and economic benefits. If the alternative is ending up single and alone, as so many divorced women do, perhaps it's the lesser of two evils.

I once tried to raise this subject with Caroline and, following her reaction, the second piece of advice I've been dispensing to men on the brink of getting married is never to repeat this mistake.

'Darling,' I began, 'have you ever wondered why the divorce rate in America is so much higher than in Europe?'

She narrowed her eyes.

'You'd better not be about to tell me it's because American women set too much store by fidelity.'

'Well, don't you think that's part of the explanation? I mean, the moment an American man strays, his wife heads straight for the divorce courts. In Italy, by contrast, where the women don't expect their husbands to be faithful, the divorce rate is only 10 per cent. I'm not saying that women should enter into marriage in the expectation that their husbands will be unfaithful, but perhaps insisting on fidelity as a condition of remaining married is setting the bar too high.'

Beat.

'Are you saying you want to be able to shag other people after we're married?'

'Oh God no. This is purely hypothetical, obviously.'

'What about me? Would I be able to shag whoever I liked, too?'

'Darling, you've got the wrong end of the stick. I was just saying—'

'Because, frankly, I'm not sure you'd be the one to profit from that arrangement. D'you have any idea how easy it is for a woman to find someone willing to shag her? I mean, compared to a man?'

'—'

'I'll tell you what, why don't we conduct a little experiment? We'll go to the nearest pub right now and see who can pull the fastest.'

'Really, darling, I think you're overreacting.'

'Then again, that wouldn't exactly be fair, would it, given our relative levels of attractiveness? To even things out, I'll give you a head start. What time is it now?'

I glanced at my watch.

'Five forty-five.'

'Okay, you go to the pub now and I won't come in until one minute before chucking-out time. Does that sound fair?'

'I've absolutely no doubt that you could pull every man in the pub in less than sixty seconds.'

'What?'

'I said—'

'Why are you still here? You're wasting valuable time. I'd get going if I were you.'

I had to leave the house and go and sit in a café for half an hour to give her a chance to calm down.

In truth, I'm not sure the prospect of an open marriage would have appealed to me even if I looked like Brad Pitt. Growing up in north London among the liberal intelligentsia, I encountered numerous examples of open marriages and they always struck me as pale imitations of the real thing. Several of them ended in divorce when either the man or the woman met someone who offered them a more conventional partnership and those that didn't tended to degenerate into the kind of arrangement that Americans call 'friends with benefits'. Without the element of sacrifice – without being willing to forgo extramarital sex as a token of their commitment to each other – their 'open' relationships lacked the moral component that makes marriage so special. And for what it's worth, the children of these couples never grew up wanting to have open marriages themselves.[1]

1 Perhaps I'm being a little priggish here. Diana Melly, who's been with her husband George for over forty years in spite of their open marriage, says the secret is not to quarrel about money. 'The combination of taking other lovers and arguing about money would be death to an open marriage,' she told the *Daily Telegraph* on 24 October 2005.

No, if I was going to marry Caroline, I had to accept that I wouldn't be able to sleep with anyone else. Some cultures might have worked out how to make marriage work in the absence of monogamy, but for two fairly conventional middle-class English people there was no alternative. It was all or nothing.

Which begs the question: Why go through with it? Why would any man in possession of a good fortune – or at least a flat in Shepherd's Bush – be in want of a wife?

Well, needless to say, there are plenty of arguments in favour of marriage, too. For one thing, you're likely to live longer. In *The Case for Marriage*, Linda Waite and Maggie Gallagher point out that 90 per cent of married men alive at forty-eight will still be alive at sixty-five, whereas only 60 per cent of single men alive at forty-eight will make it to retirement age. Married men are half as likely as single men to commit suicide and single men drink twice as much as married men the same age. Perhaps most alarmingly – at least for singletons – the authors discovered that a married man with heart disease can expect to live an average of 1400 days longer than a single man with a healthy heart.

Still, the fact that there's a statistical correlation between physical health and marriage doesn't necessarily mean there's a causal relationship. It may just be that the kind of men who get married are healthier to begin with. In any case, promoting your own physical well-being seems like a fairly uninspiring reason to get married. I expect monks live even longer than happily married men, but I wasn't about to join a monastery.

A more compelling reason is to reduce the likelihood that you'll split up – what's commonly referred to as 'security'. To paraphrase Shakespeare, marriage binds you together with hoops of steel. In the less romantic language of economics, it creates a 'barrier to exit'. Should Caroline or I wish to leave each other, there would be all sorts of hurdles in our path after we'd taken our wedding vows – not least the cost of getting divorced, which now averages £13,000.

From my point of view, that was quite reassuring. Caroline had already dumped me twice and even though there was no guarantee she wouldn't do so again she was less likely to after we were married. Since I was in love with her, that was a powerful incentive.

The fact that married couples are more likely to stay together than unmarried ones is often cited by conservatives as Exhibit A in the case for marriage. They point out that children born out of wedlock are more likely to be brought up in one-parent families and, as a result, will place a greater burden on the state.[1] This isn't just in terms of social security. There's a well-established correlation between illegitimacy and criminal behaviour. The eminent African-American sociologist, William Julius Wilson, has long argued that one of the reasons young black men are responsible for a disproportionately high percentage of violent crimes is because of absentee fathers.

One of the most important 'barriers to exit' that marriage erects is that it involves making a promise in front of those people whose good opinion you actually care about. If Caroline and I didn't get married, but simply chose to live together in perpetuity, there would be no recognised way in which we could communicate that decision to our families and friends. We could have a party, I suppose, but it wouldn't be the same as taking solemn vows in front of our nearest and dearest. There was something about the formality of a wedding, its *official* nature, which would make the decision to stay together more binding. When we promised to love and cherish one another, in sickness and in health, till death us do part, it was a promise we both intended to keep – and the fact that we would be making it in front of 130 witnesses would make it that much harder to break.

There was another, less respectable reason why I wanted to get married: my best friend, Sean Langan, was about to tie the knot and I didn't want to be left behind.

---

1 Only 30 per cent of children born to cohabiting couples in Britain will remain in a stable home until the age of sixteen, compared to 70 per cent of children raised by married parents.

I'd known Sean since he was sixteen and we'd spent a large part of our twenties trying to pick up girls together. Our role models were Bluto and Otter from *Animal House* and there was an unspoken understanding between us that being a man consisted of making an endless stream of sexual conquests. Needless to say, his strike rate was a lot higher than mine. Indeed, if we'd been a couple of single women I would have been categorised as 'the ugly friend'. The son of a Portuguese mother and an Irish father, Sean manages to combine the best of both races: he's lithe and olive-skinned, yet he also possesses the gift of the gab. Few of the women he chatted up when we were out on the razzle together could resist him. I remember one occasion, in Greece back in 1985, when he managed to get off with a member of the German Olympic swimming team in spite of the fact that she was on holiday with her fiancé at the time.

Just before I left for New York Sean had met his match in the form of a beautiful, hot-blooded Anglo-German called Anabel Cutler and it was her that he'd subsequently become engaged to. I was a bit cheesed off about this – *who was going to be my wing man now?* – and whenever I came home for the holidays I'd torture Sean with tales of my adventures as a swinging bachelor in Manhattan (all made up, naturally). Evelyn Waugh said that the great thing about living abroad is that all your friends imagine you're having a much more exciting time than them and that certainly applied to Sean. I'd refer to Anabel as the 'ball and chain' and needle him about the fact that he couldn't leave the house without asking her permission. I kept up a constant stream of malicious banter, the subtext of which was always the same: she's castrated you, you pathetic wretch.

In retrospect, it's obvious that I was jealous. Sean was in love with Anabel and, as his best friend, I felt abandoned. On one occasion, at the end of a long, drunken evening in the spring of 2000, I told Sean that he'd broken the implicit understanding between us whereby neither of us would get married until the other was ready to do so as well. It was all bollocks, of course, but best friends have a tendency to drift apart when one of them decides to settle down and I didn't want that to happen to us. I thought of Sean as being like Kipling's 'Thousandth Man':

> One man in a thousand, Solomon says,
> Will stick more close than a brother.
> And it's worth while seeking him half your days
> If you find him before the other.
> Nine hundred and ninety-nine depend
> On what the world sees in you,
> But the Thousandth Man will stand your friend
> With the whole round world agin you.

So I was relieved that we were now back on the same track. I looked forward to Anabel and Caroline becoming great friends and the four of us bringing up our children together.

2

THE WRITE STUFF

In a book called *Oscar Winning Screenwriters on Screenwriting*, edited by Joel Engel, various titans of the profession talk about that eureka moment when it first dawned on them that they wanted to be writers. The tone is set by William Goldman in the first chapter: 'What I do know is that you don't become a writer because you want to be Jacqueline Susann. You become a writer because somebody of some quality moved you when you were a kid and you thought, "Okay, I want to be Chekhov."'

Robert Benton (*Bonnie and Clyde, Superman, Kramer vs. Kramer*) traces his interest in writing to his childhood dyslexia; Ron Bass (*Rain Man, My Best Friend's Wedding, Entrapment*) attributes it to the fact that he was bedridden as a kid; Michael Blake (*Dances With Wolves*) claims it's because he felt a 'metaphysical kinship' with his grandfather and great-grandfather, both of whom were published authors. Whatever the explanation, all the contributors treat being a writer as a vocation. It was something they knew they wanted to do from a very early age.

The first sign that I wanted to be a writer, by contrast, didn't occur until I was nineteen. It was in 1983 at the launch party for my mother's second novel, *Underneath the Paradise Tree*. I fell into conversation with Karl Miller, a dour Scotsman who, in addition to being the editor of the *London Review of Books*, was a professor of English at University College London.

'So, laddie, what do you want to be when you grow up?' he asked.

'A journalist.'

Until that point, it had never occurred to me that that's what I wanted to be.

'Why a journalist?' he asked.

'Because of all the things I could do, it seems like the least amount of work for the most amount of money.'

Clearly, I knew a thing or two about journalism, but I don't think sloth or greed were my real motives. The truth is, I didn't have a motive because . . . well, I'd made it up on the spot. I didn't want to be a journalist. At least, not until that moment. Whenever I'd been asked the question before I always replied that I wanted to be an actor. But after the words had come out of my mouth the idea took root. I'd invented something about myself that I rather liked. A *journalist.* To my nineteen-year-old ears, it sounded quite cool.

Various sophomoric attempts at journalism during my university days failed to result in hordes of Fleet Street editors beating a path to my door, so I decided to try a more traditional approach: nepotism. While still in my second year, I submitted an article on the moribund state of youth culture to *New Society,* a magazine that just happened to be edited by a friend of my father's. It was published in the issue dated 15 February 1985 – I still have a copy in my attic – and, within a week, I'd been contacted by Ann Barr, the co-author of the *Sloane Ranger Handbook.* She was a section-editor at the *Observer* and, after taking me out to lunch, she commissioned an article on the new breed of 'designer' football hooligans. I submitted it on 28 May and the following day it acquired a completely unexpected topicality when thirty-nine people were killed at the Heysel Stadium in Belgium following an outbreak of violence at the Liverpool/Juventus European Cup Final. Ann Barr rewrote the first paragraph, linking it to the tragedy, and ran the article on the front page of her section four days later. To the uninformed reader, it looked as though I'd cobbled this piece together in response to the events of 29 May when, in fact, I'd been painstakingly researching it for three months. The upshot was that I was immediately branded a 'world authority' on football hooliganism and appeared on numerous television and radio programmes. The *Observer's* editor at the time was so delighted by the attention the piece attracted he offered me a contract to write fifteen features a year for the paper. He, too, was under the impression that I'd researched and written the article in four days.

The following year I received a commendation at the British Press Awards – the only journalism prize I've ever won – and on the back of that I landed a job as a news trainee at *The Times* when I left Oxford. Unfortunately, my luck didn't hold. The editor of *The Times* in those days was an old Fleet Street hand named Charlie Wilson and to pass the time I would spend five minutes every morning trying to trick the office computer system into thinking I was him. I would enter his username and then try a dozen different passwords before giving up and logging on as myself. Then, one day, I hit upon the right password: 'Top Man'. Suddenly, I had access to all the paper's best-kept secrets. It was too good an opportunity to miss. I rooted through Charlie Wilson's 'Personal' files and found a memo from the managing editor that included the salaries of every single *Times* executive. I immediately sent it to everyone in the building, making it look as though it had come from the editor's terminal. For the rest of the day, Charlie Wilson had to contend with a succession of disgruntled employees, all of whom were demanding more money after learning how much some of their senior colleagues were being paid.

It took *The Times's* systems manager a week to find the source of the security breach and in the meantime I caused as much mischief as possible. My immediate boss was a languid jazz enthusiast named Richard Williams and when he got to work fifteen minutes late one morning I sent him a message, purporting to be from the editor, saying, 'Move your fucking car. It's in my space.' He leapt out of his chair as if he'd received a jolt from a cattle prod. On another occasion, posing as the editor, I sent a memo to everyone in the building announcing that I'd taken the decision to ban smoking in the office. For the rest of the day, members of staff had to assemble in the stairwells to get their hourly fix, an inconvenience they found particularly galling given that Charlie Wilson – himself a sixty-a-day man – was wandering around with a Rothman's King Size permanently dangling from his mouth.

When the managing editor summoned me to his office to face the music I was expecting no more punishment than a slap on the wrist. After all, being able to bypass computer security systems is a useful skill for any reporter to have. Instead, I was handed the contents of my office drawer in a plastic bag and escorted from the building by a security guard.

My mother wasn't the only writer in the family. As the Secretary of the Labour Party's Research Department, my father wrote *Let Us Face the Future*, its 1945 manifesto, and he went on to produce two classic works of sociology, *Family and Kinship in East London* and *The Rise of the Meritocracy*. Between them, my parents either wrote or edited over two dozen books.

Given that my mother and father were published authors, it's surprising that it never occurred to me to go into the family business until I was nineteen. I blame it on the fact that I was a late developer. My sister, Sophie, was always considered the bright one and it was her that my parents sent to good schools and expected to do well. My education, by contrast, was a subject they didn't take much interest in. They certainly didn't spend any money on it. At the age of sixteen, having been to a succession of bog standard comprehensives, I failed all my O levels, with the exception of a C in English Literature and a grade I in CSE Drama. When I phoned my mother to give her the bad news I actually used the words 'not academically bright', a euphemism I'd heard my parents' friends use in relation to their children on numerous occasions.

My father decided to pack me off to a kibbutz. One of the reasons I did so badly at school is that I'd spent the years fourteen to sixteen in a haze of marijuana smoke – and I would have continued puffing away if I'd been able to get my hands on any of the stuff in Israel. But it wasn't available, at least not in the kibbutz I was on, and the sudden withdrawal of my daily dose had a profound effect. For the first time in my life, I began to read voraciously – Dostoevsky, Sartre, Orwell. I suddenly became interested in history, one of the subjects I'd failed at O level. I even bought the *Jerusalem Post* every morning and started energetically participating in breakfast-table discussions about the latest twists in the Arab–Israeli conflict. After several months of this, it began to dawn on me that the life of the mind might not be quite as boring as I'd thought.

I returned to Britain determined to retake my O levels and go to university. Not just any university, either, but Oxford. For someone with my academic record, this was ludicrously ambitious, but I took the view that there was no point in going back to school if I wasn't going to aim high. I promised myself that I wouldn't smoke another joint until I got in.

With a Herculean effort, I managed to scrape together another three O levels, all at grade C. That meant I was able to do three A levels and apply to Oxford. I chose Brasenose College because its admissions tutor, Harry Judge, had introduced a special scheme whereby applicants from state schools could avoid having to sit the entrance exam by submitting to a rigorous interview instead.

The subject I applied to do was Philosophy, Politics and Economics, a combination that Evelyn Waugh described as a 'self-publicist's degree', and I was interviewed by the College's three PPE tutors over the course of an hour. I must have made a favourable impression because I received a conditional offer of three Bs and an O-level pass in a foreign language. Unfortunately, this second requirement was completely beyond me so I decided to concentrate on the first instead. My hope was that if I managed to get the three Bs – still a very distant prospect at this stage – the admissions tutor would waive the O-level pass in a foreign language.

I ended up getting two Bs and a C and assumed that that was the end of the matter until I received a circular from Brasenose telling me where to pick up my room key, how to do my laundry, and so forth. It was completely impersonal – it began 'Dear candidate' – but since I wouldn't have been sent it if I hadn't got in I assumed I'd been successful. My mother was so astonished she demanded to see the letter and, after carefully scrutinising it, cautioned me not to count my chickens. She was right to be sceptical. The following week I received a letter from Harry Judge himself, this one addressed to me personally, pointing out that not only had I failed to meet their 'extremely generous' conditional offer, but I hadn't even 'made an attempt' to get an O-level pass in a foreign language. 'In view of this, I'm afraid we can't offer you a place at Brasenose College this year,' he concluded. 'Good luck in your university career elsewhere.'

It was obvious that the first letter was simply a mistake, but my father insisted on telephoning Harry Judge. He thought there was a slim chance that the admissions tutor would be so mortified once this clerical error had been brought to his attention that he'd reverse his decision and let me in. I pleaded with him not to call – it was me who'd be embarrassed, not Harry Judge – but it was no good. He had the bit between his teeth.

I was listening on the upstairs phone when my father got through.

'Which letter did he get first?' asked Judge.

'The one implying he'd got in.'

'I see. [Beat.] D'you mind hanging on a minute? I'm actually in a meeting with the three PPE tutors as we speak. I'm just going to tell them what you've just told me.'

He then placed his hand over the receiver, but in such a way that both my father and I could still hear what was being said.

'I've got some chap's father on the line – Toby Young, applied to read PPE, you probably don't remember him. Anyway, his father says he's received two letters from us, one from the College saying he's got in, the other from me saying he hasn't. Question is, what are we going to do about it?'

There followed a ten-minute discussion, dominated by the philosophy tutor, about whether the College's clerical error meant that they were now morally obliged to offer me a place.

'Okay,' said Harry Judge, when he eventually came back on the line. 'He can come.'

It turned out to be one of the most valuable lessons my father ever taught me. No matter how unlikely your chances of success, you should never give up until you've tried everything. Just occasionally, sheer, bloody-minded persistence will win out against the odds.

By the time I returned to London from New York at the beginning of 2000, I'd been a journalist for fifteen years. To say I'd become disillusioned with it is a bit misleading since it was journalism – or, rather, its gatekeepers – that had become disillusioned with me. I'd been fired from virtually every paper on Fleet Street. My efforts to set up a magazine, as well as my attempts to become the editor of an existing one, had all ended in failure. Indeed, I wasn't merely unemployed; I was regarded as more or less unemployable. One of the few newspaper executives to offer me any work at this time was a black editor at the *Observer*. When I asked him why he'd taken pity on me he said, 'Because I know what it's like to be a nigger.'

I like to think that my waning interest in journalism wasn't due to my pariah status, though I may be deluding myself. Up until this point, it had provided me with a great life and I had every reason to be grateful to the profession. As a young bachelor in London, working for a succession of gossip columns meant that I had access to an exclusive social world that I wouldn't have got close to if I'd been in almost any other profession. The fact that my responsibilities ended as soon as I filed my copy at the end of the working day meant that

I could plunge, headfirst, into London's nightlife – and having an expense account was a huge asset when it came to the dating circuit. In 1995, journalism had taken me across the Atlantic where I'd led an even more carefree, hedonistic life and, after I'd been fired from *Vanity Fair* in 1997, I was able to remain in New York by freelancing for various publications. What other profession can offer a man in his twenties and thirties such a good time?

The thing I enjoyed most about being a journalist was the sense I had of being a member of an unrespectable, but convivial club. There's an honour-among-thieves mentality within the journalistic community, a feeling that since you all belong to the same, slightly dodgy profession you ought to stick together. No doubt there's a certain amount of *esprit de corps* in all professions and I don't mean to exaggerate the loyalty of journalists to one another – I've been stitched up by my colleagues on numerous occasions – but there's a great deal of camaraderie nonetheless. It's connected with the amount of drinking you do together – and the fact that you all share a jaundiced view of the world. At social events, journalists seek each other out, eager to exchange compromising anecdotes about the rich and powerful, thereby reassuring one another that their cynical assessment of them is correct. Journalists are a curious blend of insider and outsider, laughing together at the absurdities of the world they're writing about, yet, at the same time, inescapably caught up in it. It's a way of doing business – faintly corrupt, intensely gregarious – that breeds a kind of hail-fellow-well-met companionship. As a working journalist, you can go to almost any city in the world and know that there'll be a community of fellow ne'er-do-wells who'll provide you with an instant social life. All you have to do is pick up the phone. It's almost like being a member of a criminal fraternity.

Nevertheless, it's a way of life that begins to pall as you get older. The problem with journalism as a career is that, unless you're on the fast track to become the editor of a newspaper or magazine, there's very little sense of progression. As a Fleet Street reporter, you start out writing stories for the paper and, fifteen years later, you're still doing the same thing. You might advance to a higher pay grade and you might have a fancier title, such as 'chief correspondent', but the actual work you do doesn't really change. If you have any interest in honing your talents as a writer, or even developing your skills as a reporter, this can be quite frustrating. To begin with, the learning curve is quite steep – on my first day at *The Times* I was told to go to Peterborough and file an eight-hundred-word 'profile' of the town by 5 p.m. – but within ten years you've pretty much learnt all you're going to learn. After fifteen years, you begin to feel as though you're stuck in a *Groundhog Day*-like loop. Even the stars of the profession suffer from this sense of ennui. George Bernard Shaw said that being a columnist is like standing beneath a windmill: as soon as you've dodged one blade, there's another one coming straight for you.

The feeling that you're not really getting anywhere is matched by the realisation that you're not leaving much behind, either. No article I wrote subsequently ever produced the same response as my *Observer* piece on 'designer' hooligans. With very few exceptions, writing an article for a newspaper or magazine is like dropping a stone into a well and then not hearing it go 'plop'. Old newspapers aren't used to wrap fish and chips in any more, but they might as well be for all the value that's put on yesterday's news – and the cumulative impact of doing something so ephemeral can be quite soul-destroying. You tell yourself that, as a member of the fourth estate, you're playing a vital role in the democratic process, but such platitudes aren't very comforting when you see one of your pieces blowing in the wind down Oxford Street. You begin to long for a more permanent record of your existence, something you can point to with pride and say, 'I did that.'

In my own case, this disillusionment with journalism was exacerbated by a longstanding desire for fame. I know that this is supposed to remain an unspoken longing – it's far less respectable than wanting to dress up in women's clothing, for instance – but it's always struck me as an entirely natural desire. Why wouldn't a person want to be famous? Celebrities are at the top of our society's food chain. They live in the grandest houses, dictate the latest fashions and enjoy unlimited sexual opportunities. Even if you take away the perks, the desire for fame still seems perfectly normal: it's about the struggle for recognition, a longing to be remembered after you're dead. This, surely, is at the root of why anyone wants to be a celebrity: it's a way of cheating death.

But I'm enough of a student of the subject to know that fame, as an end in itself, doesn't have the same currency it once did. Scarcely a day passes without a hand-wringing article appearing in the broadsheet press about how fame and celebrity have become the dominant values of our time, when, in fact, almost the opposite is the case. In the first decade of the twenty-first century – thanks, in part, to the phenomenal success of reality TV – we've witnessed the gradual separation of fame and status. These days, being well known doesn't automatically ensure high social standing (let alone immortality). You can be famous and still be a loser: a famous loser. The best example is probably James Hewitt, but there are countless others.

Then there's the issue of duration. All things being equal, being famous is probably preferable to not being famous, but you better make sure you remain in the spotlight for longer than fifteen minutes. Unlike love, to have had fame and lost it is worse than never having had it at all. It's like the argument about why you should never take a one-off opportunity to fly first class: once you've turned left, you'll never want to turn right again. Sometimes it's better not to know what you're missing.

In *Brewer's Dictionary of Rogues, Villains and Eccentrics*, William Donaldson includes an entry on 'Simon Dee Syndrome' named after the once-famous sixties DJ. According to Donaldson, those suffering from this condition are 'better remembered for having been forgotten than they would be if they were still remembered, which indeed they are, but only for having been forgotten, which they are not . . . specialists believe that, unusually, early detection of the disease only serves to speed up the onset of the full-blown disease.'

There was only one kind of fame I wanted: *literary fame*. Forget about journalism. I wanted to write a book or a play or a movie that would endure beyond the weekly news cycle. Arthur Koestler maintained that a writer's ambition should be to trade a hundred contemporary readers for ten readers in 10 years' time and one in 100 years, but I wasn't that ambitious. I knew I didn't have it in me to produce anything *that* good. Rather, I wanted to write something that would be regarded as a fine example of its type, like a good screwball comedy or a well-crafted thriller. Above all, it had to be a piece of work that I could produce only by using every last drop of whatever talent I had. I wanted to find out what I was capable of. If I could write something as good as *Gunga Din* – the picture, not the poem – I'd die a happy man.

3

THE BEST MAN LOST

It wasn't just Caroline I had to remain on the good side of during our fifteen-month engagement. I also had to worry about her family, a group that included two parents, an older brother and three older sisters. The manner in which they learnt of our engagement didn't help. Shortly after Caroline agreed to marry me, we flew to Manhattan where a friend of mine was hosting a farewell bash. I got up on a chair and announced our engagement at the party, forgetting for a moment that there was a *New York Times* journalist present who was doing a story about how I'd become 'an ever-present icon of defeat' in Manhattan media circles. The happy news was duly reported in that Sunday's paper. At this stage, Caroline had left a message on her parents' answering machine, but by the time they got it a colleague of Caroline's brother had already faxed the article to him. 'That's typical,' he said. 'Toby gets engaged to my little sister and the first the family hears about it is when it's in the *New York Times.*'

My only excuse for this colossal piece of mismanagement was that I was totally preoccupied with the best-man speech I had to give in Washington the day after the party. One of my oldest friends, Sean Macaulay, was marrying an American film producer called Caroline Bruce and he was relying on me to make a good impression. In addition to the bride's family – her father was a partner in a white-shoe Washington law firm – the audience was due to include the editor of *GQ*, the deputy editor of *The Times* and, rather improbably, the Chancellor of the Exchequer. (Sean's sister Sarah was engaged to Gordon Brown at the time and subsequently became his wife.)

This was 29 April 2000 – a date that will live in infamy, at least in my memory.

If I had an ounce of common sense I would have rewritten my speech the moment I set foot in the church. All my jokes were tailored to a British audience, yet it soon became apparent that only a handful of the two hundred and fifty guests were from the home country. How would the Americans respond to a best-man speech that sounded like it had been written by the Entertainment Committee of the St Helen's Rugby Club? Unfortunately, the person I chose to road-test my material on was Bruce Macaulay, Sean's younger brother. Bruce is an ex-squaddie who was then working in Australia and, after patiently listening to all my gags, he assured me they'd go over like gangbusters. 'They'll be pissing themselves,' he said.

The reception was at the Chevy Chase Country Club and, of the twenty or so tables, no more than two were occupied by Brits. As I cleared my throat, I could see Bruce grinning at me and giving me the thumbs up from the back of the room.

'It's good to see Sean looking so relaxed,' I began. 'He told me earlier that this is the first wedding he's ever been to at which he doesn't feel guilty about having fucked the bride the night before.'

A low murmur of disapproval rose from the audience, but Bruce motioned for me to carry on. His expression indicated that, while his fellow guests might be a bit on the stiff side, they'd soon loosen up.

'I'm only going to tell one off-colour joke this evening and I'm going to tell it straight away so Sean can relax,' I said. 'I understand that he and Caroline are going to be spending their wedding night here in Washington and I'd like to offer one small piece of advice . . . ' I reached into my pocket and pulled out an enormous cigar: 'When in Rome . . . '

This was a reference to Bill Clinton's method of pleasuring Monica Lewinsky, but if anyone got it they weren't about to let on.

'When I said that was the only off-colour joke I was going to tell this evening that was a shameless, barefaced lie. But, hey, when in Rome . . . '

Not only did this not get a single laugh, I could sense the audience becoming distinctly hostile. The wedding guests included Senator John Warner, one of Liz Taylor's ex-husbands, and Senator Warner and his colleagues clearly didn't appreciate being called liars by a former colonialist.

By now, I knew I'd completely misjudged the audience. The sensible thing would have been to throw away the rest of my speech, utter a few platitudes about the bride and groom and sit down as quickly as possible. Unfortunately, I was robbed of the power of decision. Successive waves of anxiety had left me lobotomised. I was on automatic pilot. I'd memorised my lines and I was going to deliver them.

'Back in Britain, we're not used to this level of hospitality,' I continued. 'When I heard how many people had been invited I asked Sean if this was going to be the American equivalent of a British Royal Wedding. He said, "Absolutely not. Caroline and I intend to stay married for longer than three minutes."'

Nothing.

The centrepiece was a bit in which I pretended I knew nothing about how to make a speech at an American wedding – very little pretence was needed, obviously – so I'd purchased a best-man speech from a website called Speech-O-Matic.com. All you had to do, I explained, was plug in the names of the bride and groom and, presto, a fully written speech was emailed to you thirty seconds later. Trouble was, I'd muddled up the bride's surname and

Christian name, so instead of 'Caroline Bruce' I'd plugged in 'Bruce Caroline'.

'It's a great honour to be the best man at Sean and Bruce's wedding,' I began, pretending to read from the speech that had been emailed to me by Speech-O-Matic.com. 'Being the best man at a gay wedding is a little like being the maid of honour at a straight wedding: if I'm the best man, how come Sean's not marrying me?'

I was confident that *this* joke, at least, would get a laugh. But once again I'd misjudged the audience. The twenty-ninth of April, I later discovered, is Gay Pride Day in the US and hundreds of thousands of homosexuals had marched on Washington that very afternoon to protest about the fact that gay marriage is still illegal in most American states. What I was doing was the equivalent of standing up in front of a white audience on Martin Luther King Day and telling a string of racist jokes.

'I'd like to thank the bridesmaids, Stan, Gregg, Ron and Brad. Brad is hoping to catch the bouquet today. Earlier he said to me, "You know what my problem is? Always a bridesmaid, never a groom."'

Embarrassed cough.

'It ends with a toast. May your hair remain thick and lustrous, may your union be blessed with a menagerie of very small dogs, and if you're ever arrested, can you make sure it's in San Francisco rather than Washington? Out there, they don't read you your Miranda rights. They read you your Carmen Miranda rights. Ladies and gentlemen, the groom and groom.'

Deafening silence.

My next 'funny' bit involved quoting from a speech that Salman Rushdie had given at Bill Buford's wedding in which the famous novelist had compared the chances of finding happiness in marriage to the odds of jumping out of an aeroplane at 50,000 feet and landing in a haystack. 'It was the worst best-man speech ever given,' I said.

'Until now,' bellowed Sean Macaulay.

It got the first laugh of the evening.

It was at this point that I broke out in what stand-up comedians refer to as a 'flop sweat'.

As I struggled on towards the end, my shirt sticking to me like a wet rag, people began to chat noisily among themselves. Some even got up and drifted out of the room. I ended by quoting from a letter Sean had written me in 1984 in which he described his ideal woman. Needless to say, she bore a remarkable resemblance to one Caroline Bruce. It was no good. By now, no one was listening. I sat down to almost total silence.

It wasn't long before the reviews started coming in.

'Well, Toby,' said the bride's mother, 'you were every bit as bad as I'd been led to expect.'

Dylan Jones, the editor of *GQ*, overheard two ex-ambassadors discussing my performance in the lavatory. 'So that's the famous British sense of humour,' said one to the other, his voice dripping with sarcasm.

'You had some good jokes,' muttered Gordon Brown, trying to be kind, 'but you should have taken your audience into account.'

The only person who seemed genuinely delighted by my performance was Bruce.

'I knew they'd react badly,' he said, slapping me on the back and roaring with laughter, 'but I had no idea it was going to be *that* badly. That was fucking priceless.'

Caroline flew back early to do some damage control on the home front, but I still had some unfinished business to take care of in New York. The moment had come to pack up the contents of my bachelor pad and transfer them to what would eventually become my marital home. I imagine that this is an experience most men go through when they get engaged, but I wasn't prepared for just how traumatic it proved to be. The process of sifting through my possessions, deciding which to keep and which to throw away, very nearly made me call the whole thing off. The sight of the remnants of my bachelor life lined up outside my flat in black rubbish bags was almost too much to bear.

I found this ordeal particularly gruelling because the place I was moving out of was so much nicer than the place I was moving in to. It had taken me eighteen months of dogged, painstaking research to find that flat and I'd lived in it for three and a half years. Real estate brokers the world over say there are three things which determine a property's value – location, location, location – and mine couldn't have been better situated: it was opposite Gwyneth Paltrow's house in the West Village.

To begin with, the packing-up process was fairly painless. I was perfectly happy to toss out the pictures of 'the cracker from Caracas', the girl I'd briefly shared with Mick Jagger; I didn't flinch when I burnt all the legal correspondence relating to Harold Evans's attempts to sue me for libel. In my mind, I already thought of the New York chapter of my life as closed; clearing out my flat was just a footnote.

I didn't get upset until the very end when I had to dispose of my most prized possession of all: my porno collection. Call me a senti-mental old fool, but there was something about this horde that made me come over all misty-eyed. We'd been through a lot together, me and these video-cassettes. We went back a long way. It was like being asked to say goodbye to a group of old friends.

Still, there was no way these tapes were coming with me. Quite apart from Caroline's reaction, which didn't bear thinking about, there was the small matter of Her Majesty's Customs. If I tried to bring any of these tapes through the 'Nothing To Declare' channel at Heathrow I'd be sent directly to jail without passing go.

I kept my collection in a large, wooden box in the bottom right-hand corner of my bedroom – an area a Feng Shui expert once identified as my 'love and marriage' corner – and when the removal men came round to pack up my furniture I decided to simply give them this box. The look of jubilation on their faces when they discovered its contents was something to behold. It was as if I'd presented them with a sack full of Acapulco Gold. One of the men spread the tapes out on my bed so he and his two colleagues could take turns to pick out their favourites. I stood in the doorway, fighting back the tears, as I watched my lovingly assembled collection being scattered to the four winds.

Suddenly, I couldn't take it any more. I leapt on the bed and scooped up all the tapes into my arms.

'Leave them alone,' I screamed, my voice choking with emotion. 'I've changed my mind.'

When I eventually regained my self-composure – about twenty-four hours later – I decided my best bet was to try and find a good home for these cassettes. At least that way, the collection wouldn't have to be broken up. I'd read in the *Sunday Times* that Martin Amis, who'd recently moved to New York, was working on a novel that was set in the adult entertainment industry. Would he be interested in housing my prized collection? I felt sure that he, above all people, would treat these X-rated videos with the reverence they deserved. I decided to place a classified ad in the *New York Review of Books*:

> For the attention of Martin Amis: One slightly used porno collection looking for a new owner. It's currently housed with Manhattan Mini Storage but if you're interested email your New York address to howtolose@hotmail.com and I'll arrange for it to be delivered in a plain, brown packing case. I'm sure it'll prove an invaluable 'research' tool.

Needless to say, I never heard from him, but the ad did produce one response: from the BBC. A researcher working for Joan Bakewell, the broadcaster once known as 'the thinking man's crumpet', called to ask if I'd be interested in being interviewed for a television programme Joan was making about pornography. A more sensible man would have immediately slammed down the phone, but I've always subscribed to Gore Vidal's maxim that there are two things in life you should never turn down: the opportunity to have sex and the opportunity to appear on television.

I realised I'd made a mistake when the researcher rang back ten minutes later and asked if I'd be prepared to play Joan Bakewell one of my 'favourite tapes' on camera. Certainly not, I told him. In any case, I'd left all of my tapes in New York. Nevertheless, any hopes I had of passing myself off as a disinterested pundit, merely commentating on the *phenomenon* of pornography, were dashed. Clearly, I was being interviewed in my capacity as a 'user', not an impartial observer. Paranoid visions of how they were going to bill me when I first appeared on screen danced before my eyes: 'Toby Young, pornography addict'; 'Toby Young, compulsive masturbator'; 'Toby – "wanker" – Young'. Unfortunately, it was too late to back out now.

'So, Toby,' Bakewell began, a cameraman perched over her left shoulder, 'when did you first develop your lifelong passion for pornography?'

I was stymied. My plan had been to appear as smooth and debonair as possible in the hope of seeming completely unembarrassed. It was being filmed at my bedsit in Shepherd's Bush and I had a copy of Philip Larkin's *Letters* at my feet, ready to flick to his dispatch to Robert Conquest in which he talks about his visit to a Soho sex shop. *You see, Joan. An interest in erotica has a fine literary heritage.* However, I immediately flushed crimson.

'Er, well, er, I'm not sure, er—'

'I have to say, Toby, I just can't see the point of it,' Bakewell continued. 'To me, it's just like watching little bits of gristle, you know? Why d'you find it so . . . *compelling*?'

As I struggled to answer this, I could see the cameraman darting about in front of me, getting the close-ups he'd been instructed to get: quivering lower lip, shaking hands, rapidly blinking eyes. This was turning into a nightmare.

'C-c-c-could I please have a glass of water?' I stammered. 'My mouth's suddenly become very dry.'

It was like being interviewed about pornography by my mum. Indeed, Joan Bakewell was actually a contemporary of my mother's at Cambridge. It wasn't her intention to embarrass me – she seemed genuinely puzzled by what an educated chap like me saw in all this filth – but I felt exactly like I did aged fourteen when my mum discovered a pile of *Playboys* under my bed.

The low point came during a discussion about who pornography is supposed to be for.

Joan: I gather from talking to people in the adult entertainment industry that these films are very popular with modern couples. Apparently, after they've put the kids to bed, they open a bottle of Chardonnay, sit down on the sofa and watch one of these tapes.

Me: That's all bullshit, Joan. The fact is, the main market for porn is sad, lonely, loveless men – men who can't get women.

Beat.

Joan: Is that you, Toby?

Me [spluttering]: Er, no, no, of course not. I mean, not any more. I'm about to get married. My interest in pornography was just a phase.

Joan: A phase? Oh, *come on.*

At this point, the cameraman swivelled round to get a close-up of the unmarked, but entirely innocent videotapes scattered in front of the television.

Me: No, really. [Beat.] A twenty-year phase.

After this ordeal, I can say with some confidence that there is an exception to Gore Vidal's rule. Have as much sex as you like and appear on television as often as you can, but for God's sake don't agree to talk about anything of a sexual nature on television, particularly with someone who reminds you of your mother. Sorry, Joan. But it's difficult to appear like a thinking man when you're talking about crumpet.

4

THE WILLIAM HAGUE LOOKALIKE

Any hopes I had of retiring from journalism to try and become a proper writer had to be abandoned when I discovered how much higher the cost of living is in Britain than America. When New Yorkers asked me how I was getting on in London my standard response was to say it was like moving to the outer boroughs, except everything was twice as expensive. Okay, that was a slight exaggeration, but according to the *Economist*'s Intelligence Unit the cost of living in London is 7 per cent higher than in New York.[1] When it comes to taxi fares, alcohol and restaurant bills, prices are almost identical – provided you substitute pounds for dollars. I soon realised I was going to have to earn considerably more in London just to maintain the lifestyle I'd been enjoying in New York – and there was scant chance of that.

The pitiful state of my journalistic career – or rather my sporadic output as a jobbing, freelance hack – was particularly hard to bear because Sean Langan's professional life had suddenly taken off.

After graduating from the University of East Anglia in 1986, Sean had landed a job as a presenter on a 'yoof' television series

1 These figures are for the year 2000.

based in Norwich. That led to a gig on an Australian chart show called *Countdown Revolution* and that, in turn, led to a presenting job on a Channel 4 motoring programme. It was steady work, but not particularly satisfying, and, like me, Sean laboured under the illusion that he was destined for greater things. Unlike me, though, he actually did something about it. In 1998, he persuaded the BBC to commission a three-part documentary that involved him going to Kashmir and trying to discover the fate of four foreign tourists who'd been kidnapped there in 1995. The resulting series, *Nightmare in Paradise*, was shown on BBC 2 in 1999 and received universally good reviews. By the time I arrived back in London, Sean had secured a second commission from the Beeb, this time to make a five-part series about the Middle East.

In the hope of competing with Sean, I had some vague notion about becoming a highbrow commentator on Anglo-American relations and even fantasised about appearing on *Newsnight* in the run-up to the US Presidential election. But it wasn't to be. The closest I came to writing about politics was a piece for the *Guardian* about the pitfalls of being the spitting image of William Hague who was then the leader of the Conservative Party. This was hardly a mark of distinction. The late Labour MP Tony Banks once described Hague as looking like a foetus and whenever he was on television Caroline would start fanning herself, pretending she was all hot and bothered – a reference to the fact that he wasn't exactly considered a sex symbol.

I first became aware of my resemblance to Hague at Sean Macaulay's wedding. On being introduced to me, Gordon Brown did an elaborate double-take and then asked if I'd be willing to do some work for the Labour Party during the next general election campaign. He suggested I tour marginal constituencies pretending to be the Leader of the Opposition and spouting right-wing gobbledegook. 'It could be very funny,' he said.

But it wasn't until I did an impromptu impression of Hague at the *Spectator* summer party in 2000 that I realised just how uncanny this similarity was. I leapt up on the editor's desk, having drunk several glasses of wine, and said I'd like to thank the magazine's staff for their unstinting support of the Conservative Party during these difficult times. 'I know the *Spectator* is the home of lost causes,' I said in my best William Hague accent, 'but this is beyond the call of duty.'

Instead of laughing, the staff received me with the air of polite boredom they reserve for visiting dignitaries. Was my impression of the Conservative leader really *that* feeble? Then the penny dropped. Hague was actually a guest at the party and my impersonation was so good they'd mistaken me for the man himself. I spent the rest of the afternoon searching for him among the drunks and has-beens crammed into the *Spectator*'s back garden. My plan was to go up to him and say, 'Don't make this any harder on yourself than it has to be, Mr Hague. On the planet I come from death by vaporisation is considered a luxury. You're being replaced.'

Writing about my resemblance to the leader of Her Majesty's Opposition was actually quite respectable compared to some of the other articles I produced in this period. Perhaps my most humiliating assignment was a piece I did for a woman's magazine about an undercover visit to a penis enlargement surgeon.

Like most men, I've always been a little anxious about the size of my penis. Is it ever so slightly . . . too big? (Only kidding, obviously. My anxiety was in the other direction.) Answering this question isn't as straightforward as it seems. Part of the problem is that there's no standard method of measurement so no one knows exactly how big an 'average' penis is supposed to be. The famous American sexologist Dr Alfred Kinsey compiled data from six thousand men, but made the mistake of letting his subjects hold the tape measure themselves, thereby dramatically inflating the results. Most urologists put the average somewhere between five and seven inches, but such a broad definition of what constitutes an 'average' penis seems designed to comfort those at the low end of the scale. An additional complicating factor is that men generally view their own penises from above so they *appear* smaller than those of other men even though they may be the same size.

Needless to say, men aren't inclined to discuss these issues with each other, at least not seriously. I once asked Sean Langan whether he thought there was any validity to the angle-of-vision point. 'Absolutely,' he said. 'When I look down I'm impressed, but when I see myself in the mirror I'm frightened.'

For years, insecure men like me have taken comfort from another of Dr Kinsey's findings, namely, that the female orgasm is clitoral rather than vaginal, so the length of a man's penis is irrelevant. Unfortunately, so many women have told me that size *does* matter I've had to abandon this salutary myth. It's not the motion of the ocean that counts, apparently, it's the size of your torpedo.

In the hope of getting to the bottom of some of these issues – as well as furnish myself with some material for a magazine article – I arranged to pay an undercover visit to Dr Roberto Viel, a Harley Street plastic surgeon specialising in penis enlargement.

Things got off to a pretty bad start when the door was answered by an extremely attractive girl.

'Yes?'

'I'm here to see Dr Roberto Viel.'

'Oh. Yes, I see. Well, er, if you'll just follow me, Mr, Mr . . . '

'Hague.'

Was I was being paranoid, or did she know what I was there for? I had no idea what percentage of Dr Viel's patients came to see him about penis enlargement, but judging from her reaction it was pretty high. She led me up some stairs and introduced me to another pretty girl, this one dressed in a nurse's uniform.

'This is Mr Hague,' she told her. Then, lowering her voice to a whisper, she added: 'He's here to see Dr Viel!'

'I see,' said the nurse, shooting me a pitying look. 'If you'd like to fill this in, sir, the doctor will be with you shortly.'

She handed me a form that had various boxes on it: name,

address, medical history, etc. I flipped it over and on the back were two additional boxes: 'Length' and 'Girth'. Was I supposed to fill in those as well?

As I was wrestling with this, I noticed that the two women were stealing furtive glances in my direction and whispering to one another. I suddenly had an overwhelming urge to tell them I was an undercover journalist, that I didn't have a 'micropenis', to use the medical term. (A 'micropenis' is one that's less than 2.7 inches when fully erect.) I wanted to whip it out and wave it around – 'Here! Look! See! It's perfectly normal.'

I flipped through the pile of magazines in the waiting room. I was expecting them to be in Japanese – I've heard the rumour – but most of them were in Arabic. Was that significant? The only magazine in English was called *Cosmetic Surgery* and, to my surprise, it contained an article on Dr Viel. Or, rather, the two Dr Viels. Apparently, Roberto has a twin brother called Maurizio and they're both plastic surgeons. Indeed, according to the article Roberto had 'already performed a procedure on his brother' although it didn't say what kind.

After about fifteen minutes, Roberto appeared and showed me through to his room. He was a tall, thin-faced man in his late thirties with a pronounced Italian accent. Without thinking, I asked him whether he and his brother were the inspiration for the twin gynaecologists played by Jeremy Irons in *Dead Ringers*.

'Of course not,' he said. 'Why you ask me this? I no like this movie.'

I cursed myself inwardly. I'd momentarily forgotten that one of the twin brothers in *Dead Ringers* is a homicidal maniac who fashions a new set of gynaecological instruments in order to torture, maim and kill his female patients. Dr Viel gave me such a hostile look I was glad I wasn't planning to go through with the enlargement procedure there and then. It's not very sensible to offend a man who's about to take a scalpel to your penis.

Dr Viel then proceeded to tell me exactly what the operation involves. Typically, he performs a two-part 'penoplasty' whereby he first increases the length and then the girth of your member. The

lengthening procedure involves cutting the 'penile suspensory liga-
ment' and pulling the penis forward, thereby adding between one
and two inches. However, he quickly pointed out that this gain
would only apply to my penis in its flaccid state; it would make no
difference when erect. Not only that, but the angle of my erection
would end up about thirty degrees shallower.

I couldn't believe what I was hearing. The lengthening surgery
was 'cosmetic' in every sense of the word. I might impress my buddies in the changing room, but it would make absolutely no
difference where it really counted – in the bedroom. On the contrary, my erect penis would flail around drunkenly instead of
standing to attention. What kind of idiot would have it done? (To
answer this, Dr Viel had an album of testimonials, accompanied by
grinning headshots.)

The widening procedure sounded even more perilous. Dr Viel
explained that it involves removing fat from the stomach or thigh
and injecting it into the shaft of the penis, thereby increasing the
circumference by approximately two inches. However, the fat has a
tendency to be reabsorbed, meaning the patient has to return for a
series of 'top-ups', and it can also result in unusual hair-growth, creating what's known in the trade as the 'hairy-donut effect'. Finally –
and this is something the good doctor omitted to tell me – the
American plastic surgeon who pioneered this operation, Ricardo
Samitier, was convicted for manslaughter after a penis enlargement
patient bled to death on his operating table.

That's right – *bled to death!*

'Hokay,' said Dr Viel at the conclusion of the consultation, 'let's
'ave a look at your pinis.'

The moment of truth had arrived. I have to admit, I was a little
nervous. Surely, the second I showed him my credentials he'd
realise I wasn't a serious patient: 'Come now, Meester Hague, you
are joking with me. Stop wasting my time. There's *nothing* I can do
for you.'

In fact, when I did show him my 'pinis', he looked worryingly unfazed. To my horror, he then pulled on some latex gloves and started manhandling it with all the finesse of a sixteen-year-old schoolgirl. Was he getting his revenge for my *Dead Ringers* question? *Pull! Stretch!! Bend!!!* At one point, I actually cried out in pain. He then got out a tape and measured the length and width of my 'pinis'. He read off the results in centimetres rather than inches, as if to cushion the blow.

'Yes, Meester Hague,' he concluded, peeling off his latex gloves. 'I think I can 'elp you.'

Sean and Anabel got married in Ibiza in the autumn of 2000 and, against his better judgement, Sean asked if I'd consider being his best man. My appalling debacle at the Chevy Chase Country Club was still fresh in my memory, but far from putting me off, that made me even more inclined to say yes. If I could pull it off, I thought, maybe that would go some way to expunging the shame I still felt. It was as if a beautiful woman was inviting me back into her bed for a second go round even though I hadn't been able to perform the first time. Here was a chance to redeem myself.

There was one surefire way to get laughs at this wedding and that was to tell a string of anti-German jokes. Anabel's mother, Lady Cutler, is German and of the one hundred and twenty guests at the wedding about forty of them were going to be Krauts. 'Lady Cutler,' I thought about saying, 'you mustn't think of yourself as losing a daughter so much as gaining the Sudetenland.' However, while I could rely on the British contingent to laugh at such infantile gags, the Germans probably wouldn't be amused. Indeed, Anabel had specifically asked me not to tell any anti-German jokes. 'Please, Toby,' she said. 'My mother will be really upset.' Consequently, I knew that if I made any reference to the beach towels strategically placed over the first three rows of seats in the church – or any other equally gratuitous remarks – I would end up antagonising at least a third of the guests, including the bride and her mother.

What was I to do?

Well, obviously, I told a string of anti-German jokes.

In deference to Anabel's feelings, though, I did make some attempt to disguise them as anti-British jokes. For instance, I pointed out that it was just as well the Germans had come with us on our boat trip to Formentera the previous day because without them the Brits would never have been able to put up the gazebo. I described the comic scenes on the beach as various pissed British hacks struggled to erect the giant sunshade that was supposed to go over the picnic table. Eventually, one of Anabel's strapping German cousins had decided to take charge: 'You, bald man, pick that up and take it over there, jah?'

Initially, this strategy seemed to be working. At one point, when I was showering the Germans with insincere praise, a blonde-haired Valkyrie leapt to her feet, punched the air with her fist and shouted 'jawohl'. However, I did get a little carried away. I related how one of the Germans had buttonholed me earlier that evening and told me that in her country weddings are organised much more efficiently. Apparently, they rank all the single people on a scale of one to fifty and then make sure that people of equivalent sexual attractiveness are seated next to each other. I then quoted the German: 'It works very well provided the margin of error is no greater than plus or minus ten points. Everybody goes home and has a nice little fuck.' After pausing for dramatic effect I added: 'I must say, I was rather surprised to hear Lady Cutler use the f-word . . . '

Towards the end of the evening, I went up to Anabel's mum and said I hoped she hadn't been too upset by my constant references to the Germans. 'At first, it was quite funny,' she said, 'but then you went too far. I'd forgotten about the obsession you British have with the Germans – always with the same stupid jokes. It's really quite boring.'

There's a postscript to this story.

The following day, Caroline and I were making our way to the airport in our rental car when a warning light appeared on the dashboard.

We were about to run out of petrol. Luckily, there was a garage nearby and even though I was suffering from an appalling hangover I thought that filling the car up with petrol was something I could just about manage. I pulled into the garage and parked alongside the nearest pump, only to realise that the petrol cap was on the other side of the car. After executing a three-point turn – or, rather, a fifteen-point turn – I was then confronted with a fiendishly difficult puzzle: how to get the petrol cap off? I wrestled with this IQ test for a good ten minutes, before finally giving up the ghost and prising it off with a penknife. After filling up the tank, I used the same tool to hammer the cap back into place. The entire performance took about twenty minutes.

As Caroline and I were leaving the garage, I noticed a group of Anabel's German relatives having breakfast in the service station restaurant and staring at us impassively through the window. They'd witnessed the whole thing.

A minute or so later, after we'd been travelling for less than a mile, the car's engine seized up and it ground to a halt. What had gone wrong? It turned out the car I'd rented was a diesel and I'd filled it up with petrol.

Sure enough, after a few minutes had elapsed, the same group of Germans came gliding past in a silver Mercedes. They slowed down to gawp at the bald man standing beside his broken-down vehicle, smoke billowing from the engine. As they disappeared over the horizon I could see them shaking their heads in disbelief: How on earth had they lost the war?

5

CAROLINE'S FROM MARS, I'M FROM VENUS

'You do realise I won't be changing my name to Young?' said Caroline as the wedding day drew near.

'But we need a common surname,' I said. 'What if we have children?'

'In that case, why not change yours to Bondy?'

My response to this was to burst out laughing – not a smart move judging from the look on Caroline's face. I realised that sidestepping this landmine was going to take some fancy footwork on my part. I gently pointed out that I needed to keep my name for professional reasons, that as a journalist I had become known as 'Toby Young'. If I changed my name to Bondy it would be like starting again from scratch. At a stroke, I'd lose all the brand equity I'd built up in my byline.

'You've "become known as Toby Young",' she said. 'Who to? Your cleaning lady?'[1]

I suddenly found myself in the awkward position of having to convince her I was better known than she thought, a case it's impossible

---

1 In fact, my cleaning lady thought I was called 'Terry'.

to make without sounding like a complete arse. At one point, thoroughly discombobulated, I made the mistake of claiming that 'everyone' read my *Spectator* column.

'*Everyone?*' she repeated incredulously. 'Okay, why don't we go outside right now and conduct a straw poll on the Uxbridge Road. We'll stop people at random and see whether they make a point of reading your *Spectator* column, every other week, because, let's be honest, it's not a weekly column, is it? This column of yours, for which you're world famous, apparently, is in fact a fortnightly column, isn't it?' I nodded. 'If you're under the impression that *everyone* reads it, I'm afraid you're in for quite a shock.'

At this point, watching me shrink to no more than six inches in height, Caroline must have felt a twinge of pity because she made what she thought of as a major concession. She offered to drop the 'y' from Bondy so I could become Toby Bond.

'That's quite a catchy byline, isn't it? "Toby Bond". Much better than "Toby Young", I would have thought.'

'But darling, if I change my name to Bond all my friends will think the whole thing is just an elaborate ruse so I can introduce myself to people as "Bond, Toby Bond". It'll sound like a pathetic attempt to pass myself off as a secret agent.'

'Yes,' she said. '*They* probably would think that.'

We discussed some of our other options. We could combine our names and become Mr and Mrs Young-Bond. The trouble with that, though, is we'd look like a couple of sad social climbers. I also didn't fancy introducing myself as 'Young-Bond, Toby Young-Bond', which would make me sound like James Bond's little brother – 003-and-a-half.

'Okay,' she said with an air of finality. 'You can choose whatever surname you want and I'll take it just so long as it isn't Young. There's no way I'm changing my name to yours.'

In the end, we decided to keep the names we were born with and not argue about what surname to give our children until we actually had a child.

This negotiation was fairly typical of the year and a half Caroline and I spent living together. It wasn't the bed of roses I'd anticipated. We argued constantly – and about petty things, too, like who should be in charge of the remote control. At one stage, I suggested we negotiate the domestic equivalent of the Camp David Agreement.

'Look at it this way,' I said. 'I'm prepared to cede control of a vital strategic area in return for long-term peace and security.'

She gave me a sceptical look.

'So you've cast yourself as Israel in this scenario, have you? I don't think so.'

In her eyes I was less like Menachem Begin, the tough, uncompromising ex-terrorist who represented Israel in the Camp David negotiations, than Anwar Sadat, the Egyptian President who was assassinated in 1981.

Where was Jimmy Carter when you needed him?

I consulted Sean Langan about this – after all, he'd lived with Anabel for over a year before they'd got married – and he recommended John Gray's *Men Are From Mars, Women Are From Venus*.

'In your case, though, I think you'll find it more useful if you think of Caroline as coming from Mars and you from Venus.'

A brief perusal of the book revealed that Sean was right: Caroline had many of the qualities Gray attributes to Martians – tough, efficient, ruthless – while I was more of a Venusian. Here was confirmation of something I'd long suspected, namely, that a gender role reversal had taken place in our relationship. As a freelance journalist, I stayed at home all day, while Caroline, who was at law school, left the house at 8.30 a.m. and didn't come home until 6 p.m. Being a writer, I was always looking for excuses not to work, so I was perfectly happy to spend my days doing household chores. Caroline, by contrast, couldn't even iron a pair of trousers.

'One of the biggest differences between Martians and Venusians is how they cope with stress,' Gray writes. 'Martians become increasingly focused and withdrawn while Venusians become increasingly overwhelmed and emotionally involved.'

At the end of her first year of law school, Caroline took her mid-sessional exams and became so focused and withdrawn she only emerged from her study – formerly my den – to watch *EastEnders*. I, on the other hand, was practically tearing my hair out with anxiety on her behalf. At least, I would have been if I had any hair. Baldness is one of the few Martian traits I do possess.

Caroline's not what you'd call a girly girl. At one point, we were discussing some of her 'anger-management issues' – she's a keen amateur boxer, among other things – when it occurred to her that she might actually have some male hormones floating around.

'D'you think I can do anything to reduce my levels of testosterone?' she asked.

'Well, you could try having your testicles removed,' I suggested.

She almost floored me with a right hook.

When I confessed to Sean that his analysis was essentially correct, he was delighted. It was an opportunity to get revenge for all the times I'd teased him about being under Anabel's thumb. He began referring to me as 'the mouse' and would make high-pitched squeaking noises whenever I did anything that could be construed as remotely pussy-whipped.

Take the following conversation that we had during the final stages of England's *Euro 2000* campaign:

Sean: Where are you planning to watch the game tomorrow night?

Me: What game?

Sean: *What game?!?* The final of the women's tiddlywinks championship. [Beat.] The England game, you muppet.

Me: Are England playing tomorrow night?

Sean: For fuck's sake. Where've you been? It's this little tournament we have every four years called *the European Championships*...

Me: Oh, Christ. Are we really playing tomorrow night?

Sean: Yeah. We are. My place. Seven-thirty.

Me: God, I'd love to do that, I really would, but I've promised Caroline I'll go to the theatre tomorrow night with her parents.

Beat.

Sean: Squeak, squeak, squeak, squeak.

Me: For Christ's sake. She'll kill me if I blow her out. We've been planning it for weeks.

Sean: Would it make any difference if I told you I have a large piece of cheese in my fridge?

Oddly enough, I wasn't too bothered by the fact that Caroline kept me on such a short leash. My late mother was an independent, strong-willed woman and, until I reached the age of fourteen, I was completely in thrall to my equally stubborn older sister. The upshot was that I'd never been interested in demure, submissive women. Nearly all my previous girlfriends had been ballsy and pugnacious, the kind of women who gave as good as they got, and I quickly lost interest in those that weren't. I didn't want to marry a woman I could dominate. I wanted someone who wouldn't concede an inch of ground without a fight, who would match me punch for punch.

No doubt I'd be more conventionally masculine if my father had been around more during my childhood. My parents remained happily married until the day my mother died in 1993, but my father spent so much time in the office I didn't see as much of him as I would have liked. He was a chronic workaholic. His base of operations was the Institute of Community Studies in Bethnal Green, a social research centre he set up in 1952, and he was at his desk by 9 a.m. every day and wouldn't come home until 8 p.m. He didn't go into the office at weekends, but he kept exactly the same hours in his second office at the top of the house. It's not an exaggeration to say that he worked eleven hours a day, seven days a week throughout his adult life. Indeed, on the day he died in 2002, he managed to do six hours work, firing off thank-you letters to various doctors, tidying up his affairs, reviewing the manuscript of a forthcoming book. Not bad for a man of eighty-six in the terminal stages of cancer.

It was this unforgiving regime that underpinned all my father's achievements as a left-wing intellectual. In addition to all the books and papers he published, he either set up or helped set up dozens of organisations/institutions, including the Open University, *Which?* magazine, the Consumers' Association, the Social Science Research Council, the University of the Third Age, the Open College of the Arts and the School for Social Entrepreneurs. His record of accomplishments was more like that of a radical government than one man. No disaster, however calamitous, could put him off his stride. In 1982, he was hospitalised with liver cancer, but he used the time to set up a patients' rights organisation called the College of Health. Saddled with responsibility for organising my mother's funeral in 1993, he became aware of the shortcomings of funeral directors and started the National Funerals College. As the historian Noël Annan put it: 'Whatever field he tilled he sowed dragon's teeth and armed men seemed to spring from the soil to form an organisation and correct the abuses or stimulate the virtues he had discovered.'

In the summer of 2001, on the eve of my wedding to Caroline. I worried about the effect my father's legacy might have on our marriage. Obviously, I could never hope to match his achievements, but I'd inherited something of his capacity for hard work and I was determined to harness it to my ambition for literary fame. The question was: Would Caroline tolerate me keeping my father's hours? She was only twenty-six, after all. She might not object to me working eleven-hour days during the week, but at weekends?

I'd seen at first hand just how much strain an addiction to work can place on a marriage. As far as my mother was concerned, the endless hours my father spent at the coalface posed the single greatest threat to their happiness. On more than one occasion, he left her in no doubt that he placed his work far above his family on his list of priorities. In family lore, the most famous example of this sort of behaviour was on Christmas Day in 1988. In the normal course of events, he set great store by family occasions and, in keeping with tradition, all his children had assembled for Christmas lunch, including three from a previous marriage. Much to everyone's annoyance, though, he was nowhere to be seen. He'd disappeared that morning to spend some time in a graveyard in Bethnal Green. He'd heard that in this particular cemetery lonely people gathered on Christmas morning to pay their respects to their recently departed loved ones, having no one else to spend the day with, and he wanted to talk to these people for a book he was then working on about death. By the time he got back, at about 4 p.m., the turkey had long grown cold and we were all furious. What the hell had he been doing? He waited patiently for our anger to die down and then began to tell us about the poor, grieving widows he'd seen pouring tea into the graves of their husbands so they could share one last 'Christmas cuppa'. Within a few minutes, everyone – including my mother – had burst into tears.

My mother was no pushover, but she'd been willing to tolerate this behaviour, at least to the extent of not divorcing my father. Would Caroline prove just as forgiving? It seemed extremely doubtful, not because she was tougher than my mum, but because the balance of power in British society had shifted slightly in women's favour. My parents had got married forty-one years earlier and, in 1960, my father still had the weight of five thousand years of tradition working in his favour. However much my mother chafed at the reality of the situation, my father was the dominant partner in their marriage. That simply wouldn't be true of Caroline and me. Once we tied the knot we'd be entering into an equal partnership and I wouldn't be able to absent myself from the marital home for eleven hours a day, seven days a week. The question was: would I be able to write something genuinely worthwhile if I didn't work as hard as my dad? Or would I eventually be forced to chose between my career and my marriage?

Any lingering doubts I had about getting married were completely laid to rest by my stag weekend.

I invited sixteen of my closest friends to join me for three days of debauchery in Marbella and – to my astonishment – ten of them said yes. I was expecting six at the most, but these ten insisted that nothing would prevent them from being present at this legendary occasion. They'd be there, come hell or high water.

Four turned up.

The excuses the no-shows came up with were breathtaking in their feebleness. My oldest friend, a man I've known since I was fifteen, got his secretary to call me on Friday morning to tell me he had a sore throat. Another man called on Saturday afternoon claiming to be stranded at Madrid Airport, having missed his connection.

'Why don't you jump in a car?' I said. 'It shouldn't take more than four and a half hours.'

'That long, eh?' he replied. 'It doesn't look like I'm going to make it then. Sorry.'

At least these men called to explain their absence. Another friend, a man I'd known for fourteen years and whose stag weekend I flew to Barcelona to attend, didn't even bother to notify me he wasn't coming. Cheers, mate.

Needless to say, the party of four did not include either of the two Seans, who were dividing the best-man duties between them, or any members of Caroline's family. True, a fifth man showed up on Saturday afternoon, which was lucky because he was supposed to be organising a tour of Marbella's fleshpots that evening, but he got sidetracked when he spotted an ex-Page Three girl across a crowded restaurant.

'You don't mind if I leave you here, do you?' he said, eyeing her distractedly.

'Actually, I'd prefer it if you didn't.'

'Great. I'll see you back at the villa then.'

The comic highpoint occurred on Sunday morning when I'd arranged to go diving with all ten of the people who'd told me they were 100 per cent certain they'd make it – 'You can take that to the bank, Tobe,' as Sean Langan put it. In the event, only two people elected to come on this trip and one of them had a panic attack in the shallow end of the swimming pool during the training session. By the time the little boat set out into the Mediterranean for what had been billed as 'the adventure of a lifetime' it was only me and one other guy and, after a cursory inspection of the waves, the driving instructor concluded it was too rough to dive. Still, all was not lost. The instructor agreed to refund part of the cost, which was a relief because the total cost of the diving trip, including the booking fee, was over £500. The refund was £16.

As a stag weekend, it was an unqualified disaster – but, in a sense, it was ideal because it was a snapshot of what my life would be like if I wasn't getting married. In my twenties I didn't think I'd ever need to start a family of my own since I could depend so completely on my close male friends. We thought of ourselves as being like the mafia – loyal to the death. But as the years passed it gradually dawned on me that this was a sophomoric male fantasy born of watching *The Godfather* too many times. Far from being a completely dependable group of soldiers, most of my mates turned out to be a bunch of unreliable bastards. The Thousandth Man? *Fuggedaboudit.* It was time for me to turn my back on 'the family', throw in my lot with my very own Attorney General and enter the civilian equivalent of the Witness Protection Programme.

Caroline and I were married on 21 July 2001. It was a very traditional wedding: the official photographer got off his face on champagne, the chief bridesmaid ended up snogging a bloke called Pete and the bride got so pissed that the groom had no choice about whether to carry her over the threshold of their honeymoon suite. If I could go back and get married all over again I wouldn't change a thing – except, perhaps, the best-man speeches.

Sean Macaulay set the tone, describing me as 'the Jeffrey Archer of weddings'.

'Pretty much every wedding Toby goes to he makes a best-man speech of which the utter social embarrassment, the acute humiliation and the legacy of marital discord he creates is tremendous. As the best man at my wedding, he humiliated me and embarrassed himself – he took everyone down with him, basically – but, to be fair, he didn't make any embarrassing revelations about my private life. He could have stuck the knife in and he didn't. [Beat.] I want to reverse that tradition this evening.'

He proceeded to tell the stories of our abortive trip to the most highly rated legal brothel in Nevada (it was closed for refurbishment), our holiday together on the Costa del Sol during which I'd paraded around the beach in a pair of see-through, white bikini briefs ('I think they were from the clingfilm company, not Speedo') and our trip to Budapest in which I was blown out by every single member of the national Hungarian volleyball team.

'There are many other stories I could tell, but of course most of them have appeared in *How to Lose Friends & Alienate People*. When Toby arrived in New York in 1995 the working title of that book was *New York: My Kind of Town*. One year later there was a new title: *Failure: It's Your Friend*.'

Sean Langan's speech was hardly any more forgiving. He pointed out that I'd caused so much ill will among his German in-laws that the only way he'd be able to restore his reputation would be to change his name to Gunter.

Still, as with Macaulay, his guns had been spiked by the fact that I'd already recounted all the most humiliating episodes in my life in print.

'How can I embarrass a man whose cannon of work includes such masterpieces as "My Life as a Bald William Hague Lookalike", "My Drug-Fuelled Life as a Skoda-Driving William Hague Lookalike" and his next piece, which he's just been typing outside, "My Wife and Her Life With a William Hague Lookalike"?'

I decided not to tell him that I'd already done a deal whereby if *Hello!* published a photograph of Caroline and me leaving the church in a Skoda I'd receive a 15 per cent discount on a new car.

PART TWO

LOSING MORE FRIENDS AND ALIENATING MORE PEOPLE

6

DON'T SAY YES UNTIL I FINISH TALKING

'D'you realise where we're sitting?' asked Mr Hollywood. 'This is the place – and I mean the exact same spot – where Darryl Zanuck, Franklin Schaffner and Francis Coppola came up with the idea for *Patton*.'

This was in the summer of 2002 at our first meeting together. Moments earlier, I'd rendezvoused with him in the lobby of the Hotel du Cap and he'd led me down to this little hideaway just above the beach, a place he identified as 'Sam Spiegel's cabana'. He was wearing a light-blue, short-sleeved shirt, some Hawaiian swimming shorts and a pair of bright-red corduroy slippers.

We were supposed to be discussing the picture he wanted me to write about the seventies record producer, but we were still at the throat-clearing stage. Or, at least, he was. I'd taken the precaution of re-reading *Adventures in the Screen Trade*, William Goldman's classic account of the writer's lot in Hollywood, the previous night. 'There is one crucial rule that must be followed in all creative meetings,' writes Goldman in chapter two. 'Never speak first. At least at the start, your job is to shut up.'

This strategy seemed to be paying off. I was amazed by how candid _____ was being. It had begun to dawn on me that I could ask him anything I liked about Hollywood – literally *anything*. In this respect, he was totally unlike anyone connected with the business I'd met before. Normally, people in Hollywood are so close-lipped that if you ask them what the time is they have to check with their attorneys before answering. Not this guy. He was fantastically indiscreet, the Hedda Hopper of the Hotel du Cap. I couldn't believe the stuff he was coming out with. It was the kind of encounter that people like me – obsessed with Hollywood tittle-tattle – dream about.

I'll give just one example here, because if I was to repeat anything else he told me I would almost certainly be sued. At the time of our meeting, *Vanity Fair* had just published its notorious interview with Mike Ovitz in which the former Hollywood agent blamed 'the gay mafia' for sabotaging his career. My question was: why did Mike Ovitz choose *Vanity Fair*, of all places, in which to launch an attack on the gay mafia? That was a bit like choosing *Pravda* to launch an attack on the Communist Party. Was Ovitz having a 'psychotic episode', as *Daily Variety* claimed?

'Mike Ovitz isn't psychotic,' explained _____. 'He's just dumb. There's no other word for it – he's just really, really dumb. People in Hollywood are either smart or dumb – that's it. Those are the only two categories. No one's really crazy. They're just smart or dumb. And Mike Ovitz is dumb.'

He went on in a similar vein, patiently answering all my queries, for what seemed like hours. Why was he being so generous with his time? I'd heard the old Hollywood adage that the first meeting is always the best – after that it's all down hill, supposedly – but this exceeded my wildest expectations. It was like meeting God: I was in a position to unlock all the secrets of the universe. All I had to do was come up with the right questions.

Was it because he was bored? He'd just embarked on what was supposed to be a one-month holiday on the Côte d'Azure – something he'd been promising himself for years – and he was already climbing the walls. On one of the tables in the cabana was a pile of

well-thumbed copies of *Daily Variety* and the *Hollywood Reporter* –
he was having his office back in Los Angeles FedEx them to him
every day – and next to them was a huge pile of scripts. He'd obviously got through all these and was now looking for something else
to occupy his time. (He'd had enough activity. He wanted action.)

Another possibility was that he simply loved to 'rap', as his assistant put it. Stories came tumbling out of his mouth like Chinese
acrobats. Indeed, in order to tell one story he'd have to pause
midway through and tell you another, just so you could fully appreciate the first. Often, it would take him half an hour to get through
a single anecdote, by which time you would have learnt some of
Tinseltown's darkest secrets.

For instance, I asked him about a rumour that was then doing
the rounds about the recent miscarriage of an A-list actress. Was it
true that the baby she'd been carrying wasn't her husband's? In order
to answer this question he had to embark on a detour that involved
a studio head, a pregnant mistress, a muck-raking tabloid hack, a
former LAPD detective and an unsolved murder. In my mind's eye,
I'd pictured Mr Hollywood as this cigar-chomping vulgarian who
was only interested in the bottom line. But he was more like a cross
between Kenneth Anger and James Elroy.

'By the way,' he said. 'If you write about any of this I will personally cut your head off.'

*'He will, too,' said Rob Long. 'Believe me, he's not someone you want to
fuck with.'*

*According to Rob, it wasn't simply inadvisable to write about my
encounter with Mr Hollywood; if I was going to repeat any of the stories he'd just told me I should avoid attributing them to him.*

*'The entertainment industry may seem like this huge global power
structure to you, but in fact it's just a village – a very small village.
Everybody knows everybody. And if you relay a piece of gossip and
attribute it to a particular person, it will get back to that person 100
per cent of the time. Mark my words, if you repeat any of the things*

_____ *said to you, and you attribute them to him, you'll get a call from* *him in less than twenty-four hours. And that is not a call you wanna* *get, my friend.'*

'What if I write about him in a way that makes it absolutely impos- *sible for anyone to identify him?'*

'What, are you kidding? Everyone in this town will know exactly *who you're talking about by the end of the first graph.'*

Beat.

'Well, I do have one thing going for me.'

'What's that?'

'No one will believe that the great _____ _____ actually called an *idiot like me and then flew me to the south of France and asked me to* *write a picture for him.'*

Beat.

'Yeah,' said Rob. 'I guess that's true.'

Twenty-four hours earlier I'd almost blown this opportunity. Mr Hollywood had bought me a first-class return ticket and it was scheduled to depart at 3.25 p.m. I didn't want to miss it because he'd arranged for his driver to pick me up at Nice Airport and take me straight to a three-star Michelin restaurant. The plan was to have a getting-to-know-each-other session over dinner before meeting again the following day to discuss the picture. He was putting me up for the night at the Hotel Belles Rives. Okay, it wasn't the Hotel du Cap, but it was still pretty swanky. According to legend, it's where F. Scott Fitzgerald wrote *Tender is the Night.* Unfortunately, when I got to Heathrow I discovered I'd forgotten my passport.

'I've got a Blockbuster Video card,' I told the woman at the British Airways check-in desk, tipping the contents of my wallet on to the counter. 'Will that do?'

'I'm sorry, sir, without a passport we can't allow you on the flight.'

'But this is France we're talking about, not North Korea. The chances of me being asked to show a passport at the airport are vanishing-to-zero.'

'Company policy I'm afraid, sir.'

'But I'm supposed to be meeting _____ _____. He's, like, one of the biggest producers in Hollywood. I'll probably never get another chance like this again.'

'In that case, sir, you should have remembered your passport.'

I called Rob from the taxi as I was racing back to my flat in Shepherd's Bush. (I'd calculated that if I was lucky with the traffic I might just be able to make the next flight.) What on earth was I going to say to Mr Hollywood?

'Automobile accident,' said Rob.

'Sorry?'

'Tell him you got in an accident.'

'But I can't say that. It would be a barefaced lie.'

'Okay, tell him you forgot your passport. But do me a favour. Call me straight back after you've spoken to him. I wanna know what he says.'

'No, no bones broken, but I'm a bit shaken up,' I told Mr Hollywood. 'My car's a total write-off.'

There was a pause on the other end of the line as he digested this information.

'So how come you didn't call me about this earlier?'

'Oh, it's only just happened. I'm phoning you from the scene of the accident.'

'I see. [Beat.] So, d'you wanna call the whole thing off?'

'Oh, God no, absolutely not. Why don't I just catch a later flight and we can meet up tomorrow?'

'But don't you have to, you know, wait by your vehicle? I mean, you can't just leave it in the middle of the street, can you?'

'Oh, it's still drivable. Heathrow's only a mile up the road.'

'I thought you said it was a write-off?'

'Er, yes, well, that's what I'll tell the insurance company, obviously, but, er, you know, it still works. Just.'

'I don't understand. If you can still drive it why did you get out of the car to make this call? Why didn't you just carry on driving and catch your flight? [Beat.] Hello? Toby? Are you there?'

Shit, fuck, bollocks.

'You're breaking up, I'm afraid. I'll call you when I get to the airport.'

Missing my original flight turned out to be a blessing in disguise. It meant that by the time I actually met Mr Hollywood the following day I'd been thoroughly coached by Rob in the art of landing a movie deal.

'It's a lot like dating,' he said. 'If he gets a whiff of just how desperate you are, you're not even gonna get to first base. You have to play hard to get.'

'But won't that be a bit implausible? I mean, in dating terms, he's a supermodel and I'm a thirty-eight-year-old virgin. He's just not going to believe it if I pretend I don't want to get into bed with him.'

'You can't think like that. You have to make out that you're like this really distinguished author who wouldn't normally soil his hands by breaking bread with a scumbag like him. You have to make him think he's seducing you.'

'But he's read my book.'

'So what? What's in the book is less important than the fact that you've actually written a book. You're a published author, for Chrissakes. To this guy, that's impressive. What you have to understand is that everyone in Hollywood, no matter how successful, has a massive inferiority complex. He may be a billionaire movie producer, but underneath he's still just this overweight Jewish guy from Queens. He probably never even went to college. You went to Oxford, for Chrissakes. As far as he's concerned, you're Anthony Powell.'

It wasn't until the late afternoon that we finally got round to talking business.

'So, I guess we ought to discuss this movie project,' said Mr Hollywood. 'Have you ever thought about turning your hand to screenwriting?'

'Whatever it is, I'll do it.'

He narrowed his eyes.

'Do me a favour. Don't say yes until I finish talking.'

Oh, God. What had I said?

Suddenly, he broke into a huge grin.

'Don't you recognise the line? It's the title of Darryl Zanuck's biography.'

'What is?'

'*Don't Say Yes Until I Finish Talking.*'

Beat.

'Oh, yes. Of course. *Duh!* Very good book. One of the classics.'

'Okay, now listen.'

Once again, he was off. He told me the life story of the seventies record producer, from his humble beginnings in Brooklyn to his coronation as 'the king of Studio 54', ending with his death from a drug overdose in a Las Vegas hotel room. No detail was considered too trivial to include. Mr Hollywood had an encyclopedic memory, placing great libraries of information at his fingertips, and it was almost as if the communicating part of his brain was at war with the archival part. He wanted to get to the end of the story, but he was incapable of leaving anything out. As each new vaguely relevant bit of information presented itself to the front of his mind he'd have to impart it before continuing. The upshot was that he spoke incredibly quickly, racing towards the end of each digression so he could return to the main narrative, only to get sidetracked again and again. Yet this was no ordinary case of attention deficit disorder; his powers of concentration were formidable. The simple process of getting through a story from beginning to end seemed to involve a gargantuan effort of will, as though he had to fight his way through all the clutter, with his whole body caught up in the battle.

For all his long-windedness, though, he was never boring. His inability to stick to the point made him seem more like an overexcited schoolboy than an easily distracted grown-up. He was extremely enthusiastic about everything he was telling me and it was this enthusiasm, above all, that he wanted to communicate. At each stage in the record producer's life story he would paint these vivid portraits in the air, trying to get across exactly why it was he found him so fascinating: 'Here's this young Jewish guy, full of hope, full of energy, really, really smart, but the most self-destructive guy in the world, I mean, like you wouldn't believe.'

Naturally, I tossed out a few ideas about how to transform this welter of information into a coherent narrative – 'Why not turn it into a musical?' – but he was surprisingly non-committal in his responses. It was as if he was saying, 'Hey, you're the writer. I'm only the producer.' But at the same time he left me in no doubt that if he did end up hiring me it would be to write a commercial picture, not some arty-farty independent rubbish. 'I'm in the business of making hits,' he said. 'I wanna make movies that 18–35-year-old young men are gonna wanna see. Of course, I'm not in that age range myself, but as far as I'm concerned, I'm still eighteen.'

When I repeated all this to Rob, he immediately launched into a note-perfect impression of Mr Hollywood: 'I'm in the business of making hits. I wanna make movies that 18–35-year-old young men are gonna wanna see . . .'

'Wow,' I said. 'That's uncanny. I thought you said you'd never met him?'

'I haven't,' said Rob. 'But they're all the same, these guys. The factory default settings never change.'

At the conclusion of the meeting, by which time he'd effectively hired me to write the picture, Mr Hollywood told me he wanted to show me something. He reached over to the pile of newspapers beside him and fished out a copy of *WWD*, the daily trade paper of the New York fashion industry.

'Check out the headline,' he said, flipping it open to an inside page.

'"Calvin Klein to Open New Flagship Store on Madison Avenue",' I read.

'Not that one,' he said, indicating a headline lower down the page. '*That* one.'

It was above an account of the New York launch party of *How to Lose Friends & Alienate People* that had taken place a week earlier.

'What d'you think of that?' he said.

I was still staring at the page, scarcely able to believe it.

'I've been waiting for that headline all my life,' I said.

There, in black and white, were the words 'Toby Takes Manhattan'.

7

PUBLISH AND BE DAMNED

In the autumn of 2001, when *How to Lose Friends* was first published in the UK, such headlines were a distant dream. The manuscript had originally been rejected by over a dozen British publishers and even though it was eventually bought by Little, Brown they clearly didn't have very high hopes for it. It was being issued as a 'paperback original' – the publishing equivalent of straight-to-video – and they weren't planning to take out a single ad to promote it. This isn't particularly unusual. The policy of most publishers is to throw dozens of books at the wall every year and hope that a couple of them will stick.

At least I'd actually got a publisher in the UK. I was initially quite optimistic about the prospects of an American sale – the book was about the five years I'd spent in New York, after all – but it had been rejected across the board. I suggested to my agent that she try and interest American publishers in the idea of a 'heroic failure': I might not have succeeded in 'taking' Manhattan, but that said as much about the hidebound, politically correct atmosphere of contemporary America as it did about me. Unfortunately, this was a concept they couldn't get their heads around. 'There's only one kind of loser in the

United States,' one publisher told her, 'and that's the big fat kind.'

The fact that I'd only been able to sell the book in one territory – and for a pretty modest sum at that – was a source of some concern because there was a chance it could wreck my career. How would Graydon Carter, the editor-in-chief of *Vanity Fair*, react? To paraphrase Mike Ovitz, would he get his foot soldiers who go up and down Madison Avenue each day to blow my brains out? While I was working at the magazine, he'd never actually hauled me into his office and said, 'If you write about any of this you'll never eat lunch in this town again', but that was mainly because I'd never got to the expense account lunch stage. If he'd wanted to deliver that threat he would have had to say, 'If you write about this you'll never eat a brown-bag lunch in your cubicle in the unfashionable part of the office ever again.' It doesn't have quite the same ring to it.

Perhaps he didn't feel the need to say anything. Condé Nast, the magazine stable of which *Vanity Fair* is a part, has a mafia-like aura that deters all but the most foolhardy of journalists from writing about it. Carol Felsenthal is a case in point. In the mid-nineties she agreed to write a biography of Si Newhouse, the owner of Condé Nast, for one of the major New York publishing houses. Felsenthal's manuscript was initially accepted, but just before publication a senior editor at the company cancelled the book, claiming it would jeopardise too many of her personal and professional relationships. Luckily, Felsenthal managed to persuade a small independent house to pick it up – Seven Stories Press – but her problems didn't end there. Not a single one of the twenty-six city papers owned by the Newhouse family reviewed *Citizen Newhouse: Portrait of a Media Merchant* and the book received a drubbing in the mighty *New York Times Book Review* from the dean of the Columbia Journalism School who described it as 'a rather dull hatchet job'. This effectively killed its prospects stone dead. Felsenthal speculates that the review was influenced by the fact that the Columbia Journalism School received a $70,000 donation from the Newhouse

Foundation in 1989 and two donations of $30,000 in 1996 and 1997.

On 15 August 2001, ten weeks before my book was due to be published in Britain, I received a call from Graydon's assistant asking me to email over those passages that mentioned him. I was reluctant to comply because I didn't want to get into a quarrel with Graydon about the book's contents, but there was no point in refusing because he could easily have obtained a copy of the manuscript from somewhere else, given his publishing connections.

After some hesitation, I decided to email him the entire book, accompanied by an explanatory note:

> Obviously, what you'll think of the book was a big question for me when I was writing it. In the end, I thought the best policy was to simply write the truth as I saw it, without any regard to how you or anyone else will react. This meant including stuff you'll no doubt object to, but it also meant including nice things without caring whether others will think I've just stuck them in in order to remain on your good side. Everyone who's read it agrees that the portrait of you that emerges is fundamentally affectionate. I hope you'll see it that way too. That's certainly the way I feel.

Two weeks later, I got an email from Graydon asking if it was too late to make any 'corrections'. I could hear the unmistakable sound of a can of worms being opened, but I also felt an obligation to hear him out. After all, he'd been a pretty generous employer for the best part of three years. So I asked him what he had in mind. I imagined that he would want to address my argument in chapter fifteen ('The 600lb Gorilla') that he had crossed over to the dark side since his days as the co-editor of *Spy*.

In fact, he was less concerned with the charge that he'd sold out and more interested in stressing just how high a price Si Newhouse had paid. I received a lengthy email back containing twenty-four corrections, of which the following – number two – was fairly typical: 'Not to be unduly picky, but on page 38, you state that Art Cooper's office was bigger than mine. I never took a tape measure to Art's office, but it was generally acknowledged within the building that I had the largest of any editor's office.'

The passage he was most exercised about was one in which I summarised a profile of him that had appeared in *New York* magazine claiming he'd fabricated a number of items in his CV, including the fact that he'd graduated from Carleton University and worked as a speechwriter for Pierre Trudeau. He thought it unfair and embarrasing to bring up those 'bogus allegations'. 'Lose that section and I'll help plug your book in any way I can,' he wrote. 'I might even throw you a book party.'

Tempting though this was, I was a bit reluctant to censor myself. (Maybe if he'd offered to hold the party in his football stadium of an office . . .) In the end, I left the passage in, but added a sentence pointing out that Graydon vehemently denied the allegations. Needless to say, he did not throw me a party and, to this day, the book has never been mentioned in the pages of *Vanity Fair*.

How to Lose Friends was not intended as an act of revenge on my ex-employer. If anything, it was an attempt to show him what I could do. My biggest regret about working for *Vanity Fair* was that Graydon had never published a longform article by me. Having only been used to write glorified photo captions, I wanted to demonstrate that I was capable of sustaining a narrative for longer than two hundred words. I wasn't naive enough to think that Graydon would read the book and offer me my old job back – I knew that by writing the book I was burning my bridges with the magazine – but I hoped he might regret not having put me to better use at the time.

Writing *How to Lose Friends* was easily the most fulfilling thing I'd done in my professional career at this point. I wasn't under any illusions about whether it would be read in a hundred years' time, but after fifteen years of writing newspaper articles it was refreshing to write something that was intended to have a shelf life of more than twenty-four hours. With a hundred thousand words at my disposal, as opposed to the usual eight hundred, I could do things like introduce characters, develop an argument and switch back and forth between different types of writing. As a journalist, the style in which you write is largely dictated by whatever genre your article falls into – the profile, the colour piece, the news feature, etc. – and you're discouraged from practising more than one type of journalism at a time. For instance, if you're writing an op-ed piece, you're not supposed to make jokes and if you're producing a piece of reportage you're expected to be objective and impersonal. But when it comes to a book, you're almost required to chop and change. In the course of writing the five-thousand-word 'Prologue' of *How to Lose Friends* I was able to combine reportage and personal anecdote, commentary and humour, in a kind of journalistic stew. I might not have done it very well, but just being able to do it at all was liberating.

Another of the reasons I found writing *How to Lose Friends* so satisfying was because it proved so difficult. Writing a book is a bit like building a house from the ground up. The hardest thing isn't the physical act of writing it or even the business of mapping out its structure beforehand, difficult though they are. Rather, it's trying to work out the elementary principles of storytelling. Hemingway said that writing is architecture, not interior decorating, and my problem was that I had to learn how to design houses in general before I could start work on my particular house. I had to teach myself the rudiments of architecture before I could get going.

Needless to say, there were lots of false starts. My first idea was to write a business book about Condé Nast. In fact, this wasn't my idea at all, but that of Morgan Entrekin, the president and publisher of Grove/Atlantic whom I happened to be seated next to on a flight to Kenya in 1999. (We were both going to the wedding of my friend Aidan Hartley.) I told him about my experiences at *Vanity Fair* and he said he might be interested in publishing a corporate history of Condé Nast. I started trying to map this out, but quickly decided that it would be more interesting to write a sociological analysis of the company, rather than a straightforward biography. In particular, I wanted to explore the issue of how the Zeitgeist was captured, bottled and sold in the glossy magazine business. However, when I started to jot down my thoughts I found it virtually impossible to express myself without referring to my own experiences as a Condé Nast employee – and as soon as I did this the book metamorphosed into something else. It became pretty clear that the book I really wanted to write was a humorous account of my disastrous career as a New York, glossy magazine journalist, but I resisted this because it seemed like such a non-starter from a commercial point of view. Who would be interested in the autobiography of a failure? It would be less like a how-to book than a how-not-to book, a hitherto non-existent genre. Other titles I considered included *The Power of Negative Thinking* and *Awaken the Dwarf Within*.

After wrestling with this problem for several months, I decided that since 99 per cent of books sink without a trace, I might as well have fun writing it. This isn't false modesty. A friend of mine who's been covering the American book trade in *Newsweek* for almost twenty years told me that the number of Americans who actually make a living from writing proper books, as opposed to text-books and so forth, is in 'the low 200s'. Quite sobering when you consider that an average of sixty thousand books are published in the States every year. Given these appalling odds, I reasoned that it was pointless to try and second-guess the market and try and write a 'commercial' book. At least if I wrote the kind of book I wanted to write and that failed I could console myself with the thought that I'd refused to compromise – and success, if it came, would be that much sweeter.

I was surprised by how time-consuming the actual business of writing a book turned out to be. Not having a deadline meant I could linger for as long as I liked on a particular passage, rewriting it and rewriting it until I completely lost sight of what worked and what didn't. I can't remember who said that books are never finished, they're just wrenched from their authors' hands, but that was definitely true of me. For almost a year, I sat in my Shepherd's Bush bedsit, burning the midnight oil, labouring over the manuscript. It was tough on Caroline – and not just because all my spare time was taken up with *How to Lose Friends*. In addition, all the hours I spent with her were devoted to the book, too. I was permanently distracted, always staring off into space, worrying away at some particular passage. After a few months of this, she told me she'd given up asking me what I was thinking about because the answer was always the same. For her, it was a glimpse of what it would be like being married to a writer – and I'm not sure she liked what she saw.

Initially, my attempts to promote *How to Lose Friends* in Britain didn't fare very well. I thought my best bet would be to appear on the *Graham Norton Show*, a popular Channel 4 programme at the time. Back in 1994, when I was editing a magazine I'd founded called *The Modern Review*, I hired Norton, who was then a jobbing stand-up comic, to perform at an event I was hosting at the Institute of Contemporary Arts. He got a bit of publicity as a result and I'd always told myself that I'd played a small part in launching his career. It was time to call in the favour.

I phoned the show and got put straight through to Tony Jordan, the celebrity booker. He paused for a few seconds after I explained who I was, clearly not used to people calling up and suggesting themselves as guests.

Tony: So, do you actually know Graham, Toby?

Me: Well, that depends on your definition of 'know'.

Tony: Put it this way, if I mention your name, will he know who you are?

Me: Er, well, er—

Tony: I see. [Beat.] Tell me, Toby, have you ever watched the *Graham Norton Show*?

Me: Oh, God yes. I watch it all the time. I'm a huge fan.

Tony: In that case, you should be aware that we only have HOUSEHOLD NAMES on the show.

Me: Oh, yes, I appreciate that, but—

Tony: Please don't call again.

Click. Dial-tone.

Little, Brown's director of publicity was a no-nonsense Scotswoman called Alison Menzies and when I told her about this exchange she was horrified. ('For heaven's sake, yer silly wee man, leave it to the professionals in future.') She explained that, with a couple of exceptions, radio is a much more effective medium for promoting books than television. If you can get your book selected for *Book of the Week* on Radio 4, for instance, it stands a good chance of becoming a bestseller. Unfortunately, that was aiming a little high for *How to Lose Friends*, but she did manage to secure me a slot on *The Fred McCauley Show*, a regional programme that went out on BBC Radio Scotland.

I appeared in the studio at the appointed hour, where I was booked in to talk about 'the art of the snub'. At least, I thought I was. What I hadn't bargained for was that the man on before me was Alan Dedicoat, a BBC announcer known as 'the voice of the balls'. His main claim to fame, I discovered, is that he calls out the winning numbers on the BBC's *National Lottery Show*. Fred McCauley found this man's tales of backstage shenanigans so rib-ticklingly funny that by the time he remembered I was waiting in the wings he had run out of time.

'So, Toby, you have exactly ten seconds to tell us about the art of the snub.'

'Er—'

'That's all we've got time for, I'm afraid. Join us at the same time tomorrow where we'll be spending a whole hour talking to Sada Walkington, the first ever contestant to be eliminated from *Big Brother*.'

Luckily, the next slot Alison secured for me was on *Broadcasting House*, the prestigious Radio 4 Sunday-morning show. At first, I was a little anxious because the date of my appearance coincided with a trip that Caroline and I were making to Wales, but Alison assured me that I didn't need to change my plans. I could simply pop into the BBC Radio Wales studio in Bangor and the station manager would connect me to London.

'Don't worry, Toby,' said Alison. 'You won't be competing with "the voice of the balls" this time.'

I was due to be at the studio at 8.30 a.m. and when I still hadn't found it by 8.25 a.m. I decided to call the station manager.

'I'm not sure I'm even in Bangor,' I told her. 'I'm looking at a road sign that says "Gorsaf Station". I think I must be in a town called Gorsaf.'

'Oh, no, Mr Young,' she said. 'All road signs in Wales are in Welsh and English. *Gorsaf* is just the Welsh word for station. You're in the right place. Stay where you are and I'll come and fetch you.'

During the broadcast I decided to tell this story, pointing out how absurd it was that all road signs in Wales had to be in Welsh *and* English. After all, the percentage of the population that actually speaks Welsh is tiny.

In retrospect, this wasn't a very wise move.

After I'd finished, the station manager came into the studio with a very grave expression on her face.

'I'm afraid I've got some bad news, Mr Young. One of our listeners has taken rather an exception to your remarks about the Welsh language and he's come down to the studio to 'ave it out with you, like. He's waiting in reception right now.'

'In that case, I think you'd better show me out the back way.'

'Oh, no, there is no back way, Mr Young. It looks as though you're going to 'ave to face the music, I'm afraid.'

I cracked open the door to see what fate awaited me. There, standing in the centre of the room, was a red-faced troll who was so steamed up he practically had smoke coming out of his ears. I counted to three and took the plunge.

'How dare you?' he said, grabbing me by the lapels. 'How bloody dare you? You come to our country – *our* country, mind you – and you have the audacity to tell us we shouldn't be speaking our own bloody language. You arrogant, carpet-bagging, southern bastard.'

It took me forty-five minutes to manoeuvre my way past him.

'Turn on the telly.'

The caller was Sean Langan and the date was 11 September 2001. I did as instructed and a few seconds later I was back on the phone, this time frantically trying to reach Cromwell Coulson, my closest friend in New York, whose office was only two blocks from the World Trade Center. After a very tense couple of hours, in which I watched first the South Tower and then the North Tower collapse, he managed to email me to tell me he was okay. He was out on the street, a few yards from the buildings, when the first plane hit. Instead of standing there, mesmerised with horror, as so many others did, he leapt in a taxi and headed uptown as fast as he could.

Every writer's biggest fear is that their book's appearance will be completely overshadowed by a great and unexpected historical event. James Joyce, for instance, was convinced that the assassination of Archduke Ferdinand was part of a conspiracy to distract the world's attention from the masterpiece he was then composing. My attitude to 9/11 wasn't quite so egocentric, but the fact that my book was about to be published certainly gave me pause for thought.

Should I postpone it until a later date?

The media became so alert to any signs of 'insensitivity' in the immediate aftermath of the attack that even to discuss such matters was taboo. For instance, Jay McInerney got into terrible trouble for reporting a conversation he'd had with Bret Easton Ellis on the day of the disaster in which they both expressed relief that they didn't have a book coming out that month. This was in spite of the fact that in the offending article – which appeared in the *Observer* – McInerney bent over backwards to appear contrite, acknowledging that his and Bret's exchange was 'a selfish and trivial response'.

Suddenly, it became deeply unfashionable to be superficial. The general attitude in the media on both sides of the Atlantic was reminiscent of the response to the Kennedy assassination forty years earlier, an event that prompted one newspaper columnist to claim that people would 'never laugh again'. Peter Kaplan, the editor of the *New York Observer*, announced that the days of 'celebrity voyeurism' were over. 'Chowing down on the shallowness of an affluent culture is going to be gone,' he said. 'It's just no longer funny.' Even Graydon felt it necessary to embrace this new earnestness. 'There's going to be a seismic change,' he said. 'I think it's the end of the age of irony.'

If *Vanity Fair* had become *Planetary Care*, where did that leave my gossipy account of working for the magazine?

At the very least, the cover would have to be redesigned. At my suggestion, Little, Brown had commissioned a graphic artist to depict a man falling through the air with the New York skyline beneath him. It was supposed to look as if he was about to be impaled on the spire of the Chrysler Building, but given that more than two hundred people had actually jumped from the burning towers after the planes had struck, that now looked in very poor taste.

More significantly, the whole tenor of the book seemed wrong. I had portrayed New Yorkers as these shallow, narcissistic creatures, primarily interested in advertising their own importance. But given their heroic response to the disaster, such views were tantamount to heresy. Ian Fleming once described New York as a city without a soul, but after the events of 11 September that was demonstrably false. The Big Apple had a core after all.

Then, just before the book was about to be published, I had a stroke of luck: I was expelled from the Groucho Club.

Under normal circumstances this wouldn't have been at all welcome. I'd been a member of the media watering hole since 1984 and still went there quite regularly. But the exact circumstances of my expulsion conspired to produce a blaze of publicity for *How to Lose Friends.*

My crime was to include a passage in the book about a cocaine-taking incident at the club involving Damien Hirst. (This was during a photo shoot for the *Vanity Fair* 'Cool Britannia' issue in 1996.) It hadn't occurred to me that the club would mind if I wrote about this. After all, it's hardly a state secret that people occasionally take cocaine at the Groucho. Indeed, if a bio-terrorist sent a suspicious-looking envelope full of white powder to 45 Dean Street it would be up somebody's nose within thirty seconds.

It wasn't as if I was snitching on Damien Hirst, either. He'd talked openly about his cocaine-fuelled nights at the Groucho in *On the Way to Work*, a collection of interviews with the artist. Far from damaging his reputation, I would have done Hirst far more harm if I'd revealed that he was a clean-living family man.

However, I hadn't reckoned on Matthew Freud, the PR guru who had bought the club earlier that year. According to a source on the membership committee, he was absolutely determined to throw me out once he learnt of the revelations in my book.

Freud's unforgiving attitude might have been because he was arrested for possession of cocaine when he was seventeen and wanted to send a message to his business partners that he was now squeaky clean. His PR company, Freud Communications, numbers several big American corporations among its clients and Matthew may have wanted to reassure them that he wasn't going to be soft on drugs at his newly acquired club.

Whatever the explanation, Freud's overreaction turned out to be a blessing in disguise. The previous week, Scotland Yard had announced it was going to clamp down on middle-class cocaine users and, as someone who'd just been banned from the Groucho Club for cocaine-related reasons, I was suddenly deluged with interview requests from radio and television producers. Here, at last, was the opportunity to publicise my book I'd been waiting for. Within seven days of the story breaking, I'd appeared on over a dozen television and radio programmes to talk about 'London's cocaine epidemic'.

I was so intent on promoting the book I didn't stop to think about the possibility that the police might take an interest in my activities. The general rule about publicity is that you're supposed to weigh it rather than read it, but what if it weighs a gram and costs £60? If Scotland Yard wanted to make an example of me, they wouldn't have to search very hard for evidence. It was right there in black and white between the covers of my book.

Needless to say, Caroline was none too pleased about the fact that I was rapidly becoming London Medialand's Mr Cocaine. Not only was she concerned about how her parents would react, she also thought it was symptomatic of my excessive interest in publicity, a facet of my character she found deeply unattractive. 'You've turned into Jordan,' she told me after I'd just appeared on the *Six O'Clock News* to discuss the latest Home Office statistics about cocaine-related deaths. 'Is there nothing you won't stoop to?'

The reviews of my book weren't kind.

'Toby Young is a balding, bug-eyed opportunist with the looks of a punctured beach-ball, the charisma of a glove-puppet and an ego the size of a Hercules supply plane,' wrote Lloyd Evans in the *Daily Mail*. 'And I speak as a friend.'

'It ought to be funny, but I felt I'd read it all before, and if I hadn't I didn't care,' drawled the *Daily Telegraph*.

'A big lint-picking session,' sniffed the *Guardian*.

Naturally, I was a bit upset about this – *Was it really that bad?* – but Alison Menzies assured me that, from a purely commercial point of view, negative reviews aren't the end of the world. Indeed, a hatchet job is better than a more balanced review, apparently, since it means the book is more likely to stick in the reader's mind. The theory is that when that same reader is next in a bookshop and sees your title on the shelf he or she will remember it without remembering the bad review and – hopefully – march it on over to the checkout.

I thought Alison was just trying to sugar the pill, but the sales figures for *How to Lose Friends* bore her out. In its first week of publication it sold 7300 copies, enough to propel it to number sixteen on the original paperback non-fiction bestseller list. Against all odds, it began to look as though my book might do quite well.

8

EUNUCH AT A BROTHEL

'Toebehhhh.'

The man on the other end of the phone was Boris Johnson, then the editor of the *Spectator*. Ever since I'd known him, this was his standard greeting. He'd make it stretch for several seconds, delivered in the kind of voice you might use while ruffling the fur of an old sheepdog: *Toebehhhh.*

Me: What's up, Boris?

Boris [cupping hand over receiver]: What's that? [Beat.] No, I fucking well don't want to talk to him. [Beat.] What? [Beat.] I don't know. Tell him I've gone to cricket practice.

Me: Boris?

Boris: Hello? Who's this?

Me: Toby.

Boris: *Toebehhhh.* What can I do for you, old bean?

Me: You called me.

Boris: Did I? Yes. Yes. I called you. [Beat.] Why did I call you?

Me: I don't know. To offer me a raise?

Boris: What? Are we not paying you enough? We are paying you enough, aren't we? How much are we paying you?

Me: £125 a column.

Boris: A fortune! For God's sake don't tell anyone round here or I'll have a riot on my hands. The natives will start coming at me in waves, brandishing their spears and baying for blood. It'll be like Gordon at Khartoum.

Me: So why did you call me?

Boris: I dunno. [Off]: Stuart?[1] Why did I call Toby? [Beat.] Oh yes. [To me]: This 'No Life' column. It's balls, isn't it? I mean, no one believes a word of it. The jig is up, old bean.

Me: So you're firing me?

Boris: Who said that?

Me: I thought—

Boris: No, no, no. I want to offer you another column. Much more prestigious. Absolute plum.

Me: What?

Boris: What?

Me: Which column do you want to offer me?

Boris: [off]: Stuart? Stuart? What column is it we want Toby to do? [Beat.] Crikey Moses, are you sure? [To me]: I think you better come in and see me, old bean.

I first met Boris – or Alexander Boris de Pfeffel Johnson, to give him his full name – when I went up to Oxford in 1983. I knew who he was since my uncle was a friend of his mother's, but I still wasn't prepared for the sight (and sound) of him at the dispatch box of the Oxford Union. It was a 'Freshers' Debate', an opportunity for politically ambitious first years to indulge in a bit of turkey-cocking before launching a campaign to become President, and Boris was proposing the motion. With his huge mop of blond hair, his tie askew and his shirttails hanging out, he looked like a typical ex-public schoolboy. Yet with his imposing physical build, his thick neck and his broad, Slavic forehead, there was also something of Nietzsche's *Übermensch* about him. This same combination – a state

1 Stuart Reid was Boris's long-suffering deputy.

of advanced dishevelment and an almost tangible will to power –
was even more pronounced in his way of speaking. He began to
advance an argument, marshalling his considerable rhetorical gifts
to ram the point home, when – a few seconds in – he appeared to
forget completely what it was he was about to say. He looked up,
startled – *Where am I?* – and asked the packed chamber which side
he was supposed to be on. 'What's the motion, anyway?' Before
anyone could answer, a light bulb had appeared above his head and
he was off, this time in an even more orotund, florid style. Yet
within a few seconds he'd wrong-footed himself again, this time
because it had suddenly occurred to him that there was an equally
compelling argument for the opposite point of view. This continual
flipping and flopping, accompanied by much head-scratching and
eye-rolling, went on for the next fifteen minutes. The impression he
gave was of someone who'd been plucked from his bed in the
middle of the night and then plonked down at the dispatch box of
the Oxford Union without the faintest idea of what he was supposed to be talking about.

I'd been to enough Union debates at this point to know just how
mercilessly the crowd could punish those who were unprepared,
yet Boris had the packed chamber eating out of his hand. The
motion was deadly serious – 'This House would reintroduce capital
punishment' – yet almost everything that came out of his mouth
provoked gales of laughter. This was no ordinary undergraduate
proposing a motion, but a brilliant music-hall turn. He reminded
me a little of Frankie Howerd. His befuddlement seemed less like
evidence of his own shortcomings as a debater and more like a
way of sending up the pomposity of the proceedings. There
was something almost postmodern about it. He left the audience
with the impression that he could easily have delivered a highly
effective speech if he'd wanted to, but was too clever and sophisti-
cated – and honest – to enter into such a silly, out-of-date charade.

This highly developed personal style, whereby he was able to use
his own lack of polish as a satirical weapon, was as effective then as

it is now. Paradoxically, even though he was always at sixes and sevens at Oxford, he was also much more evolved than the average undergraduate. His appearance and manner may have been that of an overgrown schoolboy, but he seemed at least twenty-five years older than the rest of us. Unlike the majority of our peers, who were still very much works-in-progress, Boris had the kind of comfort in his own skin that most men don't acquire until advanced middle age.

Needless to say, he was the subject of endless speculation. Oxford being Oxford, the big question was: how authentically upper class is he? On the face of it, the answer was: not at all. Other, less successful Union hacks were quick to point out that his father Stanley was a gentleman farmer of very modest means and his mother worked as a jobbing artist, painting portraits of young, buck-toothed aristocrats. The reason he and his father and all his brothers and sisters sounded like characters in a P. G. Wodehouse novel was because the Johnson family was originally Turkish and had been forced to reinvent itself as more British than the British when the patriarch of the clan, a successful politician, had had to flee the Ottoman Empire. Boris might sound as if he was to the manner born, but in fact he was a third-generation Turkish immigrant.

A variation on this theme was that Boris's Bertie Wooster-ish persona was a clever disguise, a way of concealing his towering ambition. In an age when the overwhelming majority of ambitious men and women were trying to pass themselves off as coming from less privileged backgrounds than they did, what better way to conceal your lofty aims than by taking the opposite tack? One rumour had it that Boris had once confessed to Charlie Althorp, the brother of the late Princess of Wales and his roommate at Eton, that he wanted to be President of the United States. Invariably, the person passing this on would quickly point out that this ambition wasn't as far-fetched as it sounded. Boris was born in New York, so at least he didn't fall foul of Article II, Section I of the American Constitution, preventing people not born in America from becoming President. (Cue plenty of winking and nose-touching.)

Another, altogether different theory – often put forward by the very same person in the next breath – was that, far from being an act, Boris's buffoonery was a genuine expression of his contempt for ordinary mortals. Most male undergraduates were engaged in a constant effort to impress each other by trying to appear more slick and smooth and socially confident than they were. Not Boris. By hamming up his own befuddlement, he was in effect saying, 'I'm so supremely self-confident – my social status is so much higher than yours – I have no need to try and impress you.'

Of course, there was something paradoxical about this because Boris's approach, whereby he tried to seem less polished than he was, turned out to be much more impressive than our transparently hopeless attempts to appear slick and smooth and socially confident. And at some level Boris obviously knew this so perhaps he was trying to curry favour with us after all.

Far from undercutting him, though, all this speculation just served to underline the fact that Boris was the pre-eminent undergraduate of our generation – the Biggest Man on Campus. In his four years at Oxford, he managed to become President of the Union, edit a student magazine, take a 2:1 in Classics and make off with the Zuleika Dobson of his year, a girl called Allegra Mostyn-Owen who appeared on the cover of *Harpers & Queen* in 1984 accompanied by the strapline 'The 100 Most Beautiful Women In The World'. Of all the people I met at Oxford, Boris was undoubtedly the one most likely to succeed.

'*Toebehhhh.*'

The editor of the *Spectator* sat behind his desk – an upended wastepaper basket of magazines, newspapers, orange peel, scrunched-up balls of paper and half-eaten sandwiches.

'So,' I said. 'When are you going to become the leader of the Tory Party?'

He'd been elected as the Conservative MP for Henley earlier that year.

'Never going to happen,' he said. 'They'd be mad to do it.'

'I assume you're at least going to be made a member of the front bench team?'

'Shadow Minister for Paperclips,' he muttered, casting his eyes down.

I decided to try a different tack.

'How's the atmosphere at the magazine these days? Is it a happy ship?'

'Delirious.'

I'd never found it easy to make small talk with Boris. (Was he like this with everyone or was it just me?) Whenever I asked him a direct question, he seemed to squirm and avoid eye contact, as if the give-and-take of ordinary conversation made him uncomfortable. He didn't like being asked to show his hand, even to someone who'd known him for eighteen years. He had only one mode of communicating with me: mildly affectionate piss-taking.

'So you don't think we're paying you enough, eh?' he said, looking at me for the first time since I'd sat down. 'You've become too big for us – that's the problem, isn't it? You're such a literary figure now you won't write for us unless we pay you a king's ransom. That's it, isn't it?'

I assured him that that wasn't the case. Meagre though my *Spectator* salary was – £6500 per annum – it was still my only regular income.

Suddenly, he changed the subject.

'When was the last time you went to the theatre?'

'I'm not sure. Why?'

At that moment the phone rang. It was Lloyd Evans, a mutual friend of ours from Oxford. One of Boris's first appointments as editor of the *Spectator* had been to make Lloyd the poetry editor.

'Lloyd, old bean. I've got the Honourable Toby D. M. Young sitting here looking as wise as a tree full of owls.'

As they were talking – Boris kept saying 'triffic, triffic' – it dawned on me that the job he was thinking about offering me was that of drama critic, a post then occupied by Sheridan Morley. Did I want to do it? It would involve going to the theatre three or four times a week, hardly something that was likely to endear me to Caroline. And it would be a great deal of work for very little money. On the other hand, I harboured a sneaking ambition to become a playwright and seeing all those plays would be an invaluable form of research. I'd tried to write a play in New York about the rivalry between Graydon Carter and Tina Brown – its title was *Liberté, Egalité, Publicité* – and while it hadn't come off I wasn't ready to give up this ambition quite yet. Even if being a drama critic didn't result in a career in the theatre, it would be useful nevertheless in terms of honing my screenwriting skills. I hadn't received the call from Mr Hollywood at this stage, but becoming a screenwriter was still my fondest hope. It would also be an opportunity to familiarise myself with a whole area of classic literature. Just think: within a few years I'd be able to boast that I'd seen *all* of Ibsen's major works.

On balance, I thought I did want to do it.

When Boris had hung up, I rattled through the various plays I'd seen in the past twelve months, saying which ones I'd liked and which ones I hadn't – and why – in the hope that I'd sound like a suitable man for the job. But he wasn't listening. Another thing that makes it hard to have a proper conversation with Boris is that his attention is constantly wandering.

Stuart Reid popped his head round the corner.

'I don't want to hassle you, but we're going to need that column in fifteen minutes.'

'Hell's teeth. Really? Better get on with it, I s'pose. *O tempora! O mores!*'

This had the effect of forcing him to come to the point. He offered me the job and I told him I'd be willing to do it provided he paid me £500 a column.

'£500?!? Stone the crows. That's more than Conrad's paying me.'

We eventually settled on £225.

As he was walking me out, he said that if anyone asked could I say I was only being paid £200? Apparently, Mary Wakefield, the *Spectator's* drop-dead gorgeous associate editor, had bet him a bottle of champagne that he wouldn't be able to get me to do the column for £200.

'You know how it is, old bean. Beautiful, brainy gal and all that. Don't want to lose a bet to her.'

I told him I would keep *schtum*.

Kenneth Tynan said that a critic is a person who knows the way but cannot drive the car. Alas, this doesn't apply to me. In my first outing as the *Spectator's* drama critic I got lost on my way from Waterloo Station to the National Theatre, making me five minutes late for the beginning of the play. It was an inauspicious start to my new career.

When Tynan became a drama critic, he pinned a note above his writing desk to remind himself of the effect he wanted his reviews to produce: 'Rouse tempers, goad and lacerate, raise whirlwinds.' I achieved this almost instantly, but not quite in the way Tynan had in mind. The tempers I roused were those of my fellow critics who, almost to a man, took it as a personal affront that someone who knew as little about the theatre as me should have been promoted to their ranks. I thought that was a little unfair – after all, most of them probably didn't know much about the subject when they first started – but they were a fairly tight-knit bunch and it was inevitable that they'd resent the new arrival.

My chief tormentor was Sheridan Morley, the man I'd replaced at the *Spectator*. I always knew he'd be a ticklish customer – he'd been doing the job for ten years – and in the hope of smoothing things over I offered to take him out to lunch on the eve of my first review. I thought that if I appeared before him, forelock in hand, and told him what a huge honour it was to succeed such a distinguished critic, I might succeed in drawing his sting.

He agreed to the lunch, though he insisted that we go to his local watering hole about five yards from his front door. I'd had somewhere more like the Ivy in mind for this august occasion – the passing of the baton from one generation to the next – but I couldn't very well object. After all, the point of the lunch was to butter him up.

He was a little prickly at first, but after the publican had unscrewed a bottle of white wine he loosened up and began to regale me with funny stories about John G. (John Gielgud), Larry (Laurence Olivier) and Johnny Lahr (John Lahr), among others. His store of theatrical gossip was formidable. He was like an anecdote jukebox: all you had to do was plug in a name and out would pop some hair-raising story.

After his ploughman's had been cleared away, he asked me why it was that Boris had replaced him with someone who clearly knew 'next to nothing' about the theatre. I was a little taken aback – I thought he'd appreciate having finally come across someone who hadn't heard any of his anecdotes before – but I was determined to maintain the convivial atmosphere.

'I think it's because we were at Oxford together,' I said. 'It's absolutely no reflection on your abilities as a critic. Just a case of the Old Boy Network at work.'

Needless to say, I didn't actually believe this. I could think of a dozen reasons why 'Sherry' had been sacked. But I wanted to spare the old boy's feelings.

When the bill arrived he insisted on paying it and it was only then that I realised why he'd brought me to this dive. His pride wouldn't allow me to pay for his lunch, but he wasn't going to waste too much money on mine.

On the tube heading back to Shepherd's Bush, I thought it had gone quite well, all things considered. It wasn't until I opened the following week's copy of *Private Eye* and read the following item in the 'Street of Shame' column that I realised my mistake:

Boris Johnson seemed on the brink of tears when he sacked the *Spectator*'s veteran theatre reviewer Sheridan Morley. 'I'm going to have to let you go,' he sobbed. 'I didn't want to, but Conrad Black insisted.'

Shortly afterwards Morley had a call from crazed self-publicist Toby Young. 'I'm your successor,' Young announced, 'but I don't know anything about the theatre. Can we have lunch?'

Rather charitably, Morley agreed to meet and give the tyro critic a lengthy briefing on the history of drama. As the meal was ending, Young said he was glad there were no hard feelings: 'It's just that Boris and I were at Oxford together, and I told him I needed a job.' Whereupon the shameless scallywag departed – leaving Morley to pick up the bill for lunch!

Similar stories began appearing in various gossip columns and I suspected all of them of bearing Morley's fingerprints. (The item in Nigel Dempster's column in the *Daily Mail* began: 'The splendid Sheridan Morley . . . ') Then the letters started rolling in. Every time I made a factual error in one of my reviews, Morley would fire off a letter to the *Spectator* pointing it out. He even wrote a letter on the subject to the *Observer*, a paper neither of us worked for, as though the fact that he'd been deprived of his column in the *Spectator* was an event of national importance: 'After nearly forty years as a drama critic, I am more than used to being hired and fired; but I have never before been replaced by a writer so cringingly and embarrassingly unqualified for the job.'

No doubt I'd wildly overestimated my ability to charm Morley over a bottle of Liebfraumilch, but it still struck me as a slightly odd way to behave. At this point in my career I'd had numerous columns taken away from me on both sides of the Atlantic, but it had never occurred to me to bear a grudge against any of my successors. After all, it was always the editor's decision to fire me, not the person who'd been given my job.

Someone told me that when Morley was replaced as the drama

critic of *Punch*, a job he'd held for twelve years, he waged a similar campaign against Rhoda Koenig, an American expat who inherited his *Punch* column. A few months into the *Spectator* job, I found myself sitting next to Koenig at a press night and I thought I'd take the opportunity to introduce myself and find out if there was any truth to what I'd been told. In addition to having an alleged common enemy, we had a mutual friend in the form of James Wolcott, a columnist for *Vanity Fair*. I was also a big fan of her writing.

Me [turning to her and smiling]: You're not Rhoda Koenig, by any chance?

Rhoda [staring straight ahead]: My name is Rhoda Koenig, yes.

Me [proffering hand]: Hi, I'm Toby Young.

Rhoda [not taking it]: Yes, I know who you are.

Me: I believe we have a mutual friend in the form of Jim Wolcott?

Rhoda: To quote Dickens, we don't have a mutual friend so much as a friend in common.

Beat.

Me: What's the difference?

Rhoda [still without looking at me]: Look it up in a dictionary. Don't you get it? I don't want to talk to you. I'm doing my best to ignore the fact that I'm sitting next to you. I find the fact that you're doing theatre criticism an ABSOLUTE DISGRACE.

With that, she got up and shuffled to the end of the row, placing herself as far away from me as possible.

9

WHO WANTS TO BE A MILLIONAIRE?

One of the consequences of *How to Lose Friends* selling a respectable number of copies was that I got a call from a film and television production company wanting to option the movie rights. Not only that, but when I told them I wanted to adapt it for the screen, they didn't blink. They made me an offer of $8000 for a twelve-month option and $50,000 for the screenplay, which included a treatment, a first draft, a second draft and a polish. Admittedly, the $50,000 wasn't guaranteed. The only money I'd definitely receive would be $5000 for a fifteen-page outline. If they liked that, they'd pay me to write a first draft, and if they liked *that*, they'd pay me to write a second draft, and so on. Still, it was better than a poke in the eye with a sharp stick.

I wanted to accept this offer immediately, but my agent told me to sit tight. Sure enough, over the course of the next few days, a succession of other production companies threw their hats into the ring, including Miramax, Working Title, Fragile Films, Company Pictures and FilmFour – and they all said they'd be willing to let me have first crack at the screenplay. I began to fantasise about the possibility of a bidding war.

Then things got really exciting.

An American friend of mine living in London got in touch and asked if I'd mind if he showed the book to a few of his contacts in Hollywood. The catch was that he wanted to attach himself as the screenwriter. I told him to go ahead. In the extremely unlikely event of him persuading a big studio to buy the rights, I was prepared to give up the chance of adapting it myself.

Within forty-eight hours he'd managed to get the book to Rachel Horovitz, then an executive at Revolution Studios, and twenty-four hours later she notified my agent that she intended to make an offer. Rachel Horovitz is a legend in London and New York literary circles. Not only is she the sister of Adam Horovitz (Adrock of the Beastie Boys) and the daughter of the playwright Israel Horovitz, she had been the person responsible for acquiring the rights to *About A Boy*, Nick Hornby's book. This was back in 1998 when she was working as a literary scout for Tribeca Productions, Robert De Niro's company. The amount Tribeca had paid for *About A Boy* was reported to be $2.5 million. Suddenly, I was in the running for what my agent called 'silly money'.

Horovitz was aware of the other offers I'd received and she asked my friend how much it would take to persuade me to 'take it off the table'. She didn't want to get into a protracted bidding war; she wanted to make me an offer I couldn't refuse.

My friend discussed this with me and I in turn discussed it with my agent. There were two ways Horovitz could go in this situation. Either she could make an offer to option the movie rights for a year, which we estimated would be somewhere in the region of $70,000; or she could make an offer for the rights in perpetuity – what's known in Hollywood parlance as an 'outright sale' – in which case the sky was the limit. The problem was, if we sent a message to Horovitz telling her that only an offer for an outright sale would be acceptable, there was a chance she'd simply walk away. Should I, effectively, bank the $70,000 or go for broke? It was exactly the kind of dilemma that contestants on *Who Wants to Be a Millionaire?* face every week.

'Sod it,' I told my agent. 'Let's roll the dice.'

My American friend conveyed this to Horovitz and she told him that in order to make me a 'Hornby-esque' offer she'd have to persuade Joe Roth, the head of Revolution, that this was a project worth investing in. And the only way to do that, apparently, was to attach a couple of movie stars. I thought that was probably the end of the matter – *Why hadn't I taken the $70,000, goddamnit?* – but a few days later my friend called to tell me that Horovitz had managed to interest a star in playing Caroline.

'Who?'

'If I tell you, do you promise not to tell anyone? If this gets out it could completely scupper the deal.'

'Cross my heart and hope to die.'

'Julia Roberts.'

'You're kidding?'

'Nope.'

'Jesus H. Christ.'

As you can imagine, I was cock-a-hoop. *Julia fucking Roberts!* But her interest wasn't sufficient to persuade Joe Roth to get his chequebook out, apparently. After all, *How to Lose Friends* was principally a story about a man – an overweight, balding, middle-aged man. In order to get Roth to authorise a 'Hornby-esque' offer, Horovitz would have to interest a star in *that* role as well.

Naturally, I had plenty of suggestions. How about Jack Black? He had the right kind of pugilistic energy. Or Philip Seymour Hoffman? In addition to being a terrific actor, he looked a lot like me. Or Mike Myers? He could play me as a cross between Wayne Campbell and Austin Powers. Any one of them would be perfect.

Unfortunately, Julia Roberts had her own ideas about who should play me: Hugh Grant. According to Horovitz, she'd enjoyed working with him in *Notting Hill* and wanted to recreate their onscreen chemistry.

As soon as my friend passed this information on, I got a terrible sinking feeling. It wasn't so much that I thought he was wrong for

the part – I'd be happy to be played by Richard Griffiths if it trig-
gered a 'Hornby-esque' offer – as the fact that he didn't like me very
much. This all stemmed from a fight I'd had with Elizabeth Hurley
in 1994.

Elizabeth and I used to be friends, but we fell out over a talking
book she read that I was intending to give away free with a special
issue of *The Modern Review*. More specifically, we quarrelled over
the photographs I wanted to use on the front and back of the cassette.

After making the audio recording, Elizabeth put me in touch
with a photographer called John Stoddart. He'd taken some pictures
of her posing at the Dorchester Hotel in various states of undress
and I selected two of these and sent them along to our printer,
imagining she wouldn't have a problem. Not only had she given me
Stoddart's number, but pictures from this same set had appeared in
Loaded, *Esquire* and *GQ* – and it's a work of moments to find them
on the Internet. However, in between me printing the cassette
covers and the magazine hitting the news-stands Elizabeth wore
'that dress' to the premier of *Four Weddings and a Funeral*. To paraphrase Byron, she awoke the following morning to find herself
famous. Suddenly, her career prospects had dramatically improved
and she decided her image needed protecting.

She called me twenty-four hours later to tell me she didn't want
me to use the Dorchester pictures I'd selected on the cassette cover.

'Too late,' I said. 'It's already been printed.'

'In that case, you'll be hearing from my lawyer,' she said.

Click. Dial-tone.

The next day I got a call from a firm called Schilling & Lom
threatening to throw the book at me if I allowed the cassette to
appear in its present form. I hemmed and hawed – Elizabeth didn't
own the copyright in the pictures, John Stoddart did – but in the
end I decided to capitulate. After all, now that her boyfriend was
earning £5 million a movie, he could afford to fund a nuisance suit

against me if Elizabeth wanted to bring one. In any case, the whole point of giving away the talking book was to publicise the latest issue of the magazine and I could do that just as easily by leaking the whole story to the press.

So I went to town with it. I wrote a piece for the *Mail on Sunday* in which I pointed out that it was a bit rich for Elizabeth to object to me printing these pictures when she'd appeared nude in virtually every film she'd made up until that point. It was only because she was now famous, having worn 'that dress', that she didn't want these pictures to appear. In effect, Elizabeth was the first actress in history who didn't get noticed until she put her clothes *on*.

Shortly after this story appeared, I got a strange phone call in the middle of the night. I let my answering machine intercept it and heard the following words in a woman's voice. 'Just because you couldn't dip your wick, you've dipped your pen in poison ink. Elizabeth Hurley's much more famous than you'll ever be—'

'Elizabeth,' I said, picking up the phone. 'I know it's you.'

Click. Dial-tone.

I waited by the phone, hoping the woman would call back. My plan was to record as many of these messages as possible and then stick them on a second audio-cassette that I could give away with the next issue of *The Modern Review*. Alas, the phone didn't ring again so I never found out if it was Elizabeth. Nevertheless, I went round telling all our mutual friends that I was the first fan to be harassed by an obsessed actress.

A few weeks later, I found myself at a party that Hugh and Elizabeth were at. As the evening wore on and the alcohol began to flow, Hugh decided to enlist the help of a friend to throw me out. We scuffled for a bit, but before it could escalate too far the hostess intervened and whisked me off to another room. I wrote about that incident, too, pointing out that the experience could have been a lot worse: Hugh might have hit me with his handbag.

In short, of all the journalists in the world Hugh Grant might consider playing, I was probably the most unlikely.

Sure enough, when Rachel Horovitz tracked him down – he was on holiday in Mustique at the time with Elizabeth – his response was pretty definitive.

'No fucking way,' he said.

The following day Horovitz notified my agent that Revolution wouldn't be making an offer for *How to Lose Friends* after all.

The thing I regretted most about Horovitz's withdrawal was it meant that Caroline wouldn't now be played by Julia Roberts. I thought of this as the ultimate wedding present – what girl wouldn't want to be immortalised by America's sweetheart? – but Caroline turned out to be hugely relieved.

'If I was played by Julia Roberts it would mean that, for the rest of my life, whenever I was introduced to someone at a party they'd look at me and think, "*You* were played by Julia Roberts?" Quite frankly, I'd prefer to be played by Julie Walters.'

My agent invited all the remaining companies to make formal offers, but, rather disappointingly, Miramax pulled out. My mole inside the company's London office told me that Harvey Weinstein had decided against putting in a bid because *Talk*, the Miramax-funded magazine edited by Tina Brown, had just gone belly up and he didn't want it to look as though he was seeking to vent his rage by making a satirical film about *Vanity Fair*, *Talk*'s chief rival. According to the *New York Times*, *Talk* lost $54 million over the course of its two-year life, half of which came out of Miramax's pocket. My mole told me that Weinstein might change his mind further down the line, but for the time being he didn't want to be involved in anything that reminded him of his ill-starred foray into the New York magazine business.

That didn't surprise me. According to Graydon Carter, Weinstein had always felt a bit ambivalent about *Vanity Fair*. Just before I left New York at the beginning of 2000, I had dinner with Graydon and he related a bizarre tale about his last meeting with Weinstein. It had taken place at a party given by Michael De Luca, then the President of Production at New Line Cinema, at a Los Angeles restaurant called the Atlantic. Graydon was leaving the party with his friends Mitch Glazer and Kelly Lynch when he spotted Weinstein sitting at a table surrounded by models. Graydon went over to pay his respects and Weinstein immediately started threatening him in a loud voice so all the models could hear. Jabbing Graydon in the chest, Weinstein said he'd heard that he was planning to run a piece attacking him in *Vanity Fair* and that if he did he'd retaliate by running a negative piece about Graydon in *Talk*. Graydon was stunned. He assured Weinstein that he had no intention of doing any such thing, pointing out that it wasn't his style 'to trash the opposition'. (This was shortly after *Talk* had launched.) But the Miramax heavyweight refused to be placated. According to Graydon, having put on such a macho display for the benefit of the models, he could not now back down.

'Come on, Carter,' he said, raising himself to his full height. 'Let's take this outside. You and me.'

Graydon said he had no choice but to leave the party with Weinstein.

As they were exiting, Weinstein looked back over his shoulder and said, 'Stick around girls. This shouldn't take long.'

However, the moment they were outside, Weinstein's demeanour changed completely.

'I love your magazine,' he said, pumping Graydon's arm. 'I think you're the greatest magazine editor in the world.'

According to Graydon, he went on flattering him for about fifteen minutes before finally returning to the party.

'I bet he got back to the table, cracked his knuckles and said, "I took care of him".'[1]

I don't know how much of this was embellished, but Graydon and Weinstein clearly had a complicated relationship and it may

---

1 A version of this story appeared in a profile of Harvey Weinstein by Ken Auletta in *The New Yorker* ('Beauty and the Beast: Does Hollywood Hate Harvey Weinstein?', *The New Yorker*, 16 December 2002, p. 78).

have been for that reason that Miramax declined to participate in the auction. In any event, five companies *did* submit offers and when my agent and I sat down to examine them it was clear that FilmFour's was the best. Not only were they offering the most money – it wasn't 'Hornby-esque', but it was nothing to sniff at – they also had a great track record, having produced *My Beautiful Laundrette*, *Trainspotting* and *East Is East*, among other films. However, just as I was about to accept their offer, an American independent called GreeneStreet Films threw its hat into the ring. GreeneStreet didn't have FilmFour's illustrious history, but a movie it had made called *In The Bedroom* had just been nominated for five Oscars, including Best Actor and Best Actress. That meant they would have no problem attracting 'above-the-line talent' when it came to future projects.

I decided to meet with the heads of both FilmFour and GreeneStreet, partly because I thought it would help me to make up my mind, and partly because I thought it would be nice to be courted by a couple of veteran movie producers. Here was a chance to meet with two powerful people in an industry I wanted to work in without having to prostrate myself before them. On the contrary, they'd be petitioning me. It was an opportunity that would probably never come up again.

The chief honcho at FilmFour was a man called Paul Webster who'd previously headed up Miramax's London office. He began the meeting by telling me the reason he liked *How to Lose Friends* was because it reminded him of *Money*, Martin Amis's book. He added that he'd tried to get *Money* off the ground as a movie three times, but without any success. I asked him if Amis himself had been involved in trying to adapt the book for the screen and he said no: 'As far as I know, Amis has never written a screenplay.' I should have bitten my tongue at this point, but I couldn't resist pointing out that much of the material in *Money* had been drawn from Amis's experience as the screenwriter on *Saturn 3*, a science fiction film starring Kirk Douglas, Harvey Keitel and Farrah Fawcett.

Why did I do something so idiotic? What was I trying to prove by demonstrating that my knowledge of Martin Amis trivia was more encyclopedic than Webster's? It was hardly the best way to get off on the right foot with a man I was thinking seriously about doing a deal with.

The meeting with John Penotti, the head of GreeneStreet, took place in New York and, if anything, was even less successful. Having read my book, he thought it would be fun to rendezvous at a party in the meatpacking district being thrown by Louis Bacon, the reclusive hedge-fund manager who owns GreeneStreet Films. We had a couple of drinks at the bar and were just getting down to business when Harvey Weinstein came barrelling through the front door. He had a model on each arm, the kind of eye candy Frank Sinatra used to refer to as 'cufflinks'.

Having sunk two double whiskies, I got it into my head that this was a heaven-sent opportunity to pitch Weinstein on the merits of my book. Didn't he realise it was *Less Than Zero* and *Bright Lights Big City* rolled into one? (Hic!) It was time to put his feelings about Graydon to one side and get out his chequebook.

I told Penotti I had to use the bathroom and made my way over to where Weinstein was standing. I convinced myself that the next few seconds would constitute one of the defining moments of my life.

'Mr Weinstein—'

'Back the fuck up,' said a security guard, interposing himself between me and the movie mogul.

'But—'

'NOW.'

I lingered for a few seconds, labouring under the illusion that if only I could catch Weinstein's eye it would all be okay.

'Okay, that's it,' said the security guard. 'You're leaving.'

With that, he placed an enormous paw on my shoulder and frog-marched me towards the exit.

'Don't let this guy back in,' he told the doorman after he'd deposited me on the street. 'He's bothering Mr Weinstein.'

To his credit, John Penotti didn't withdraw GreeneStreet's offer after I'd left him dangling that night, but I decided to throw in my lot with FilmFour nevertheless. The deciding factor was that FilmFour was a British company and, in the absence of 'Hornby-esque' levels of temptation, I liked the idea of *How to Lose Friends* being a British film.

Caroline and I went to Le Caprice to celebrate the closing of the deal and talked about how radically my life had changed since the book's publication. Overnight, I'd gone from being 'an ever-present icon of defeat' to a 'published author'. Not only that, but a respectable production company had optioned the movie rights and hired me to write the screenplay. Suddenly, I was a success.

Psychologically, I wasn't prepared for this turnaround in my fortunes. I joked to Caroline that success would be a much tougher test of character than failure. Not giving up in the face of adversity isn't all that tough if you have a modicum of self-belief. Not allowing success to go to your head is an altogether different proposition.

Fortunately, the universe usually finds a way to bring you crashing back down to earth.

On 7 July 2002, less than two months after concluding my deal with FilmFour, *Variety* published a story saying that Channel 4 had decided to shut down its film division. All fifty-five members of staff were to be made redundant, including Paul Webster.

10

THE NAKED SELF-PUBLICIST

'Hello? I'm looking for Margie Beck. Do you have any idea where I might find her?'

It was the afternoon of 15 July, 2002, less than four hours before my New York book party. After the modest success of *How to Lose Friends* in Britain, I'd finally sold it in America and I was desperately trying to get in touch with a woman I'd heard about who ran a celebrity lookalike agency. It was part of an elaborate publicity stunt I was planning.

'This is she.'

Aha!

'I wonder if you can help me. I'm trying to get hold of a Graydon Carter lookalike.'

'Who?'

'Graydon Carter. He's the editor-in-chief of *Vanity Fair*.'

My plan was to have the Graydon lookalike gatecrash the party, beat the crap out of me, and then make a getaway in a waiting limo. If that didn't merit a mention in 'Page Six', the city's pre-eminent gossip column, I didn't know what would.

'Oh, boy,' she said. 'Not somebody I've ever, ever had. You know, that's going to be a tough one. I don't think that anyone has ever had that request.'

I racked my brains. There had to be a proper celebrity whom Graydon looked vaguely like. His weight went up and down, but as far as I knew he was going through a 'heavy' phase at the moment . . .

'How about Barbara Bush?'

'*That* I can do. But I should warn you: she's eighty-two years old and has a little trouble getting around. Can you supply a wheelchair?'

Clearly, this wasn't going to work out.

I got the idea for this stunt when I discovered just how angry Graydon was about the American publication of *How to Lose Friends*. My first inkling of this was when I read a piece by a journalist named Alessandra Stanley in the *New York Times* called 'Revenge of the Underlings'. Citing my book alongside *The Nanny Diaries* and *The Devil Wears Prada*, she claimed to have identified a new literary genre called 'boss betrayal'. Graydon was one of the few bosses prepared to go on the record about this new trend. 'You're forced into playing it cool when all you really want to do is throttle them,' he said.

Another indication that Graydon had soured on the book was a comment he made to the gossip columnist Lloyd Grove, then at the *New York Daily News*. After I'd done the deal with FilmFour, Grove called Graydon and asked him who he'd like to be played by if *How to Lose Friends* was ever made into a film.

'I don't know about me,' he said, 'but for Toby Young Verne Troyer.' (For those of you who don't know, Verne Troyer is the dwarf who plays Mini-Me in the Austin Powers films.)

Why had Graydon suddenly taken such a dislike to the book? Was it because I'd refused to make the 'corrections' he'd suggested in his twenty-four-point email?[1] Possibly, but his animus seemed to

---

1 Point number five read: 'Throughout the book you have me saying "doncha" and "betcha", "lemme" and "ya" and suchlike. This is not the way I speak and I think it weakens the book.'

postdate that. Shortly after the book came out in Britain, he made a number of comments in the press that, while they weren't exactly enthusiastic, betrayed a certain lingering affection. 'Toby's a piece of gum that stuck to my shoe five years ago and that I still can't get off,' he told a reporter for *WWD*. 'He had a worm's-eye-view, as it were, of what goes on at *Vanity Fair* – which explains the book, which has a little fact and a lot of fiction. He was on chemical substances most of the time, and no one ever let him near anything. Every day I make a list, and the last two years Toby was here there'd be an item on the list that read "Fire Toby". I guess I never got far enough down the list to do it, and I did have a soft spot for the guy. I basically forgot to fire Toby Young every day for two years.'

Why had this (broadly) good-humoured attitude changed? According to my sources at *Vanity Fair*, whenever my name came up he now flew into a rage, referring to *How to Lose Friends* as an 'unauthorised biography' and describing it as 'a gross violation' of his 'privacy'. That was a strange way to react to a book that, while it might not have been unreservedly complimentary, was pretty even-handed. I was under the impression that the Graydon Carter who emerged from *How to Lose Friends* was a fundamentally sympathetic character and, since the book had come out, I'd received a number of emails confirming this. 'I think your portrait of him is not only accurate, but quite positive in an unexpected way,' wrote one contributing editor at the magazine. 'In fact, I don't think anyone's going to portray Graydon any better.'

One of our mutual acquaintances tackled him about this, pointing out that the book was essentially 'good PR'.

'It's not the things he's written about me that I object to,' Graydon explained. 'It's more the fact that he's written a book at all. It's a breach of trust.'

This was essentially the same argument that Alessandra Stanley put forward in her *New York Times* piece: that books like mine, written by 'servants and office assistants' trying to 'cash in' on the fame of their employers, were the literary equivalent of kiss-and-tell stories in tabloid newspapers. 'They are a variation on the tell-all exposé,' she wrote, 'written not by peers or rivals or the principals themselves but by subordinates, books that all could be subtitled, "You'll Never Serve Lunch in This Town Again."'

The problem with this argument is that, while it might apply to a book written by, say, Frank Sinatra's valet, it doesn't apply to books written by professional journalists. If a person of some notoriety employs a journalist to work for him or her they have to accept that at some point that journalist may write something about it.

In any case, if he was opposed to my book on principle, why had he initially been quite sanguine about it? Why the sudden change of heart?

I think the real reason Graydon soured on *How to Lose Friends* is because my agent managed to sell it in America. He wasn't particularly bothered when it was being published in the UK, but he didn't like the idea of it being read by people he knew in New York and Los Angeles. Like most men who are fond of dishing it out – particularly journalists – Graydon is remarkably thin-skinned. Number sixteen in his twenty-four-point email read as follows: 'On page 113, you say that I expect to be treated with the same fawning reverence as any other *macher*. In fact, I'm not that way at all. I love a joke at my expense. But it has to be from someone who knows me well and it has to be funny.' That sounds reasonable enough, but the reality is that no joke at Graydon's expense would ever pass the second of these tests. His reaction to the book reminded me of the reaction of Clive James when I wrote an irreverent profile of him for the *Evening Standard*. 'I wouldn't have minded,' James told my editor, 'but it just wasn't funny.'

Judging from my American book tour, Graydon didn't have much to worry about.

Two weeks earlier I'd flown to Washington where my arrival coincided with the largest demonstration in the nation's capital since Vietnam. It was something to do with the IMF and the World Bank, both of which were holding their annual meetings in Washington that weekend. I was supposed to be giving a reading at a large, independent bookshop and when I arrived – having fought my way through an army of protesters – the manager greeted me with the news that only eighteen people had turned up. 'That's pretty good, under the circumstances,' he said. I nodded and smiled politely while putting an imaginary gun to my head. I quickly calculated that if every person in the room bought a copy of *How to Lose Friends* my American publisher, Da Capo Press, still wouldn't make enough money to cover my hotel bill. It would have been more cost-effective to have stayed in London, picked eighteen people at random out of the Washington telephone directory and simply read them an extract over the phone.

Next stop was Cambridge, Massachusetts – Da Capo's home town. After the low turnout in Washington, I was anxious that no one would show up. This was particularly worrying because my editor, John Radziewicz, had threatened to put in an appearance.

Thankfully, when I arrived at Barnes & Noble in Harvard Square I counted twenty-four people in the audience. Admittedly, four of them, including Radziewicz, were from Da Capo, but still. It could have been worse. Then, just as I was about to start reading, a man in the front row leapt to his feet and started waving his arms around. 'What's going on here?' he said. 'Who the hell is *this* guy?' It turned out that I'd been double-booked with the authors of *Living in the Dead Zone*, an academic tome about borderline personality disorder.

Radziewicz and I had a quick confab. I was worried that if the other authors disappeared they'd take half the audience with them. Why didn't we just share the podium? 'No, no, that's not gonna work,' said John. He explained that the majority of the people present were from a local homeless shelter and the only reason they'd come was because Da Capo had promised them a hot meal. 'If they have to listen to those other guys as well I'm going to have a riot on my hands,' he said.

It took me several seconds to realise he was joking.

Dallas was a bit more promising. I was put up free of charge at the famous Adolphus Hotel, having been invited to speak at a series called 'Authors at the Adolphus'. The hotel's publicity director, David Davis, was convinced I'd draw as big a crowd as the authors of *The Nanny Diaries*. I thought that was unlikely, not least because the hotel was charging $45 a head. (It included a three-course lunch).

On the morning of my appearance Davis arranged for me to be interviewed by the local Fox affiliate in the hope of drumming up a bit of business. However, it didn't go quite as planned. About half way through the interview, the presenter cocked her head to one side, touched her earpiece and then nodded vigorously.

'Sorry to cut in, Tony,' she said, 'but I've just been told that the Dallas Desperados Dancers are here in the studio and they've agreed to show us one of their latest routines. Y'all don't mind, do ya?'

At that point, a cheerleading troupe came bouncing into the studio and started waving their pompoms and flashing their knickers. I must have looked pretty crestfallen – *What about the rest of my interview?* – because after a couple of minutes the producer asked me if I'd like to join in. I thought he was joking, but it turned out he wasn't. 'Go 'head,' he said, shoving me in front of the studio lights. 'Break a leg.'

I ended up dancing a jig alongside the Dallas Desperados Dancers, holding my book aloft like some second-hand car salesman.

Incredibly, all seventy-five tickets to the event later that afternoon were sold. I was extremely flattered – *They love me, they really, really love me* – but my euphoria was short-lived. The local journalist who'd been saddled with the task of interviewing me kicked off by asking how many people in the audience had read my book. Not a single person raised their hand. They were all there for the three-course lunch.

The interviewer then asked me to name my most difficult

journalistic assignment and, without thinking, I said, 'That would be when I dressed up as a woman in the hope of getting off with a lipstick lesbian at a bar called the Clit Club.' The ladies in the audience stared at me in open-mouthed disbelief. I'd been warned by David Davis not to use any 'curse words' – 'Dallas is the buckle of the Bible Belt,' he explained – and, judging from the look on his face, 'clit' fell into that category. Nevertheless, I ploughed on. The punch-line involved me being pursued through New York's meat-packing district by a group of rampaging bull dykes: 'Forget about Bosnia. That was the most dangerous journalistic assignment of the nineties.'

It didn't get a single laugh.

The climax of the book tour took place on the roof of the Standard Hotel in Los Angeles where I'd organised a book party in conjunction with the LA Press Club. Initially, I'd resigned myself to picking up the tab for this shindig, but at the last minute a helpful publicist offered to put in a few calls and – miracle of miracles – she found a sponsor in the form of Stella Artois. Only later did she explain that, in order to keep the sponsor happy, I would have to invite some movie stars. Consequently, I spent my entire time in LA frantically working the phones, trying to persuade my friends to trawl through their Rolodexes in search of 'names'. By the time the party started, I had copper-bottomed commitments from Josh Hartnett, Courtney Love, Tobey Maguire, Eric Stoltz and Quentin Tarantino.

In the event, none of them showed up.

I arrived early at Serena's, the venue for the New York launch party. A rumour had spread that Si Newhouse was going to show up and I wanted to be there to greet him in person. Needless to say, this rumour turned out to be false, but it did provide me with the opening gag of my speech:

For all the *Vanity Fair* people who are here tonight, I have good news and bad news. The good news is Si Newhouse isn't coming.

So you needn't worry about being spotted by the man who pays your bills. The bad news is there's a photographer stationed across the street with a high-powered telephoto lens trained on the entrance. So you're all going to be fired!

I thought I was exaggerating the extent to which I'd become radioactive – but I wasn't. One of the few well-known journalists who did put in an appearance was Richard Johnson, the editor of Page Six, and he told me afterwards that a succession of people had come up to him over the course of the evening and begged him not to mention they were there. 'I'd really appreciate it if you kept my name out of it,' said one ex-magazine editor. 'I do want another job some day.'

Still, not every editor in Manhattan was terrified of Condé Nast. I got a call the following day from a journalist at the *New York Observer* asking me if I'd be willing to pose nude to promote the book. He assured me that while it used to be just attractive women who disrobed to promote their books, these days men did it too. When it comes to getting noticed, apparently, the sword is mightier than the pen – even if the sword in question is actually smaller than a pen.

I was a little sceptical, but at this point my book needed all the help it could get. The American critics hadn't been any kinder than their British counterparts.

'The summer of Eurotrash continues,' wrote one. 'First there was *The Sexual Life of Catherine M* and now this whiny, bitchy and gossipy tripe from British writer Toby Young.'

'He wore out his welcome on the job and he does the same on the page,' wrote another.

'Okay, I'll do it,' I told the *New York Observer*.

I was back in London by the time the relevant issue of the weekly came out, but my friend Euan Rellie called to give me a full report.

'Two words,' he said. 'George Costanza.'

'You're not serious?'

'Look on the bright side. If your book's ever reprinted you can stick this photo on the cover and rename it *You'll Never Get Laid In This Town Again.*'

Later that day, John Radziewicz called from Cambridge to give me his verdict.

'I've only seen a faxed version,' he said, 'but I asked a girl in our New York office to take a look at it on the news-stand and she said it wouldn't have been so bad if the *Observer* wasn't printed on pink paper.'

The imaginary gun was back at my head.

'How does the faxed version look?' I asked.

I was hoping Radziewicz would say something nice – *anything* – to cushion the blow.

'Well, Toby, let me put it this way: I hope that some of these distortions are due to the telephonic transmission of the image.'

PART THREE

FROM HERE TO PATERNITY

11

BLOODY HELL!

'Look, bubby.'

It was 6.45 a.m. and Caroline was sitting on the side of the bed holding what looked like a lollipop stick. What was going on? Why had she woken me at this ungodly hour?

Then the penny dropped.

'That's not what I think it is, is it?'

'Yes.'

'Well, what does it say?'

She indicated two pink lines.

'Does that mean you're pregnant?'

I'd rehearsed this moment a hundred times in my head. I knew that the right thing to do was to jump for joy, to reassure her that I wanted a baby as much as she did. But she'd caught me off guard.

'*Bloody hell.*'

My mind immediately went back to the argument we'd had two weeks earlier about whether to continue having unprotected sex. We'd never *decided* not to use protection – it was just something we'd drifted into in the past few months. Or, to be more precise, she was quite keen to get pregnant and, without ever having said as much, I was just passively going along with this. To utilise a concept that the philosopher John Locke came up with, I'd *tacitly* consented to it simply by not objecting to it. However, I'd finally decided we ought to have a grown-up conversation about it. I wasn't necessarily opposed to the idea – at least, that's what I told Caroline – but I thought it was something we should discuss out in the open.

My main concern, I explained during this conversation, was the negative impact it would have on her career. Caroline was halfway through her two-year training contract at a prestigious law firm and if she got pregnant – still a wholly notional concept at this point – she wouldn't be able to complete it. A recent change in the Law Society's Code of Practice meant that trainee solicitors were now eligible for maternity leave so Caroline could take the last few months off and still technically complete her training contract. But if she qualified as a solicitor by default, so to speak, she was bound to alienate the firm in question who'd chosen her from among hundreds of ambitious applicants. For wannabe solicitors, securing a full-time position at the firms where they've done their training is often their best hope of full-time employment. There was nothing to prevent Caroline from applying for a job at another firm at some point in the future, but what decent law firm would take on a woman who had a small child at home and no experience as a practising solicitor?

Apart from the financial implications – I'd been looking forward to splitting the bills with Caroline for several years to come – I was worried about the effect it would have on our relationship. I told Caroline about the regrets that my mother had had about giving up her job at Radio 3 when she got pregnant with my older sister. After she left the BBC she went on to do a number of high-powered part-time jobs, including editing the educational magazine *Where*, but the organisations she worked for were nearly always connected to my father and it was a cause of considerable frustration that she never had an independent source of status. She often said, only half jokingly, that if she hadn't given up her broadcasting career in order to have my sister and me she could have become the BBC's first woman Director-General – and, on some level, she blamed my father for this disappointment.

Wouldn't Caroline find it equally emasculating to be so dependent on me? And wasn't it at least possible that this would become a source of resentment later in our marriage?

'First of all, I'm not particularly ambitious,' she said. 'It's not like I'll feel deeply unfulfilled if I don't have a high-flying career. And second of all, you're not pressurising me into having children. If anything, it's the other way round. Oh, and by the way, being a solicitor isn't the most exciting job in the world.'

'It's all very well for you to say that now, but you don't know how you'll feel after you've spent five years buried in nappies. That may turn out to be *even more boring* than being a solicitor. In those circumstances, it's inevitable that you'll end up resenting me. It won't matter that it was your decision to start a family. You'll blame me for not persuading you to change your mind.'

She thought for a moment.

'Listen, you do want to have children, don't you? I mean, that's a given, right?'

'At some point, yes, but I don't want you to foreclose any of your other options by getting pregnant now.'

'Okay, suppose I complete my training contract, get a full-time job and then put off having children until I've been made a partner. Let's put to one side the fact that I'll be at least thirty-five by then and may have difficulties conceiving and, even if I do, the chances of something going wrong will dramatically increase. Let's suppose it all goes like clockwork. What then? Am I supposed to go back to work three months after I've given birth? Have you ever talked to women in this situation? Women trying to juggle motherhood and a career? I have and, believe me, they're miserable. They hate not being there when their child takes its first steps. They hate the fact that the nanny has a closer relationship with their child than they do. And do you realise how much a full-time nanny costs?

Practically all my salary would go on childcare. I mean, what's the point?'

'The point is you'd have an independent source of social status. You'd be a professional person in your own right. At dinner parties, you wouldn't just be Mrs Toby Young.'

She stared at me in disbelief.

'Let me get this straight. You want me to work my arse off all day, do a job I hate and feel really, really guilty about the fact that I'm a crap mother just so when someone asks me what I do at a dinner party I can say, "I'm a solicitor"?'

'Basically, yes.'

She narrowed her eyes.

'This isn't about my status, is it? It's about yours. You're the one who'll be embarrassed about being married to someone who's "just a housewife". You want me to have a career because you have this pathetic fantasy of wanting to be part of a' – she put air-quotes around it – '"power couple".'

She had a point.

When I thought about it, I did want to be married to a successful career woman and, undoubtedly, one of the reasons for that was because I thought it would reflect well on me (not least in the eyes of other career women). And, of course, that was a ridiculous reason for wanting Caroline to postpone getting pregnant. Why should Caroline sacrifice her own happiness just to satisfy my own insatiable desire for status?

But there was another part of me that wanted Caroline to become a lawyer because I knew she'd do it so well. It was only when it began to seem more and more unlikely that she'd pursue a legal career that I realised how much I'd been looking forward to seeing her blossom in that profession.

'The thing is, darling, you're so good at arguing. I mean, just listen to yourself. You may not have any burning desire to be a lawyer, but you'd be really, really good at it.'

'Wait a minute,' she said, leaping on this point in her typical lawyerly fashion. 'This is an argument I can't win. Either I fail to persuade you I shouldn't become a lawyer, in which case I should become a lawyer, or I succeed in persuading you, in which case I should become a lawyer.'

As usual, she'd won the argument. If starting a family was what she really wanted, and she was absolutely convinced that being a wife and mother would make her more happy than having a career, then we should continue to have unprotected sex.

'Don't worry,' she said. 'I probably won't get pregnant for at least a year.'

Over the next few weeks, as the news that I was going to be a father gradually sank in, I began to worry about the effects it would have on *my* career, too. As an aspiring writer, shouldn't I try and reduce the demands on my time rather than increase them? Of the various enemies of promise identified by Cyril Connolly, I already had to contend with journalism and drink. Wasn't it a bit rash to throw in the 'pram in the hall' as well?

Then again, perhaps Connolly wasn't the best guide in these matters. Anyone even vaguely familiar with his dissolute life knew that these were just the excuses he came up with for not producing the masterpiece he thought he was capable of. (At one stage, he even blamed his love of conversation, referring to it as 'a ceremony of self-wastage'.) Connolly's real vice wasn't avarice, gluttony or lust; it was his addiction to displacement activity, the fact that he'd prefer to do almost anything other than write. In a diary entry made shortly after she married Connolly, Barbara Skelton wrote: 'Feel very restive and dissatisfied, saddled with a slothful whale of a husband who spends his time soaking in the bath and then plods despondently to White's where he studies the racing form.'

Still, even if the 'pram in the hall' wasn't responsible for Connolly's failings, shouldn't aspiring writers still try and avoid having children, particularly in the twenty-first century? Connolly probably never had to change a nappy in his life, whereas I could envision an endless series of chores: bath time, bedtime, night feeds. Caroline might not be intending to share any of the financial burden of running the household, but she'd still expect me to share the domestic burden. Up until now, the only time I'd found to write the things I really wanted to write was after midnight, when the phone had stopped ringing and Caroline had gone to bed. How could I continue to burn the midnight oil if I was going to be woken at 6 a.m. by the pitter-patter of tiny feet? Given the need to earn a living – a need that would only increase as my family grew in size – where on earth would I find the time to write anything worthwhile?

I was reminded of Thomas More's letter to Peter Gilles that forms the preface to *Utopia* in which he apologises for not finishing the work sooner:

> You see, when I get home, I've got to talk to my wife, have a chat with my children, and discuss things with my servants. I count this as one of my commitments, because it's absolutely necessary, if I'm not to be a stranger in my own home.
>
> Thus the days, the months, the years slip by. You may ask, when do I write then? Well, so far, I haven't mentioned sleep or meals and in fact the only time I ever get to myself is what I steal from sleep and meals.

Of course, not all writers find the trappings of domesticity so burdensome. For some, it's only when they're settled in a stable and loving relationship – with the children playing happily in the garden – that they're able to let their imaginations run wild. 'It is the reverse of the Cyril Connolly dictum,' Zoë Heller told an interviewer in the *Observer* after her second novel had been short-listed for the Booker Prize. 'The pram in the hall has been very good to me. Instead of all the psychic energy expended on "Where am I going out tonight? Does he love me? Who am I really?" – happiness, domesticity and routine has freed up an awful lot of mental energy. I know it is an anti-romantic image of the creative process, but I really believe it.'[1]

Nevertheless, I was nervous. In order to make it as a writer – particularly of screenplays, which are incredibly labour intensive – I'd have to be completely ruthless when it came to choosing between my laptop and my family. I'd have to find that splinter of ice in my heart that Graham Greene said all writers must have if they're going to produce anything of merit. But was it there to be discovered? I wasn't sure. I was reminded of something Martin Amis had said during a Q & A at a New York bookshop I'd attended. It was back when I worked for *Vanity Fair* and I'd gone along to hear him with James Wolcott. Someone in the audience asked Amis how he managed to be so prolific, given that he had an illegitimate daughter with an ex-girlfriend, two sons by his first wife and two daughters by his second.

'Well,' he said, rather sheepishly, 'the work tends to come first.'

'No shit,' whispered Wolcott.

I didn't have to study Amis's life to appreciate the costs associated with this strategy. My friend Sean Langan, who had recently become a father, was also putting the work first and it wasn't going down particularly well with his wife.

Anabel's pregnancy coincided with a three-part documentary series Sean was making that involved travelling across South America on a motorbike. The idea was to duplicate the journey Che Guevara had made thirty years earlier, though it wasn't identical in every respect since Sean's beautiful Anglo-German wife had her arms wrapped around his waist. After she got pregnant, Anabel told Sean she was determined to stay by his side – or, rather, behind his

1 The interviewer didn't ask Heller what effect the birth of her two children had had on her partner, the screenwriter Lawrence Konner. Judging from his recent output – *Planet of the Apes* (2001), *Mona Lisa Smile* (2003) – it hasn't 'freed up' the 'creative process' for him.

back – for as long as she possibly could and he said that was perfectly okay, provided she didn't expect him to slow down. *Travels of a Gringo* had been commissioned by Channel 4 and he was already several months behind schedule.

The low point, according to Anabel, was when they were filming an interview with Hugo Chavez, who was then in his first term as President of Venezuela. She was standing to one side, observing her husband at work, when, quite unexpectedly, she fainted.

'Santa Maria!' exclaimed the President. 'Your wife! She just collapsed.'

'Oh, don't mind her,' said Sean, squinting at Chavez through the viewfinder. 'She's pregnant. Now, Mr President, about these oil tariffs . . .'

Anabel returned to London shortly after this incident and, among the couple's friends, it became a source of much speculation as to whether Sean would complete the film before her due date. In the end, he made it back in the nick of time, but he did little to redeem himself in the maternity ward of Queen Charlotte's Hospital. After Anabel had been in labour for less than half an hour, following a mad dash to the hospital, he told her he was so traumatised and exhausted by the experience he felt as if he'd personally had twins. Twenty-six hours later, when she finally gave birth to their son, she still hadn't forgotten this remark.

Not surprisingly, Caroline was aghast at Sean's behaviour. The final straw, as far as she was concerned, was when he returned to South America to film some additional scenes just six weeks later, leaving Anabel to contend with their newborn alone. I made a great show of agreeing with Caroline that Sean's behaviour was completely unacceptable – 'I'm shocked, *shocked*!' – but, secretly, I rather admired him. Anabel was every bit as tough as Caroline, yet Sean had simply refused to modify his behaviour. It was if he was sending her a message: *On this and all future occasions, my career comes first.* Sean may not have been a writer, but he undoubtedly possessed the splinter of ice that Graham Greene was talking about. He had a powerful sense of vocation and, by ruthlessly pursuing it, not only had he made a name for himself, he'd discovered himself, too. The charming Irish-Portuguese rogue I'd grown up with had become a *homme serieux*, a great foreign correspondent in the tradition of James Cameron and Nicholas Tomalin. As the television critic of the *Financial Times* wrote: 'Whether openly or secretly, most stay-at-home journalists are in awe of those lone wolf reporters such as Sean Langan who keep us informed about the forbidden parts of the world.' Sean wasn't about to jeopardise that reputation by remaining in London and changing nappies.

The price he paid, though, was that Anabel became more and more disenchanted with their marriage. At first, she was fairly good-humoured about Sean's uncompromising professionalism – she enjoyed telling the Chavez story at dinner parties – but when it became apparent that this wasn't going to be an isolated incident, that this was how he intended to carry on, she began to seethe. When she'd married Sean, she envisioned a future in which they'd travel the world together, living a nomadic, romantic existence, and keeping body and soul together by making documentaries. But the birth of their child immediately rendered that fantasy impractical. The alternative, whereby she stayed in London and looked after the kids while he criss-crossed the globe picking up awards, was significantly less attractive. She was willing to put up with it for the time being, telling herself that his career was particularly hot right now and he had an opportunity to make a series of films that would really consolidate his reputation, but there was a limit to her tolerance.

If their marriage was going to last, Sean would have to compromise.

'Listen to this,' said Caroline. It was a few days after she'd taken the pregnancy test and she was reading aloud from a book called *What to Expect ... when you're expecting*. This American pregnancy manual – 'by mothers, for mothers' – had become a source of constant amusement to us on account of the way in which it tried to sugar-coat its puritanical advice by presenting it in a non-judge-mental fashion. This comes under the heading 'An Early Baby Present': 'Chances are quitting smoking won't be easy, as you probably already know if you've tried to do it in the past. But a smoke-free environment – in utero and out – is the very best gift you can give to your baby.'

She looked up at me and mimed sticking her fingers down her throat.

'It's enough to make you want to take up smoking,' she said.

Flipping to another section, she proceeded to itemise the long list of horrors that a woman can look forward to during pregnancy. They sounded so absurdly grim, in spite of the authors' efforts to soft-pedal them, that we both laughed almost continuously. I told her, half jokingly, that it might have made more sense to read the book before deciding to get pregnant. It was as though she'd made an enormous effort to get on a ship, even though she knew next to nothing about the on-board conditions and even less about the destination.

'Welcome aboard HMS *Pregnancia*,' I said. 'During the voyage, you'll have to urinate more frequently than normal, you'll suffer from increased flatulence and you'll vomit repeatedly. When we arrive at our destination – after nine months at sea – the process of disembarkation will be almost unendurably painful and, once there, you won't be able to go anywhere else for the next eighteen years. For the first year at least, your sleep will be constantly interrupted by a great deal of noise and, even when it isn't, you'll have to get up every three hours and spend forty-five minutes performing a task that will make your nipples feel like they're on fire. You will always have the option of getting back on board HMS *Pregnancia*, but bear in mind that after another nine months of incontinence, flatulence and vomiting, you will return to exactly the same place, only this time you'll have at least twice as much work to do as you did before.

'Have a good trip!'

'I want to get off,' she said.

12

SCHMUCKS WITH UNDERWOODS

I can pinpoint the exact moment I fell in love with Robert McKee, the famous Hollywood screenwriting 'guru'. It was on the final day of a three-day seminar entitled 'Robert McKee's Story Structure' that he was giving in London's Scientific Lecture Theatre. I was sitting in the auditorium with about two hundred other people, most of them aspiring screenwriters, when he suddenly veered off into a digression about Charlotte Rampling. My ears pricked up because, quite by chance, I happened to be sitting next to Carmen Callil, Britain's leading feminist publisher. During the previous two days, McKee had often launched into soliloquies about actresses he admired, praising them as much for their physical attributes as their technique, and on each occasion I'd noticed Callil bridling slightly. Clearly, she suspected McKee of being a Male Chauvinist Pig, though up until this point he hadn't said anything too self-incriminating. He'd merely sailed very close to the wind. I was hoping he'd finally cross the line.

'Charlotte Rampling,' he said, concluding his five-minute eulogy. 'She can sit on my face ANY TIME.'

I immediately cut a sideways glance at Callil. For a second or two, her mouth hung open in astonishment. Then, suddenly becoming aware that several people in the auditorium were monitoring her reaction, she adjusted her seating position too quickly and slid forwards.

The founder of Virago Press had fallen off her chair.

On the face of it, this story doesn't reflect particularly well on McKee. The cost of the three-day course was £411.25 and it isn't clear why a group of impoverished writers should pay that kind of money to listen to the sexual fantasies of a portly, middle-aged man. As for his credentials as a screenwriting 'guru' – a breed of snake-oil salesmen that dates back to the birth of the motion picture industry – they're laughably unimpressive. On the IMDb (Internet Movie Database), a definitive online reference source, he has only three credits: as the writer of a four-part television series called *Abraham*; as one of twenty writers on a short-lived *Columbo* spin-off called *Mrs Columbo;* and as the 'story consultant' on a straight-to-video 'animated feature' (i.e., a cartoon) called *Barbie as the Princess and the Pauper.*

Yet his former pupils include Peter Jackson, Kirk Douglas, John Cleese, Julia Roberts, Lawrence Kasdan, Eddie Izzard, Joel Schumacher and David Bowie, to name but a few. Pixar, the digital animation studio, sends ten people to take the Story Structure course every year. He has been hired to teach CEOs how to write better speeches. He's even been invited to speak to NASA. Between them, his students have won 26 Oscars, 124 Emmies, 20 Writers Guild of America Awards and 17 Directors Guild of America Awards and, according to the *New York Times*, the only Hollywood notable *not* to have taken his seminar is Steven Spielberg.[1]

So what accounts for McKee's success? Well, to begin with, he knows his onions. As an undergraduate at the University of Michigan, he fell under the spell of Kenneth Rowe, the creative writing professor who taught a legendary seminar on playwriting. (His most famous student was Arthur Miller.) After graduating,

1 These figures were up to date at the end of 2005.

McKee embarked on a career in the theatre, as both an actor and a director, but he returned to Ann Arbor, first to take a Masters in Theatre Arts and then to study for a Ph.D. at the Cinema School.

McKee owes his career to his insight that Rowe's teaching, summed up in his masterful book *Write That Play*, could equally well be applied to screenwriting. 'The basic structure of a play,' Rowe maintains, 'is the beginning of a conflict, the movement by complications to a crisis or turning point and the movement to the resolution of the conflict.' If you substitute the word 'screenplay' for 'play', that's the kernel of McKee's teaching, too.

Then there's his take-no-prisoners style, as illustrated by the Charlotte Rampling remark. On day one of his seminar at the Scientific Lecture Theatre he swaggered on to the stage with all the macho self-confidence of a gunfighter. Indeed, he was dressed a little like Lee Marvin in *The Man Who Shot Liberty Valance* – black boots, black pants, black shirt (though without the black hat). He spoke in a low, stentorian voice, laying down the basic principles of screenwriting in tablets of stone, and daring anyone to challenge him. ('Bad movies are sometimes made from good scripts, but good movies are never made from bad scripts.') Those foolish enough to do so got very short shrift. 'If you interrupt me one more time you're gonna have to leave,' he told a woman in the front row. He had a messianic quality, as if he was bringing down the Holy Word from Mount Hollywood and he wasn't about to tolerate any heretics. He actually summed up his entire screenwriting philosophy in ten bullet points and referred to them as 'McKee's Ten Commandments'.[1]

---

1 Not to be confused with the eleven rules Preston Sturges came up with to ensure box office success: 1. A pretty girl is better than an ugly one. 2. A leg is better than an arm. 3. A bedroom is better than a living room. 4. An arrival is better than a departure. 5. A birth is better than a death. 6. A chase is better than a chat. 7. A dog is better than a landscape. 8. A kitten is better than a dog. 9. A baby is better than a kitten. 10. A kiss is better than a baby. 11. A pratfall is better than anything.

Such extreme pedagogy can easily come across as arrogant and self-important, but McKee has the personal magnetism to pull it off. He's what's referred to as a 'charismatic teacher', a male version of Miss Jean Brodie. At first, I resisted the gravitational pull emanating from the podium – *Who is this wanker?* – but after a brief struggle I gave up the fight. There are many different ways of teaching, all with something to be said for them, but the great thing about the charismatic teacher is that he can *inspire* his students.

The thing I found most appealing about McKee was his belief in traditional storytelling. Not for him the avant-garde experimentalism of small, independent filmmakers like Derek Jarman and Peter Greenaway. He's a firm believer in the craft of storytelling – a craft that can be learnt only by studying genre masters like William Goldman and Robert Towne. According to McKee, a good screenplay should transcend its individual subject matter and communicate eternal truths about the human condition – and the only way it can do that is by conforming to certain universal principles of storytelling.

McKee's insistence that there are guidelines that all screenwriters have to master before they can produce good work shouldn't be confused with the belief that there's a time-tested formula for making commercially successful pictures. In the course of giving his Story Structure seminar, McKee repeatedly quoted William Goldman's famous maxim, namely, that when it comes to predicting which films are going to light up the box office each year, 'No one knows anything.' To describe the principles of storytelling McKee subscribes to as a blueprint for making hit movies would be the equivalent of dismissing Aristotle's *Poetics* on the grounds that the Greek philosopher reduces all great narrative art to one, catch-all formula. McKee is absolutely insistent that he teaches form, not formula.

By the same token, McKee's claim that in order to 'work' a film has to be properly crafted shouldn't be mistaken for the belief that commercial movies are superior to non-commercial ones. On the contrary, at the seminar I attended McKee was incredibly scornful about a whole raft of successful pictures, including *Titanic* and *The English Patient*. Rather, he believes that all screenwriters, no matter how ambitious, should be aware of the storyteller's craft and only when they've mastered it can they then start to experiment with different forms. Even the most celebrated art-house directors, he pointed out, began as successful genre filmmakers.

If all this sounds a bit didactic it's because McKee has been teaching his course since 1981 and has had constantly to contend with his students' knee-jerk dismissal of 'Hollywood' movies. The thing I really liked about McKee's seminar was that he had taken up the cudgels on behalf of an unfashionable approach to movie-making and wasn't afraid to take the fight to the opposition. He was constantly raining blows on trendy European directors, who are second to none when it comes to creating 'pretty pictures', but completely clueless about 'deep structure'. In effect, McKee provided me with a way of fleshing out my own prejudice in favour of traditional narratives. If I was going to become a screenwriter, I didn't want to write small, European films that would make the rounds of the festival circuit and then be seen no more. I wanted to create great, popular entertainment that would endure for decades to come.

When FilmFour went belly up, I assumed the movie rights to *How to Lose Friends* would revert back to me. Indeed, I regarded the closure of FilmFour as a blessing in disguise since the book was now selling quite well in America, prompting renewed interest in Hollywood. My plan was to claw back the rights from FilmFour's parent company and hold another auction. Given the book's 'hot' status, I began to fantasise once again about a 'Hornby-esque' offer.

After talking it over with my agent in the autumn of 2002, I decided my best strategy was simply to arrange a meeting with Mark Thompson, the newly appointed chief executive of Channel 4, and ask him to give me the rights back. Thompson, formerly a high-ranking BBC executive, had taken the helm at Channel 4 the previous December and it had been his decision to shut down the broadcaster's loss-making film division. At the time of its closure, FilmFour had sixty or so films in development and the word on the street was that Thompson was planning to return the rights to all of them in due course. The point of the meeting was to try and expedite the process.

Paul Webster, the former head of FilmFour, was still an employee of Channel 4 at this stage and, since he was feeling a little sheepish about having acquired the rights to *How to Lose Friends* just six weeks before the company closed, he agreed to come along to the meeting to help me press my case. I managed to schedule a 12 o'clock appointment with Thompson at Channel 4's Horseferry Road headquarters and Webster and I arranged to have a quick chat beforehand so he could coach me on what to say.

I'd been planning to make a financial argument, offering to repay Channel 4 for the unexpired portion of their eighteen-month option. This struck me as a good way of speeding things up since the quicker they returned the rights, the more money they'd get back. However, Webster told me he didn't think this would be necessary. He thought that Channel 4 would accept the 'moral case' – that I had done the deal with FilmFour under the impression that the company was a going concern and would shortly put the movie into 'fast-track' development. Given that the story was set in New York in the years 1995 to 2000, the project had a limited shelf life and I now had an opportunity to get the film made by doing a deal with one of the eight major studios. But I needed to strike sooner rather than later because the book wouldn't remain on Hollywood's radar screen for ever.

'That should be enough,' Webster said. 'Mark doesn't want to get a reputation as the ogre of Horseferry Road.'

In fact, Thompson already did have a reputation as a bit of an ogre, thanks to an incident many years earlier when he'd bitten a junior BBC colleague. 'It hurt,' said the victim. 'I pulled my arm out of his jaws, like a stick out of the jaws of a Labrador.' (The BBC dismissed the incident as 'high jinks' and 'horseplay'.)

We entered Thompson's office at 12.15 p.m. and the first thing that struck me was his air of power. I was reminded of something Conrad Black had once said about Max Hastings: he looked as though he wouldn't have any qualms about drowning kittens. Thompson's office was very different in appearance from Mr Hollywood's – no plasma, no water feature, no trophies – but it had the same, slightly oppressive atmosphere. I had the sense of being in the dragon's den.[1]

'So, where are we on this?' he asked Webster.

'Toby and I were just having a conversation downstairs and I think Toby should repeat to you what he's just said to me,' he replied.

The ball was in my court.

I pressed the 'moral case' as forcefully as I could, but I was inhibited by Thompson's slightly intimidating presence. He kept a poker face throughout, regarding me with Olympian detachment.

'This is something I want to hang on to, I'm afraid,' he said after I'd set out my stall. 'I know that's not what you want to hear, but I'm very keen to take this forward.'

He explained that FilmFour would shortly be resurrected, though on a much more modest scale, and this was one of half a dozen projects he wanted to continue to develop.

'So,' he said, apparently changing the subject, 'how's the script coming along?'

That floored me. Back when FilmFour still existed, I'd turned in a preliminary treatment which had then been politely eviscerated by a development executive. I'd been working on a second draft of the treatment when *Variety* announced that the company had been 'shuttered' and since then I'd consigned it to my bottom drawer. Technically, I was supposed to have completed

1 Less than two years later, Thompson became the Director-General of the BBC.

a full-length screenplay within six months of signing the contract, but I'd assumed that that deadline could be safely ignored.

'I've written a first draft, obviously, but I'm not quite ready to show it to anyone yet,' I said. 'It still needs polishing.'

'Can you get me something by the end of January?'

That was less than six weeks away.

'Sure, no problem.'

'Good. I look forward to reading it.'

The possibility of meeting that deadline was pretty remote, not least because the screenplay I was supposed to be writing for Mr Hollywood was also due at the end of January. How on earth was I going to produce *two* scripts by then? Ben Hecht, the legendary American screenwriter, claimed that he wrote over half his scripts in under a fortnight – but he was a certified genius. In 1939, ten films that he'd worked on were released, including *Gone with the Wind, Stagecoach, His Girl Friday, Gunga Din* and *Wuthering Heights.*[1] Judging from the progress I'd made on the biopic about the record producer, by contrast, I had almost no aptitude for screenwriting. It had taken me a fortnight just to write the word 'Untitled' at the top of the first page.

At this stage, the only textbook I'd read on the subject was *Screenplay* by Syd Field. Written in 1979 – and peppered with references to films like *Jeremiah Johnson, Three Days of the Condor* and *Dog Day Afternoon – Screenplay* is a how-to book for the complete beginner. 'A screenplay is a STORY TOLD WITH PICTURES,' Field informs us on the first page (his emphasis). Like Robert McKee, his credentials as a screenwriting 'guru' are pretty threadbare. He's certainly no literary critic. On page 160 of *Screenplay* he includes a brief aside about Shakespeare's supposed difficulties in mastering his chosen form. 'Only when he completed *Hamlet* did

---

1 Hecht said: 'Anybody with a good memory for clichés and unafraid to write like a child can bat out a superb movie in a few days.'

he transcend the limitations of the stage and create great stage art,'
he tells us. In Field's view, then, all of the plays Shakespeare wrote
before *Hamlet*, including *The Taming of the Shrew, Richard III, Titus
Andronicus, A Midsummer Night's Dream, Romeo and Juliet, The
Merchant of Venice, Henry IV* parts I and 2, *Much Ado About
Nothing, Henry V, Julius Caesar* and *Twelfth Night*, do not constitute
'great stage art'.

On the face of it, the rudiments of screenwriting, as set out by
Field, are fairly simple. To start with, you've got to divide your story
into three acts, otherwise known as the beginning, the middle and
the end. 'Act I' has to start with a 'setup', in which you introduce
the main character and set your story in motion, and it has to end
with a 'plot point', an incident that spins your story off in a new
direction. 'Act II' has to contain the bulk of the action, in which the
protagonist must confront a series of increasingly difficult obstacles
and, like 'Act I', end with a 'plot point'. And, finally, 'Act III' has to
contain the 'resolution' of your story in which, typically, the main
character either kills his chief antagonist, saves the planet from space
aliens or gets the girl (or, ideally, all three). And it doesn't really
matter if it's all been done before.

So far, so good. But as soon as I began to think about screenwriting in any depth, the rules quickly became more complicated.
For instance, the main character cannot simply react to a series of
external events; he has to be proactive. The plot must be driven by
the choices he makes. These choices have to be organic – they have
to be the kinds of choices that this particular character *would*
make – and yet, at the same time, they have to move the story forward in a dramatically satisfying way. That is, the narrative has to
develop in the strict, rule-bound way that is required by whichever
genre you've chosen to work within.

If it's a romantic comedy, for instance, the third act has to climax
with a scene in which the male lead is seen racing through the
streets, whether on foot or in some kind of motorised vehicle, to
rendezvous with the female lead, preferably against the background

of a 'ticking clock' – this is actually a screenwriting term of art – such as a plane about to take off or a wedding about to take place. And his final declaration has to be made in a very public way, such as over the public address system in a football stadium or bellowed from one end of a crowded railway platform to another. He can't just call her on his mobile and tell her to jump in a cab.

Even taking all that into account, you've barely scratched the surface. Few films have just one main character – a hero in the classical sense. Rather, they have a set of characters – some good, some bad, most somewhere in between – and not only do they all have to interact in a way which is both organic and dramatically satisfying, but each one has to have an 'arc' (another term of art). That is to say, they have to be transformed by their experience – and in a good way, too, as if they've undergone an extremely effective form of therapy.

And this is before you've even begun to think about the sub-plot.

In the course of mapping out the script for Mr Hollywood, I found it impossible to make all these different elements dovetail together. I'd imagined, naively, that writing a screenplay would be a matter of getting my creative juices flowing and then sitting back as a set of fully formed characters leapt out of my unconscious and started dictating their own dialogue. In fact, it was much more like doing a Rubik's Cube, only a cube with many more than nine squares on each side.[1]

The thing that really puzzled me, though, wasn't the issue of how anyone managed to get all the bits of the cube to line up correctly,

---

[1] For some screenwriters, the characters really do start dictating their own dialogue. According to Robert Benton, the writer of *Bonnie and Clyde*, *Kramer vs. Kramer* and *Places in the Heart*: 'What happens to me a lot is that the characters themselves take over; they acquire a heft, a size, a life of their own, and at some point they're often determined to do what they want to do regardless of what I have in mind. I listen to them – sometimes to my detriment, because sometimes the characters I write aren't smart enough to be in a movie.'

difficult though that was. Rather, it was the question of how someone was able simultaneously to 'do' the Cube *and* create a genuine
work of art. Merely producing a piece of work that ticked all the
boxes was hard enough, but managing to write something that was
also pretty good . . . How was that possible? How was it done?[1]

I experienced a similar sense of bafflement when I reviewed a
production of *Hedda Gabler* for the *Spectator*. I was struck dumb by
Ibsen's artistry. His characters lived and breathed – everything they
did seemed completely in keeping with exactly who they were – yet
they also managed to interact in a way that produced an exquisite
piece of drama. How did Ibsen pull it off? How was he able to
shunt his characters around like chess pieces – for that's what's
required to produce a satisfying dramatic narrative – and yet simultaneously foster the illusion that they were moving entirely under
their own steam? Somehow, he was able to combine the kind of
finicky, mathematical intelligence required to put together a play as
well constructed as *Hedda Gabler* and, at the same time, not stifle
the creative flow that enabled him to produce such fully realised,
three-dimensional characters as George Tesman, Mrs Elvsted, Judge
Brack, Eilert Lövborg and Hedda herself. Ibsen said that at the
moment of conception a playwright must be on fire, but at the time
of writing, cold. Yet, in being cold, don't you extinguish the fire?
How is a playwright – or a screenwriter – able to access his unconscious while doing a Rubik's Cube?

In a classically designed screenplay, according to Robert McKee, the
story is set in motion by an 'inciting incident', a dynamic event that
radically alters the balance of forces in the protagonist's life. In
Casablanca, for instance, it's the moment Ilsa walks into Rick's bar,
while in *Kramer vs. Kramer* it's Mrs Kramer's decision to walk out

---

1 'All you do,' said Gene Fowler, the writer of *White Fang, The Call of the Mild and What
Price Hollywood*, 'is stare at a blank sheet of paper until drops of blood form on your forehead.'

on Mr Kramer and their child. After an 'inciting incident' has occurred the story then becomes about the protagonist's pursuit of whatever will restore his life to equilibrium, a quest that, if successful, will result in a deeper, more satisfying state of balance than the one he started out with at the beginning of the film. By the end of *Casablanca*, Rick doesn't merely achieve closure in his relationship with Ilsa, he rediscovers his sense of humanity – and at the conclusion of *Kramer vs. Kramer*, Mr Kramer hasn't simply learnt to cope with being a single parent, he's taught himself how to be a proper father as well.

One of the ironies of McKee's Story Structure seminar is that this doesn't just apply to the stories – it's true of the storytellers as well. Like most of the people taking the course, I had a sense that my life wouldn't be complete – wouldn't be *in balance* – until I'd produced a piece of writing that I could be proud of. In spite of everything, I was dissatisfied with my lot and I'd focused on screenwriting as a source of salvation. I was convinced that I wouldn't be truly happy until I'd joined the exclusive club of people who make a living from writing screenplays. To use a bit of McKee jargon, becoming a successful screenwriter was my 'deep desire'.

McKee himself is all too aware of just how personally the people in the lecture theatre respond to his course. 'The students realise that it's their life I'm talking about: it's out of balance, they're struggling to put it into balance,' he told *The New Yorker* in 2003. 'How are they going to do it? They have conceived of that object, that something, that if they could get it, would restore the balance of their life. Now, for the character, it could be that he needs to right the injustice that was done to his family; it could be to find something worth living for to get him up in the morning. Right? But for the students it's a successful piece of writing. And until they achieve a successful piece of writing, their lives will be perpetually out of balance.'

There was no doubt that at the end of McKee's three-day seminar I did feel genuinely inspired. I couldn't wait to get home and turn on my computer. In that respect, 'Robert McKee's Story Structure' was well worth £411.25. But even equipped with the 'McKee's Ten Commandments', I still wasn't confident I could actually sit down and write a screenplay. Taking a screenwriting course, I realised, was a little like taking a course in how to be a chess grandmaster. Boning up on the theory was all very well, but it didn't help much if you lacked any innate ability. I began to suspect that being able to write a good script – like the ability to play chess at a very high level – was one of those rare talents that you're either born with or you're not.

And I didn't think I had been.

13

WELCOME TO PARENTHOOD

The moment I saw Caroline's face I knew something was wrong. We were spending the Christmas holidays in Verbier, a Swiss ski resort, and I'd arranged to meet her for lunch at a mountain-top restaurant called Cabin de Mont Fort. I'd spent the morning 'guiding' – skiing with a mountain guide – while she'd been piste-bashing with a friend.

'What's the matter?' I asked.

'I think I might have injured the baby,' she said.

It turned out she'd had a bad fall earlier that morning, landing on her stomach. Twenty minutes later she felt a 'violent twinge'.

'What if I've killed it?' she asked.

I told her not to be silly. The unborn child is an incredibly resilient creature. It can survive car crashes, falls from second-floor windows, extreme temperatures. There have even been instances of babies being born to mothers who've experienced such terrible head trauma they're clinically 'brain dead'. It would take more than a minor skiing accident to cause any serious damage.

But she was far from reassured. On the contrary, she was angry that I was being so blasé about it.

'How do you know it's going to be okay?' she said. 'I don't

understand why you aren't more worried. It's as if you don't care. Why did you let me come skiing in the first place?'

The answer to that question, regrettably, was that I'd been too much of a skinflint to cancel the holiday. By the time Caroline had dropped her little bombshell, I'd paid for the flights and put down a deposit on the chalet and I was damned if I was going to write that off. Caroline was understandably a little anxious about doing something so risky, but I pointed out that she was an extremely competent skier and the only danger she faced was the possibility that someone might crash into her. After she still wasn't convinced, I told her to ask our family doctor whom I knew to be very broad-minded.

'It's not advisable,' she told Caroline, 'but if it was me I probably would.'

We arrived in Verbier on Boxing Day and went skiing for the first time on 27 December. As I watched Caroline gingerly pick her way through a mogul field I began to worry that my insistence on not cancelling the trip might have been a mistake. I've had enough skiing accidents in my time to know that there's a long moment between something going wrong and the impact of the crash when your life flashes before you. As Caroline was falling through the air she'd be gripped with terror, not only for herself, but for our unborn child as well. Then, just before hitting the deck, she'd probably think: *This is all Toby's fault. As soon as I'm out of traction I'm going to divorce the little cunt.*

In the twelve weeks since Caroline had announced she was pregnant, I hadn't reacted in the way expectant fathers are supposed to. I was constantly being asked by Caroline's friends how I *felt* about the prospect of becoming a father and, before I could respond, the answer was always provided for me: 'You must be thrilled.' Well, no, actually, I wasn't. My male friends who'd already had children took enormous pleasure in telling me how my life was going to be 'completely destroyed' by the arrival of the baby, and yet they expected me to look forward to it as if it was the domestic equivalent of winning the lottery. The truth was, if becoming a father automatically turned you into a baby bore, I didn't find the prospect all that exciting.

Dipping into *What to Expect . . . when you're expecting* hadn't done much to reassure me. Its relentlessly politically correct tone is guaranteed to drive even the most liberal, easy-going men into frothing-at-the-mouth reactionaries. Take what is says about sex: 'Expectant fathers, like expectant mothers, can experience a wide range of reactions when it comes to interest in sex during pregnancy – all of them "normal".' Oh, yeah? What if it makes you want to put on an enormous nappy, climb into a giant cot and stick your thumb in your mouth? Is that 'normal'?[1]

The general tone of the book is one of breathless condescension, something Caroline had had to get used to since becoming pregnant. When she first announced her good news, several people told her how 'brilliant' and 'clever' she was, as if she'd passed an exam. I wanted to point out that getting knocked up doesn't involve much in the way of intellect. People who are really quite poorly educated manage it. Even animals have been known to pull it off. In fact, IT INVOLVES ABSOLUTELY NO INTELLIGENCE WHATSO-EVER. You might as well congratulate someone for managing to use the lavatory. (On second thoughts, I was probably going to be doing a lot of that over the next few years.)

The only time my ears had pricked up at the mention of paternity was when two of Caroline's friends, a beautiful lesbian and her twenty-five-year-old Spanish girlfriend, told me they were interested in having a baby. Did I know of any potential sperm-donors? I told them that provided they didn't mind the sperm being delivered in the old-fashioned way, I could think of at least one man who might

1 It isn't all bad news. In a chapter entitled 'Oral Sex' the authors write: 'Fellatio . . . is always safe during pregnancy and for some couples is a very satisfactory substitute when intercourse isn't permitted.'

be interested in the job. Needless to say, this went down like a cup of cold sick with Caroline. When your wife's pregnant, you're not supposed to get excited at the prospect of going to bed with a couple of gorgeous lesbians. That's not 'normal', apparently.

'So, you want to see if we can see your baby move, ja?'

The speaker was the German doctor at the local medical centre. He had an amused, long-suffering air, as if he thought we were being absurdly overcautious in asking him to check up on our baby after such a trivial incident. Indeed, when Caroline initially described the accident to the nurse on duty she was told a scan probably wouldn't be necessary. The nurse pointed out that a consultation with a qualified doctor would cost 100 Swiss francs (£40), a fact that weighed quite heavily with me given that I'd forgotten to take out any travel insurance. Still, Caroline wanted to go through with it and it seemed a small price to pay for her peace of mind.

At first, the doctor's manner remained extremely light-hearted. After getting Caroline to lie on her back, he asked her to pull up her sweater and roll down the top of her trousers. He then applied some gel and started trying to detect a heartbeat. The Doppler Machine was on the equivalent of speakerphone so we could hear everything the doctor was hearing.

As soon as the sensor touched her stomach, the sound of a rapid heartbeat filled the room and I beamed at Caroline. *You see! Everything's fine.* But it was a false dawn. The doctor explained that what we were hearing was Caroline's heartbeat. 'You are nervous, ja?' he said, flashing her a sympathetic smile. 'This is your first baby, ja?' Clearly, as far as he was concerned, there was absolutely nothing to worry about.

Ten minutes later, and still no heartbeat, he'd turned into Dr Mengele.

'Who told you it was okay to ski?' he asked crossly.

'Our doctor did,' said Caroline.

'Well, I don't know what kind of doctor would tell you a thing like this.'

He continued trying to detect a heartbeat, but to no avail.

'How reliable is that machine?' I asked, pointing to the Doppler. 'Is there some other test you can do?'

'You must go to the hospital in Martigny right away,' he said, referring to the town at the bottom of the mountain. 'I will call you an air ambulance.'

At this point I know I should have been thinking about Caroline and the baby – what if the foetus had actually died as a result of the accident? – but the words 'air ambulance' started alarm bells ringing. A friend of mine had been airlifted off the mountain and taken to Martigny the previous year and he'd ended up with a bill for nearly £30,000.

'Is an air ambulance strictly necessary?' I asked. 'I mean, you can drive to Martigny in thirty minutes. Why don't we just hop in my rental car?'

Doctor Mengele gave me a withering look.

'This is an emergency,' he said.

I wanted to reply that if the baby's heart really had stopped when Caroline had felt a 'violent twinge', getting to the hospital in fifteen minutes rather than half an hour wasn't going to make much difference. On the other hand, if it was perfectly all right and he simply didn't know how to operate the Doppler Machine properly – by far the most likely explanation – I was damned if I was going to take out a second mortgage to get airlifted to the hospital.

However, one look at Caroline made me bite my tongue. Even though these seemed like perfectly logical points, I didn't want her to think I cared more about the contents of my wallet than our unborn child. More importantly, I was worried about how she'd react if she knew I was capable of such cold-blooded reasoning at a moment like this. It would confirm her suspicion, often voiced, that I was suffering from some form of Asperger's syndrome.

Surely, it was worth spending £30,000 just to avoid the potential fall-out?

Then again, that was more than I earned in a year . . .

As I piloted the Fiat Uno around a series of hairpin bends, Caroline and I barely exchanged a word. I knew that if I made any attempt to reassure her she'd just snap at me. ('How do you *know* it's going to be okay?') At one point, when we stopped at a traffic light, I reached out for her hand, only to have it snatched away. It was as if she was saying, 'Don't let's waste our time going through the motions. This is too serious for that.'

I couldn't help wondering how this episode would affect our relationship. Obviously, that would depend on how bad the news was when we arrived at the hospital. In my mind's eye, I could picture this hatchet-faced paediatrician telling us that he could have saved the baby if only we'd arrived fifteen minutes earlier. Alas, it was now too late. He'd then inform us that the foetus had to be removed immediately and, as Caroline was being wheeled into the operating theatre, I'd be presented with a bill for £30,000.

Okay, maybe that scenario was a bit far-fetched, but there were other, more likely outcomes that would be almost as bad. Suppose the baby had been long dead by the time we arrived at the hospital? Caroline would still blame me. After all, if I hadn't been so parsimonious and insisted on going through with this blasted holiday . . .

Even if she didn't remain furious with me for very long, our relationship still might not survive the death of the baby. I would need to call on reserves of compassion I wasn't sure I had. For a couple to get through something as calamitous as this, the burden has to be shared. What's required is a cohabitation of the spirit, an ability to take on one another's suffering. Would I be capable of such a thing? Nothing in my make-up suggested I would. I was a jester, a cynic, a cut-up. I didn't have the emotional vocabulary to deal with the death of an unborn child. I could easily imagine the aftermath of this tragedy being exactly like the lead-up: the two of us sitting side by side, staring straight ahead, not exchanging a word.

Then a completely left-field thought occurred to me: What if Caroline was experiencing a phantom pregnancy? Okay, there was pretty compelling circumstantial evidence – we'd had unprotected sex, Caroline stopped getting her period, a pregnancy test yielded a positive result – but we'd never actually *seen* the baby. We were scheduled to go in for the first ultrasound two days after we got back to London. What if the reason Dr Mengele hadn't been able to detect a heartbeat was because the baby didn't exist? If that was the case, then this whole anxious car journey, with the two of us consumed with fear, would turn out to be absurd – comic, even.

I tried to imagine how Caroline would react to the news that there was no baby. Would she be frightened by her ability to manufacture so many of the symptoms? Or would she see the funny side? And what about my reaction? Would I be able to resist the urge to tease her about it in the car journey back to Verbier? Poor Caroline would be in the unfortunate position of having had a very traumatic experience, but getting very little sympathy – from anyone, not just me.

No. That was ridiculous. Of course the baby existed. And, thinking about it, I felt reasonably sure everything would turn out to be fine. But how did I *know* the baby would be okay? At bottom, it was nothing more than a hunch, a gut feeling. And what if I turned out to be wrong? Not only would Caroline lose faith in me – distrust all such bland assurances hereafter – but I would, at some level, lose faith in myself. I'd been relying on a kind of precognition when deciding how much to worry about the baby and it began to dawn on me that I depended on this sixth sense across the board. I got an intuitive feeling about something almost every day, whether it was the real story behind a series of events I was writing about or an idea about how a particular scenario was going to play out, and I placed an enormous amount of confidence in that hunch. Was this a form of extreme egotism – a belief that I was blessed with some sort of supernatural gift – or were such gut feelings a central part of everybody's decision-making process?

I was terrified that if I was wrong in this instance – if everything *wasn't* okay – I would never be able to place any confidence in my intuition again. In addition to having a dead baby, an estranged wife and a bill for £30,000, I'd be a broken man.

For the first time in my life, I began to pray.

Please God, don't let anything have happened to our baby. Grant me this wish and I promise I'll repay the debt by doing at least two good deeds of equivalent worth . . .

We arrived at the hospital at 5.15 p.m. and after I'd handed over my credit card to the receptionist we were whisked up to the maternity ward on the third floor. After a brief wait, a handsome young doctor appeared and told us to follow him. He led us into his surgery and, when we'd told him what had happened, he began to arrange the ultrasound monitor so we'd both be able to see whatever he was seeing.

This immediately produced a cry of protest from Caroline.

'If it's dead, I don't want to see it,' she said, holding her arms up in front of her.

Suddenly, I was plunged into a crisis. Would she mind if I saw it? Should I ask her if she minded? Or would the sensitive thing be to simply look at her and not make any attempt to see it? In the end, the doctor set up the monitor in such a way that, while Caroline could just about avoid seeing it, I couldn't.

Caroline asked him what the likelihood of the baby being dead was, given that the other doctor hadn't been able to detect a heart-beat. He told her that Doppler Machines were notoriously unreliable and there was every chance the baby was okay. He seemed wonderfully – reassuringly – unconcerned, as if he saw two or three couples a day who were racked with anxiety because their baby's heartbeat hadn't shown up on a Doppler scan.

He applied some grease to Caroline's stomach, folding a flannel over the top of her trousers so it wouldn't stain the material, and then ran a device that looked like a Braun travel shaver back and forth across her womb. I reached out for her hand and this time she let me take it. She looked away, biting her lip.

Almost immediately, a foetus popped up on the monitor. Was it alive? I couldn't tell. Then, in answer to my question, it suddenly went into a spasm, as if it had been jabbed with a cattle prod.

'Look,' said the doctor, turning the monitor towards Caroline.

Caroline jerked her head round and stared intently at the screen.

'You see that?' he said, pointing to a tiny blob in the baby's chest. 'That's its heart.'

'Is it beating?' I asked, but I already knew the answer.

I began to smile uncontrollably.

'Of course it's beating,' he said.

Both Caroline and I started laughing – gleefully, insanely, like a couple of demented fools. Suddenly, now that I knew everything *was* going to be okay, being an expectant father *did* feel like winning the lottery.

'Stop laughing,' the doctor told Caroline. 'You're making it harder to see the baby.'

'I like you much better than the other doctor,' she said.

I bent forward and kissed her forehead.

'You see?' I said. 'What did I tell you?'

In the car on the way back up the mountain, we couldn't stop talking. I felt light-headed – tipsy, almost. I told her about my phantom pregnancy hypothesis and she said the next time she was suffering from morning sickness she was going to vomit all over me. We compared notes about what we'd been thinking on the way to the hospital and, like me, she was worried about how our relationship would bear up if anything had happened to the baby. The mood in the car was so sunny now it was almost as if we were two different people. Who were those tight-lipped depressives who'd come down the mountain a couple of hours earlier?

'You do realise it's going to be like this from now on,' said Caroline.

'What is?'

'Parenthood. The next fifty years of our lives are going to be filled with episodes exactly like this. This is just the beginning.'

Oh, Christ, I thought. *You're probably right.*

14

THOU SHALT NOT PROCRASTINATE

According to Syd Field, one of the greatest obstacles to writing a screenplay is something he refers to as 'resistance': 'After you write FADE IN: EXT. STREET – DAY, you'll suddenly be seized with an incredible "urge" to sharpen your pencils or clean your work area. You'll find a *reason* or *excuse* not to write. That's resistance.' Other examples of 'resistance' given by Field include cleaning the fridge, washing the kitchen floor, changing the sheets and having sex. All writers are familiar with the urge to engage in this kind of displacement activity – and I'm no exception. My favourite way of avoiding having to put pen to paper (apart from having sex, obviously) is to spend hours on the Web searching for out-of-print books that I've convinced myself are absolutely essential for 'research purposes'. When they arrive, shipped to me from some second-hand book dealer in Dubuque, I carefully remove them from their envelopes, place a protective cover over their dust jackets . . . and then never look at them again.

In order to avoid writing the screenplay about the seventies record producer I went one further and actually flew to New York to interview the septuagenarian author of the biography that _____ _____ had acquired the rights to. Incredibly, I even managed to persuade Mr Hollywood to pick up the tab. He sent me a business-class ticket and put me up for three nights at the Parker Meridien Hotel on W57th Street. It was my first real taste of Hollywood extravagance.

The reason I was able to convince _____ to go to these lengths is because the screenplay was supposed to be 'based on' the biography. I hadn't realised this until I received the 'Writer Employment Agreement' – the forty-eight-page document Mr Hollywood sent over after our meeting at the Hotel du Cap. Technically, I'd been hired to *adapt* this book for the screen, rather than produce an original screenplay.

At first, I was relieved. I cracked open the biography in a state of high excitement, hoping I'd be able to turn it into a film script with very little alteration. Every screenwriter's dream is to do what John Huston did with *The Maltese Falcon*. According to legend, after Warner Bros hired him to adapt and direct it he got his secretary to retype the book in screenplay form, labelling each scene as either 'interior' or 'exterior', and preserving the dialogue verbatim. When she'd finished, she mistakenly sent the pages to Jack Warner and he immediately gave Huston the thumb's up. 'I love it,' he told him. 'You've really captured the flavour of this book. Shoot it just as it is – with my blessing.'

Alas, the book I was supposed to be adapting was no *Maltese Falcon*. To be fair, this wasn't the biographer's fault. If you laid out the most dramatic events in the record producer's life in chronological order, they didn't add up to a movie. Few people's lives do. Indeed, some of Hollywood's most successful biopics, such as *Citizen Kane*, are about fictional characters, and those that aren't – *Spartacus, Lawrence of Arabia, Patton* – take a very cavalier attitude to the facts. (The old Fleet Street adage applies: if you can't make it, fake it.)

As far as I could work out, the secret of writing a successful biopic about a real person was to confine yourself to just one episode in that person's life, hopefully one that unfolded in a particularly dramatic way. Ideally, it should both reveal their character and define their lives, so that by the end of the film the audience has a sense of who that person was and what they achieved and – in the best of all possible worlds – how those two things were connected. A good example is *Amadeus*, which manages to have an epic, Oscar-winning grandeur in spite of confining itself to the last ten years of Mozart's life.

The problem was, no period in the record producer's life immediately sprang to mind – certainly not the last ten years, which were spent in and out of the Betty Ford Clinic. My reason for wanting to meet his biographer, apart from furnishing myself with an excuse for further delay, was to see if he could think of an episode in the man's life that would make a suitable subject for a movie.

'Sure, go meet him, pick his brain,' said Mr Hollywood. 'He probably has a ton of stories he left out of the book. Get him to tell you about the time our friend booked the Elvis Presley Suite in the Las Vegas Hilton and took exactly the same cocktail of drugs Elvis took the night he died. He had some assistant get hold of the autopsy report and go through it line by line, making sure he didn't forget anything. Fucking lunatic. The same assistant ended up taking him to the Emergency Room at five o'clock in the morning.'

'Hi, I'm Toby Young,' I said, extending my hand. 'Thank you very much for agreeing to see me.'

In addition to being a biographer, the man I'd flown three thousand miles to see was a retired drama critic and, at his suggestion, we'd arranged to have lunch at Joe Allen's, the legendary Broadway restaurant on West 46th Street. By the time I arrived – a few minutes late – he was already sitting in what I imagined was his regular booth.

He took my hand very reluctantly.

'I was beginning to think you weren't coming,' he said.

'Oh, God, sorry. Have you been sitting here long?'

I glanced at my watch. I was less than three minutes late.

'No, it's not that,' he said. 'It's just that there wasn't a reservation.'

I looked around: the place was virtually empty. Why would I need a reservation?

In the hope of discovering some common ground, I told him I was the *Spectator*'s drama critic and he asked me whether I'd managed to catch any shows on this trip.

Aha, I thought. *Here's my chance to impress him.*

'As a matter of fact, yes. Last night I went to see *Imaginary Friends*.'

'Imaginary what?'

'*Imaginary Friends*. It's a musical by Nora Ephron about the feud between Lillian Hellman and Mary McCarthy.'

'Is that it? Surely there must be something else worth seeing?'

I was stumped.

I decided to get on to the subject of the record producer before things deteriorated any further. After a bit of throat-clearing in which I told him what a masterful biography he'd written, I outlined the problem I was having writing the screenplay.

'I need to find some episode in his life that would work as a movie,' I explained, hoping he might suggest one.

'Well, that's why they're paying you the big bucks,' he said.

With that, he let out a little chuckle and asked the waiter to bring him another iced tea. We'd already established that I was paying for lunch.

'Yes, of course, but I was wondering if you could perhaps tell me some of the stories you left out of the book. You know, the really juicy stuff, the kind of thing you might not have been able to completely stand up as a biographer, but which I'd have no qualms about using in the film. You know, dramatic licence, and all that.'

'You want me to make stuff up?'

'No, no, no, I was just, you know, hoping you might tell be able to tell me some of the more risqué stories you didn't see fit to include in what is – obviously – a very serious biography.'

He took a gulp of his iced tea.

'Sorry,' he said. 'Everything I know about him is in the book.'

I decided to switch tack.

Maybe if I could start him off by discussing his subject's character, he'd automatically launch into a few anecdotes to illustrate the points he was making.

'The thing I can't figure out,' I said, 'is why this hugely successful man was such a self-saboteur? I mean why, having achieved everything he'd set out to achieve, did he throw it all away? What was the wellspring of all his self-destructive behaviour?'

My dining companion perked up.

'Now you're getting to the nub of it. That's the six-million-dollar question.'

I nodded enthusiastically.

'So? What's the answer?'

'I don't profess to be a psychologist,' he said, raising himself to his full height. 'I have absolutely no clue why he behaved the way he did. I just deal in the facts.'

He said this in an incredibly dismissive way, as if to speculate about what made the record producer tick would be the kind of airy-fairy bullshit that only a pretentious arsehole would attempt.

Who am I talking to? I thought. *His biographer? Or the police officer who discovered his body?*

Less than five minutes had elapsed and we'd completely exhausted the subject of one of the most colourful characters in the history of the music business. I faced at least another hour in this man's company. What on earth were we going to talk about?

The other surprise in the 'Writer Employment Agreement' was that I'd been hired to produce a 'Rewrite', rather than a full-length screenplay, even though Mr Hollywood had never mentioned this before.

What was that about?

'It's a fairly standard ruse,' said Rob Long when I asked him about it. 'All Hollywood producers are required to stick to the Writers Guild of

America's rules when it comes to compensating screenwriters – they're not allowed to pay you less than the amount stipulated in the WGA's "Schedule of Minimums". The way they get around this is to pretend they've only hired you to do a "Rewrite" – or, worse, a "Polish" – when, in fact, they want you to write an entire screenplay from scratch. The WGA minimum for a "Rewrite" is $25,000, whereas the WGA minimum for a "Non-Original Screenplay" is $80,000. [Beat.] How much is he paying you?'

'$35,000.'

'Well, for a "Rewrite", that's not bad. But for a full-length screenplay, it's lousy.'

I told Rob the name of the writer whose script I was supposed to be rewriting.

'Him? Oh, my God. He's an incredible hack. How d'you know it's him?'

'Because his name is right here on page one of the Writer Employment Agreement.'

'Uh-oh.'

'What?'

'Well, if his name's on the contract that means he's probably already been guaranteed a credit.'

'What, even if I don't use a single word of his screenplay?'

'Welcome to Hollywood, my friend. I've won Golden Globes for episodes of Cheers *I haven't even* seen, *let alone written.'*

'So this guy could win a "Best Adapted Screenplay" Oscar for my script? That's outrageous.'

Rob laughed.

'Did I ever tell you the story about the imp?'

'No.'

'Okay, so there's this blocked screenwriter. He sits in front of his typewriter all day, staring at a blank sheet of paper . . . nothing. He goes to bed, convinced he'll never write anything again and when he wakes up he's amazed to discover this full-length, perfectly typed screenplay sitting on his desk. He starts reading it and, straight away, he realises it's a brilliant piece of work, the best screenplay he's ever read. So he gives

it to his agent and tells him to sell it. There's an auction and, before the day is out, it sells for three million dollars. That night, the screenwriter thinks, Maybe I wrote this screenplay in my sleep or something, *so he sits down in front of his typewriter and starts tapping away at the keys – but he's still completely blocked. So he goes to bed and, sure enough, the following day there's another perfectly typed screenplay sitting on his desk. He gives it to his agent – and this one sells for six million dollars!* Okay, *he thinks,* I'm going to get to the bottom of this. *So that night he pretends to go to sleep, but he keeps one eye open and, in the middle of the night, this imp appears and starts dancing on the typewriter keys, banging out a script. The screenwriter leaps out of bed, runs over to his desk, and holds out his palm. "Don't worry," he says. "I'm not gonna hurt you. I just wanna know if there's any way I can reward you for these fantastic screenplays you keep writing?" "That's very kind of you," says the imp, jumping on to the screenwriter's palm. "What did you have in mind?" "How about a car?" "No, I don't need a car." "How about a house?" "No, I don't need a house." "Well, there must be something I can do for you. Whatever it is, you've got it. Anything." [Beat.] "How about credit?" At this point, Toby, if you were standing next to me, you would see me make a sledgehammer of my fist and bring it crashing down into the palm of my hand.'*

'So, have you ever written any books of criticism?' I asked the biographer.

We were struggling through the first course at this point and the second one loomed ominously.

'Theatre criticism isn't proper writing,' he said as he chewed his way through a stack of pancakes.

'Aha. So you're familiar with my work?'

I was hoping for a laugh, but he gave me a blank look.

'What d'you wanna be a drama critic for? [Munch, munch.] It's a lousy profession.'

'Well, I thought it would be a great way to learn about the theatre. [*Sotto voce*]: I have this secret ambition to become a playwright.'

Beat.

'You wanna piece of advice, Toby? Get another ambition. You work for years on something, you don't receive a dime, and then . . . nothing. No one wants to put it on. Producers won't return your calls. Believe me, it's very, very hard to get a play produced.'

I knitted my brow and nodded, doing my best to pretend I'd never heard this before.

'Tell me, Toby, you married?'

'Yes.'

'Kids?'

'Not yet, but my wife's pregnant.'

He shovelled another pancake into his mouth.

'Congratulations. [Munch, munch.] You got a private income?'

'No.'

'There's your answer,' he said, wiping his mouth with his napkin.

What about my fee?' I asked Rob. 'It says here in the Writer Employment Agreement that if the picture gets made I'll get an additional $175,000 if I receive a sole "screenplay by" or "written by" credit. What'll happen if my name doesn't appear anywhere?'

'I wouldn't worry about that.'

'But—'

'You don't have to worry about your compensation at this level, not when you've been contracted to write something by a studio. That's an amateur's mistake. The truth is, it's always going to be cheaper to just pay the writer. A script fee, even a really high one, is roughly half of the catering budget on some pictures, so it's not a big deal. I mean, what's $175,000 to a big Hollywood studio? That's the cost of redecorating the Chairman's private bathroom. In any case, credit is entirely the province of the WGA Credits Committee. Credits are assigned by them, never the producer and never the studio.'

'But I'm not a member of the WGA.'

'Ah, well, in that case, you might have a problem.'

*

Towards the end of my lunch with the record producer's biographer, he adopted a let's-cut-the-bullshit-and-lay-all-our-cards-on-the-table tone and asked me how far I'd got with the screenplay.

'Well, I've mapped out the structure . . . '

'I see. How long you been working on it?'

'Well I first met with _____ back in July.'

'JULY? You've been working on this thing for nine months and all you've done is "map out the structure"? That's pathetic, Toby.'

'Yes, well. [Beat.] I suppose it is, rather.'

'There's no supposing about it. IT'S PATHETIC. Listen, this is a real opportunity, Toby. Don't blow it. You wanna be writing theatre criticism the rest of your life?'

'Er—'

'Of course you don't. This is an opportunity to make big money. BIG MONEY. How tough can it be to be a screenwriter? Take William Goldman. He started out as a second-rate playwright on Broadway. And now look at him? I always think of that Woody Allen line: "90 per cent of it is just showing up." Don't blow it, Toby. Stop fucking around. What the hell are you doing flying out to New York to talk to me anyway?'

He leaned in so his nose was only inches from mine and, for a second, I thought he was going to grab me by the lapels.

'START WRITING, TOBY.'

15

DON'T PANIC, MR MAINWARING

Saturday, 26 July 2003

5.15 A.M.

I'm woken by a call from one of the midwives at Queen Charlotte's to tell me that Caroline has gone into labour. I immediately start trying to yank on my trousers – 'Tell her I'll be there in five minutes' – but the midwife says there's no need to panic. She advises me to have a shower, get something to eat and then make my way in.

Caroline was admitted to the Edith Dare Ward at 8 p.m. yesterday and given a tablet in order to kick-start the whole process. (The baby is twelve days overdue.) The fact that she's gone into labour is good news. If nothing had happened by 8 a.m., Caroline was due to be given another, more powerful drug called oxytocin and this, in turn, would have made it more likely she'd end up having a caesarean. She wants to avoid this if she possibly can because: (a) something is more likely to go wrong; (b) it means she'll have to spend a minimum of three days in the hospital afterwards instead of twenty-four hours; (c) it will take her longer to get her figure back; (d) it'll leave a scar; and (e) she doesn't fancy being conscious while her stomach is cut open and the baby scooped out.

6.00 A.M.

I arrive on the Edith Dare Ward, only to be told Caroline has been moved to a delivery suite on the third floor. I bound up the stairs, two at a time. As I walk down the corridor, looking for her room, I can hear the occupants of the neighbouring suites crying out in pain. Poor Caroline.

When I enter the room she's locked in the loo. I knock on the door and say 'Hi, bubs' as solicitously as I can, but she says 'Hi' back in a very perfunctory, irritable way. I later discover that at this very moment she's leaning over the lavatory bowl, waiting to be sick. It turns out that her first contraction occurred at about 11 p.m. last night so she's been in labour for seven hours.

When I left her on the ward at 10.30 p.m. (partners aren't allowed to stay overnight), she said she wanted to avoid an epidural if she possibly could. Ostensibly, this is because an epidural makes it more likely that she'll have to have a caesarean, but I suspect the real reason is because she doesn't want to seem like a softy. I was amazed by how macho the atmosphere was in the antenatal classes. I attended these sessions under duress, expecting them to be a bit girly, but I couldn't have been more wrong. Virtually the sole topic of conversation was whether or not to have an epidural and woe betide the expectant mother who said she was considering it. Testosterone, not oestrogen, was coursing through these women's veins. Their unacknowledged role model was Rambo in *First Blood*. If he could stitch up his own leg without an anaesthetic they could jolly well give birth without any pain relief.

*

In the event, the first thing Caroline says when she emerges from the bathroom is, 'I'm having an epidural.' If I had to sum up the expression on her face I'd say she looked shocked. She was expecting the contractions to be painful, but not *this* painful.

7.00 A.M.

Risi – the midwife – appears. She's a large, no-nonsense West Indian woman who looks a bit like Hattie McDaniel in *Gone with the Wind*. After a quick examination she uses something called an 'amniohook' to break Caroline's waters.[1]

This reminds me of a Mars/Venus conversation we had about 'internal examinations' last week.
Me: Doesn't it make you feel a bit squeamish?
Caroline: No.
Me: It does me. I find it the hardest thing to deal with when thinking about what you have to go through – the *invasiveness* of it all.
Caroline [irritably]: So do I, obviously, but I'm pretending it's no big deal. Can you not say how horrible you think it is, please?

Caroline's waters are a bit brackish and Risi immediately turns to the trainee midwife and says, 'Meconium'. She explains to Caroline that the baby has 'passed a stool' inside the womb, something that could be a sign of 'fetal distress'. These are the two words you don't want to hear in a delivery suite. Caroline asks if that means she'll have to have a caesarean, but Risi tells her to relax. 'If there's anything to worry about I'll tell ya, darlin'.'

---

1 'Amniohook' was just one of a dozen new words I learnt during Caroline's labour and its aftermath that I've been trying to forget over since. Others included 'episiotomy', 'lochia', 'meconium', 'transverse' and 'pessary'.

7.15 A.M.

The anaesthetist arrives to administer the epidural and, wouldn't you know it, he's the spitting image of Dr Kovacs on *ER*. Caroline and I each have a 'freebie list' of the five celebrities we'd allow the other to sleep with and Goran Visnjic, the actor who plays him, is at the top of hers.[1] I can't believe how flirtatious he is. 'You have really strong ligaments,' he says, as he probes for an opening between two of her vertebrae. 'Do you exercise a lot?' Then, a moment later, having failed to get the needle in, he adds: 'You have *really* strong ligaments.' When he's finished he says, 'A less experienced anaesthetist might have put the needle in too far, but I could tell from looking at your back that you're really skinny.'

'Sorry for being such a wimp,' says Caroline.

'Don't be silly. It's the same level of pain as acute appendicitis and if someone came into hospital with acute appendicitis and we said "Just grin and bear it" and refused to give them an anaesthetic we'd be sued left, right and centre. Believe me, if men went into labour, they'd all have epidurals.'

These are the magic words. Caroline actually laughs for the first time this morning. What a smooth-talking bastard.

While she's waiting for the epidural to take effect, Caroline turns to me and says, 'It took you a long time to get here. What were you doing?'

---

1 Caroline's full list is Goran Visnjic, Matthew McConaughey, Josh Hartnett, Matt Dillon and David Beckham ('Provided he didn't open his mouth'). Mine is Kelly Brook, Angelina Jolie, Rosario Dawson, Eva Mendes and 'Nicole' from the Renault ads.

7.45 A.M.

Risi examines Caroline again and says, 'Oh, my. I can see baby's head.'

Caroline's ready to start pushing, but Risi tells her to hang on while she conducts a more thorough examination. As she's doing this she asks her whether she wants the baby delivered on to her stomach. Caroline can't reply because she's got a thermometer in her mouth, so I speak for her: 'I don't think she wants you to plonk it straight down on top of her when it's still covered in all that white gunk. If it was me, I'd want you to clean it first, then put it on my stomach.'

Risi looks at me as if I'm Dr Niles Crane.

8.00 A.M.

The baby is 'transverse', which means its head is in the wrong position. Risi says she's going to get a doctor to come and take a blood sample from the baby's scalp to determine its oxygen level. If the level is below a certain threshold, they'll have to perform a 'section'. This is exactly what Caroline doesn't want.

8.15 A.M.

The consultant appears. Caroline and I are both quite anxious – how much danger is the baby in? – but his manner is so brusque we don't get a chance to ask him any questions. He talks to us as if he's a colonial officer addressing a couple of natives in some far-flung outpost of the British Empire: 'We'll take a blood sample to see if baby's well. If baby's not well, we'll get baby out. Okay?'

Yes, sahib.

Why do all the doctors dispense with the indefinite article when referring to the unborn child? It adds to the impression that they're talking to you in pidgin English.

8.35 A.M.

The test results are back and *baby's* oxygen level is fine. But for some reason Caroline's contractions have stopped. Risi decides to give her some of the dreaded oxytocin. Yikes!

8.50 A.M.

When Risi's out of the room, Caroline sits bolt upright, grabs my arm and says, 'Under no circumstances must you let them give me a caesarean. Do you understand? *Under no circumstances.*' I promise her I'll do everything in my power to prevent this, but what can I do? One of the hardest things about being in hospital is not knowing exactly what the power relationship is between doctor and patient. It's not a democracy, obviously, but is it a constitutional monarchy or a dictatorship? Suppose the consultant strides in, takes one look at Caroline, and says, 'Baby's not well so we're going to cut baby out. Okay?' How will he react if I say, 'Actually, we'd like this baby to be delivered through the vaginal canal. Okay?' Presumably, he'll summon Dr Kovacs and get him to administer the chloroform.

8.55 A.M.

Caroline's contractions are now occurring about once a minute and Risi decides to have a crack at a normal delivery. (Hooray!) It's time to start pushing.

In *What to Expect . . . when you're expecting* there's a chapter entitled 'Fathers are expectant, too' in which it says: 'Your being beside her, holding her hand, urging her on and providing the comfort of a familiar face and touch will do her more good than having Dr Lamaze himself at her bedside.'

In the event, no sooner have I taken up my station by the bedside than Caroline turns to me, points to a chair in the far corner of the room and says, 'Go and sit over there and don't move until I say so.'

9.20 A.M.

'Keeppushingkeeppushingkeeppushingkeeppushingkeeppushing,' says Risi.

'Is that the right action?' asks Caroline.

'Yes. That's right.'

9.30 A.M.

After half an hour of pushing and no sign of the baby, Caroline asks Risi if a caesarean is inevitable. Risi says she doesn't think so. 'I think you will have a baby in your arms by 10 a.m.'

Caroline and I look at each other. She manages a weak smile, but I actually squeal with delight.

9.35 A.M.

'Really hard . . . push now . . . keeppushingkeeppushingkeepphusing . . . keep it up now . . . as long as you can . . . nearly there, Caroline, nearly there.'

9.40 A.M.

Risi asks Caroline if she's sure she doesn't want the baby delivered on to her stomach.

'Who told you that?' says Caroline, shooting an angry glance in my direction. 'Of course I want the baby delivered on to my stomach.'

9.45 A.M.

After a monumental pushing session, and still no baby, Caroline tells Risi she doesn't know if she can carry on.

'Darlin', don't say that. You need to be positive at this stage. It isn't coming – woosh, woosh – like you see on the telly. Even a woman who's having her sixth baby has to do a bit of pushing.'

'Not much though,' says the trainee midwife.

9.50 A.M.

A paediatrician appears. A doctor has to be present at the delivery because of the meconium.

This is it!

9.51 A.M.

'Getting ready to catch baby now,' says Risi, knees bent, hands cupped together like a wicket keeper. 'Take a deep breath in and push right down into your bottom . . . Keep it coming . . . that's it, keep it coming . . . BRILLIANT.'

9.52 A.M.

IT'S A GIRL!!!

9.53 A.M.

Instead of delivering the baby on to Caroline's stomach, Risi hands her to the paediatrician who, after a very cursory examination, hands her to me. I've been slightly dreading this moment. What if I don't feel what I'm supposed to? But it turns out I needn't have worried. The baby opens her eyes and stares into mine and I instantly feel a huge surge of paternal love. I think: *Even allowing for the fact that I'm biased, this baby is an absolute knockout.*

I hand her to Caroline and her reaction is exactly the same. 'Oh, my God,' she says, gazing at her in disbelief. 'She's *so* beautiful.'[1]

---

1 Needless to say, she looked like Winston Churchill.

9.55 A.M.

Risi weighs her: 7lb, 15 ounces.

'It was like shitting a football,' says Caroline.

Sunday, 27 July 2003

9.15 A.M.

I arrive at the hospital clutching my digital camera. (Spot the dad!) My plan is to take a picture of Caroline and the baby and email it to all our friends, but as I'm making my way across the delivery ward I can't help noticing an adorable-looking black baby. This gives me an idea. If I can just persuade Caroline to let me photograph her holding *this* baby, I can email *that* picture to all our friends instead. No explanation, just the words, 'Marcellus was born yesterday at 9.52 a.m. He weighs 10lb 3 ounces and Caroline reckons he's going to be a boxer.'

'You are joking, aren't you?' says Caroline.

At this point I notice that my mother-in-law is sitting on the bed beside her. She doesn't look any more amused than Caroline.

'Yes, yes, of course I'm joking.'

9.45 A.M.

We have to wait for a paediatrician to give the baby the thumbs up before we can leave so I go in search of some coffees. Incredibly, I bump into two couples we know – and not from the antenatal classes, either. Having babies really is *de rigueur* within our peer group.

10.30 A.M.

As we're walking out Caroline and I can't quite believe that we're allowed to take the baby home. The extraordinary care taken by the staff at Queen Charlotte's leaves you in no doubt about how passionate they are about the welfare of the babies in their charge, and yet, after having gone to such painstaking lengths to ensure a healthy delivery, they then simply plonk them in their parents' arms and send them on their merry way. It would be much more consistent if they kept the babies in the hospital and made the parents attend course after course for at least a year until they were fully qualified care-givers. Only then could they take their babies home, and those that failed any of these courses would be deemed unfit parents and never allowed to see their babies again.

10.45 A.M.

I carry the baby into the house, saying, 'Look, it's your home.'

8.35 P.M.

During a brief respite, Caroline and I manage to have a quick conversation about what to name her. (We'd promised ourselves we wouldn't decide on a name until he or she had actually appeared.) I want to call her after my mother, but – surprise, surprise – Caroline wants to call her after *her* mother. We compromise and name her after both of our mothers: Sasha Rose Bondy Young.

11.20 P.M.

I'm relieved we've had a girl. I've just been flipping through a copy of Kenneth Tynan's *Diaries* in the lavatory and found the following passage about the birth of his son Matthew:

> I do not like male competition – in fact I am not all that crazy about men *per se* – so I was much relieved to find that Matthew is sensitive, almost girlish-looking – resembles Roxana when she was born. So long as he develops my feminine streak he will be very welcome. I shall shortly buy him a few pretty frocks and enter him for Sadler's Wells Ballet School.

Monday, 28 July 2003

3.20 A.M.

I'm completely exhausted – and in a new way, too. I feel strangely absent and egoless, as though my sense of self has had the volume turned down. I know becoming a parent is supposed to make you less self-absorbed, but this is more like taking a pill designed to cure you instantly of narcissistic personality disorder. Sean Langan said he felt the world shift on its access when his son was born as Anabel's attention switched from him to their son. (Not surprising, considering he buggered off for six weeks after the birth.) I feel the same way, but it's not Caroline's love I feel being transferred to Sasha – it's my own self-love. I haven't quite reached the stage where I'd be willing to throw myself in front of a runaway horse to save her, but it probably isn't far off. She feels at least *as* important as me, if not more so.

I remember being sceptical when other fathers have reported feeling this way about their children. I thought it would be like having an exotic pet that you're particularly fond of – a monkey, say, or a pot-bellied pig. But it's different from that, and it's a difference in kind, not degree. Sasha feels so infinitely precious, a tiny, delicate little creature who's been entrusted to my care and it's my duty to see she has the best possible life.

The corollary of all this, of course, is a feeling of almost non-stop terror. The thought of any harm coming to her chills me to the marrow. When I move her around I'm terrified that I might bash her head against a sharp corner and when I'm putting on her Baby-gro I worry that, in bending her arm or leg to squeeze it into one of the holes, I might break it. Caroline says she feels this too, and so intensely she doesn't know how she's going to bear it.

Welcome to parenthood.

PART FOUR

WHAT GOES UP MUST COME DOWN

16

THE TREATMENT

'Is this Toby Young?'

'Yes.'

'I have _____ _____ for you.'

This was it. The call I'd been waiting for. Almost a year had elapsed since my first meeting with Mr Hollywood at the Hotel du Cap and I'd finally submitted a piece of work.

He was calling to give me his reaction.

Needless to say, I hadn't written an actual screenplay. I'd just given him a very detailed treatment. In my contract with the studio, it hadn't asked for a treatment. Rather, it had simply stated that I would be paid $35,000 for a 'Rewrite' – that much was guaranteed – and, if Mr Hollywood thought highly enough of that, $20,000 for a 'Polish'. But it occurred to me that it would be sensible to include an intermediate stage, whereby I submitted a treatment. Only when we'd discussed this and he'd signed off on it, would I then go on to write a full-length screenplay.

This wasn't merely another excuse to procrastinate – though, God knows, it was that. In addition, it meant that the screenplay I eventually turned in would have a far better chance of being made. But the best thing about this arrangement – the thing that made it really ingenious, as far as I was concerned – was that it would necessitate a number of lengthy conversations between _____ and me. That, more than anything, would help me forge a lasting relationship with him.

Rather surprisingly, Mr Hollywood had warmly embraced the idea – 'That's smart, really smart' – and I couldn't stop congratulating myself on what a canny operator I was.

'You idiot,' said Rob Long when I told him about my masterstroke. 'That's such an amateur's mistake. You only get paid for a draft, so write the draft.'

I was flabbergasted.

'But, surely, if the screenplay I write is based on a treatment he's already signed off on, it's much more likely to be made?'

'Do you have any idea how unlikely it is that your script will get made? I mean, statistically? The major studios release, on average, 225 pictures a year. Most of these are schlock: sequels, remakes, big-screen adaptations of TV shows . . . lowest-common-denominator stuff. Only 10 per cent are based on original screenplays. So that's between twenty-two and twenty-three pictures a year. Now, do you know how many screenplays are registered with the Writers Guild of America, West every year? I'll tell you: about fifty thousand. [Beat.] You do the math.'

'But this is a project close to _____'s heart. He really wants to make this.'

'Do you understand the words "vanity project"? Do you have any idea how much fun it is – really fun – to sit around and give a writer notes on a treatment, because you can be vague and contradictory and incredibly irritating and you never have to refer to a script, or a page number?'

'But the longer he and I spend talking about this, the more likely it is that we'll end up forging a close relationship.'

'Why? I've talked about it quite a lot with you and, I have to say, I'm thinking of taking you off my Christmas card list. [Beat.] Listen, the smartest thing to do is write the draft – quickly – and write a good one,

because the only way to be this guy's friend – and that's an insane thing to want, by the way, but you seem to want it, so off you go – is to either have a lot more money than he does – which you don't – not need anything from him – which you do – or write an incredible script that he – or his designated subordinate – reads and loves. Notice what's not there? Right. A treatment.'

Beat.

'So what should I do?'

'Since it's highly unlikely, as a matter of pure statistics, that the script will ever get produced, why not just write it well and interestingly and get paid for it, rather than expose yourself to a lot of unpleasant encounters with him and his development people that will only end up leaving you both convinced that the other is a no-talent fool? That's what I'd do.'

'Have you seen *Chicago*?'

Typically, Mr Hollywood's opening remark was something completely out of left field. Why on earth was he asking me that?

'Yes,' I lied.

'What did you think?'

Rob had actually warned me about questions like this. If anyone in Hollywood asks you what you think of a particular movie, and you don't know what the relationship is between that person and the director/producer/star of the movie in question, just say, 'I fucking loved it.'

'I . . . er . . . fucking loved it?'

'Why?'

Oh, shit.

'Well, to begin with, I absolutely adore musicals.'

'You do?!?'

Ah, what tangled webs we weave, when first we practise to deceive.

'Er, well—'

'Wanna know what I thought?'

'Yes. *Yes.* YES. I'd *love* to know what you thought.'

He immediately launched into a fifteen-minute monologue that began with an analysis of Kander and Ebb's writing partnership, segued into the story of how Bob Fosse came to direct *Cabaret*, double-backed into an exegesis of *I Am A Camera* and then spun out into an endless series of anecdotes about Christopher Isherwood's adventures in Hollywood. As usual, it was riveting stuff – but what it had to do with my treatment was anyone's guess.

Eventually, he came to the point.

'The thing I liked about *Chicago* is that Rob Marshall managed to relate all the events in Roxy Hart's life to show business. Every time something big happens to her – bang – there's a song-and-dance routine about it. So it's not just a story about this woman who shoots her husband and has to stand trial and is eventually acquitted. It's also a story about how every aspect of our society, particularly the criminal-justice system, has been completely permeated by show business. You know, in a society in which everyone's famous for fifteen minutes, everybody, not just you and me, is in the entertainment business. [Beat.] That's what's missing from your treatment.'

'But—'

'Look, what you've written is in many ways very smart and well organised, but what I don't get from it is how this particular record producer, more than anyone else, is responsible for this obsession we all have with celebrities. I mean, he created this world we all live in. *He created it*. [Beat.] I don't get that from your treatment.'

'Yes, but—'

'Tell me, Toby, when was the last time you were in the United States?'

'Er—'

'Have you seen *US* magazine?'

'Yes, I think I have. Is that the one that—'

'It's the hottest magazine in America. And you wanna know why?'

'—'

'Because it's full of pictures of celebrities. Celebrities, celebrities, celebrities. On every fucking page. It's unbelievable.'

Beat.

'If we could just get back to my treatment for a second . . . '

'Can you hold for a moment? I have to take another call.'

As I was waiting for Mr Hollywood to come back on the line, I tried to gauge what he really thought of my treatment. He clearly didn't think it was a suitable template for the picture he had in mind – that much was obvious. But did he regard it as a noble first effort or a complete waste of space? Was he regretting hiring me – or did he still believe in me?

'Contrary to popular myth, this is a very polite business,' Rob had told me. 'There's this patina of niceness in Hollywood and it's a breach of the code to be openly mean about anything or anyone. The definition of "friend" is so elastic in Hollywood that it includes the definition of "enemy". People don't have enemies, they have "frenemies". Of course, beneath the surface, it's full of the meanest, most horrible people you're ever likely to meet, but whereas it's totally acceptable to screw people over in business, in public everyone has to pretend to be very nice. You know that line from The Godfather? *"It's not personal. It's just business." Everyone in this town uses that line all the time. [He put on a whiney voice.] "It's not personal. It's just business." In reality, of course, it's always fucking personal.'*

'Three things about this treatment,' said Mr Hollywood, coming back on the line. 'You never sense his genius. You never feel his passion. And you never like him.'

Ouch! So much for the patina of niceness.

'I want to feel the glamour and the excitement and the pizzazz of a new era. I want to see how this guy brought it about – his genius – and I want to see his passion . . . and I want to like him.'

'But—'

'Listen, I know he's not a likeable guy – I *know* this – but we have to make a movie so you have to find a way for the audience to like him.'

'Yes, I realise that, but—'

'When I read your book, you did it, that's the movie. You like that guy. You like him. He does stupid things, he fucks up, but in the end you like him. When I got to the end of the book, I liked you. That's why I called you. Shit, that's why I *hired* you. That's what you have to do for this guy. You have to make him likeable.'

Beat.

'So you want me to do another treatment?'

'Hey, don't get disheartened. I'm not a big reader. I can barely read a billboard. But I read your treatment. I read it the moment I got it because I really care about this project. I really want to do it. And I know you can write this, Toby. This is your story. You'll lick it next time.'

17

STAGESTRUCK

On the face of it, there was nothing particularly unusual about the evening I spent at the Soho Theatre in the summer of 2003. I did what I'd been doing every Wednesday night since being made the *Spectator*'s drama critic – I went to the opening of a new play. I took my place alongside my fellow critics and, with some trepidation, waited for the curtain to rise.

The only difference was that the play in question was all about me.

The story of how I found myself in this situation began the previous year when I was approached by a young playwright called Tim Fountain to see if I'd be interested in making a cameo appearance in a piece he'd written about Julie Burchill. (Julie and I used to be old friends but we had a very public falling out in 1995.) It wasn't a permanent role. Rather, he wanted me to put in a one-off performance on press night in the hope of garnering a bit of publicity. The part he wanted me to play was that of Daniel Raven, Julie's twenty-seven-year-old boyfriend.

I told him I'd be delighted to help.

At first, I patted myself on the back for being such a nice guy. *It's a terrible chore*, I told myself, *but I'm happy to give a leg up to a struggling young playwright.* As the press night drew near, however, I got more and more excited. I began to talk about getting into character. I asked Daniel's sister, the journalist Charlotte Raven, to tell me all about him. I forbade Caroline to mention the Scottish play.

Then, just before *Julie Burchill Is Away* was about to open, Tim emailed me to say he'd cut my line. 'It was really kind of you to offer, but it just didn't work,' he wrote. I was crestfallen. It took a superhuman effort of will not to email him back and beg him to reconsider. I didn't care about not having a line. Couldn't I just have a non-speaking role? I WANTED TO BE ON STAGE.

Alas, it was not to be. But the upshot was that Tim and I became 'theatre buddies'. (No, that isn't a euphemism.) We started going to plays together and, afterwards, he'd tell me what he thought they were about. I found this quite helpful when it came to writing reviews since Tim's knowledge of the theatre was so much greater than mine. In addition to the Burchill play, he'd written a very successful one-man show about Quentin Crisp called *Resident Alien*.

In the spring of 2003, I asked Tim if he'd like to collaborate on a one-man show based on *How to Lose Friends & Alienate People*. It was a foolish thing to do since I should have been spending all my spare time on the two screenplays I'd been commissioned to write – but that's probably what made it so appealing. (It was a form of resistance.) I also saw it as another opportunity to slap on the greasepaint. After all, who was better qualified to play me than me?

As a boy, it had been my ambition to become an actor. I appeared in numerous school productions and, from the age of eleven to fourteen, went to Anna Scher's drama school in north London. Admittedly, it wasn't a proper 'school' – it only involved one evening a week – but I was good enough to land a small part in a television adaptation of *Cranford*, Elizabeth Gaskell's novel. As a floppy-haired nineteen-year-old, I even appeared as an extra in the film version of *Another Country* and it was only when I failed to make any headway as an actor at Oxford that I eventually turned to

journalism. Here was my chance to realise my boyhood dream –
twenty years after I'd abandoned it.

By the end of May, Tim and I had condensed the book into a fifty-
five-minute stage show and I performed it in front of a couple of
dozen people in a draughty church hall. In addition to various loyal
friends that I'd dragooned into turning up, the audience included a
go-getting young producer called Olivia Wingate. Tim and I were
hoping she might think highly enough of the play to come on board.

'So,' I said to Olivia afterwards. 'What did you think?'

'I liked it.'

'Does that mean you want to produce it?'

'That depends.'

'On what?'

Beat.

'Tell me, Toby, have you and Tim considered bringing in a professional actor?'

My face fell. Actors have this expression they use about other
actors: 'He's so crap, he couldn't even get a job playing himself.' In
my case, that was literally true.

'Was I *really* that bad?'

'It's not your acting abilities that concern me, so much as your
physical presence on stage. You have to remember, a large percentage of theatregoers are women.'

So *that* was it: I wasn't good-looking enough to play myself.

Olivia suggested the play would have a much better chance of
succeeding if an up-and-coming young star was cast in the part. I
agreed, but what actor with half a career would want to waste their
time playing me?

'How about Jack Davenport?' she said.

I was flabbergasted. That was like suggesting that Cameron Diaz,
Lucy Liu and Drew Barrymore should play the 3am Girls. Jack
looks like a genetically engineered movie star – not surprising, given
that his parents are Nigel Davenport and Maria Aitken. In fact, he
practically *is* a movie star. In addition to appearing in *The Talented*

Mr Ripley, he'd just finished filming *Pirates of the Caribbean* in which he played Keira Knightley's fiancé and would go on to appear in the sequel.

What planet was she on?

'What's this I hear about you being played by Jack Davenport?'

The caller was an ex-girlfriend who'd just read the news in a gossip column. Miraculously, he'd agreed to do it.

'It's completely ridiculous,' she continued. 'I mean, if you looked anything like Jack Davenport I never would have chucked you.'

She had a point.

About a fortnight after he'd come on board, Jack and I spent an evening together and, as gently as I could, I broached the subject of why he'd accepted the part.

'I'm still trying to work out an answer to that one,' he said. 'In order to do this I had to turn down a very lucrative offer that involved going to Cuba. Actors are usually happy to do as little work as possible for as much money as they can get, but the situation's been reversed here.'

'How have your friends reacted?'

'They think I'm barking.'

'Have any of them said, "You're far too good-looking to play this guy"?'

'Oddly enough, no. How have your friends reacted?'

'They've all said, "This guy is far too good-looking to play you."'

Jack may have been playing me, but the truth was I'd much rather have been playing him. I got a taste of what it would be like to be Jack Davenport during the evening we spent together. We started out at Zilli Fish on the Cut, then went to see *King Lear* at the Old Vic and, finally, ended up at a restaurant called Chez Bruce in Wandsworth. No matter where we went, women stopped and stared. It was like hanging out with Tom Cruise.

'So,' I said. 'Are you going to do anything about your appearance to make your portrayal of me more plausible?'

'Like what?'

'I dunno. Shave your head? Cultivate acne? Gain twenty pounds?'

'Absolutely not.'

'Why?'

'Because I don't want to ruin my chances of getting any other work when this thing closes on the first night.'

I laughed nervously.

'But, surely, if you don't do anything to alter your appearance, no one's going to believe you're me?'

Beat.

'With the greatest of respect, Toby, it's not like you're this public figure who everybody has a clear picture of in their head. Ninety-nine per cent of the people in the audience won't have a clue what you look like.'

This observation was brutally confirmed during the interval of *King Lear* when Jack and I were milling about outside the Old Vic. A beautiful girl approached and asked him, rather breathlessly, if he was *the* Jack Davenport.

'For my sins,' he said, raking his fingers through his hair.

'Is it true you're going to be playing Toby Young?' she asked.

'That's right,' I said, shouldering Jack out the way. 'Of course, he's not nearly good-looking enough, but unfortunately Brad Pitt wasn't available.'

The girl gave me a blank look.

'I'm sorry, who are you?'

Quod erat demonstrandum.

Unfortunately, while the character Jack was planning to play might be a better-looking version of me, he wouldn't necessarily be more attractive. Much to my chagrin, Tim had resisted all my efforts to make myself more appealing than I am in real life.

'It would be a grave mistake to sugar the pill,' he said.

Jack agreed with this.

'I feel very strongly about not pandering to the audience,' he told me. 'Initially, I want them to think, "Who the fuck is this guy?" But gradually, bit by bit, I want to win them over. I want them to come away liking you in spite of their better judgement.'

At this point he paused and looked me in the eye.

'I may have my work cut out.'

I found the experience of adapting my book for the stage far less painful than trying to adapt it for the screen. No doubt this was partly because I was collaborating with someone else, but I still ended up doing about 75 per cent of the work. What made it so much easier was the fact that it was a collective endeavour. To my amazement, everyone concerned with the production, not just Tim Fountain, seemed to think it was expected of them to help write the play. For instance, Jack Davenport arrived at rehearsals one morning and announced that he'd completely rewritten the script from top to bottom. Having never had a play produced before, I had no idea whether this was normal or not, but Tim seemed to take it in his stride so I followed his lead. A typical rehearsal would begin with Tim, Jack and me having an animated discussion about a particular passage in the script, with the director, Owen Lewis, acting as a referee. These arguments frequently became quite heated, with voices raised and tempers frayed, and would often end in a kind of stalemate.

At first, I found the absence of a clear chain of command quite frustrating. I wanted someone to be in overall charge and, not surprisingly, I thought that person should be me. But after a couple of weeks I began to relish these endless discussions, not least because, after going over the same ground again and again, a consensus on various points began to emerge. The conclusions we eventually reached seemed like pretty good ones, too.

This decision-making process was in stark contrast to Fleet Street, where the editor's word is law and there's rarely enough time to debate anything. According to the playwright David Ives, it's no accident that the theatre emerged from the birthplace of democracy: 'Consider the theatrical process. A group gets thrown together to put up a play. Over weeks of planning, weeks of rehearsal and weeks of performance, *all the people in that group have to agree.*' In the run-up to the opening night of *How to Lose Friends*, every decision had to be debated – at length – before a conclusion could be reached. As a way of working, it took some getting used to, particularly after the absolutism of Fleet Street. But I grew to appreciate it more and more as the weeks passed.

It goes without saying that I'd never tried to write anything in these circumstances before. Up until this point, writing had always been a solitary process, just me sitting in front of a computer and staring at the screen. I'm naturally a pretty gregarious person, so I found this enforced solitude quite hard to bear. Typically, I wouldn't be able to sit at my writing desk for longer than half an hour at a time, constantly inventing excuses to pick up the phone or meet people for coffee. The upshot was that I was a very slow worker. I found the act of writing almost physically painful and was only able to produce anything by a colossal act of will. At the end of a day in which I'd written no more than five hundred words I was completely exhausted.

Adapting *How to Lose Friends* for the stage, by contrast, was a breeze. After reading Tim's first draft and talking it over with the director, I went home and produced a completely new draft from scratch. I sat down at 9 p.m. and, by the time I looked at the clock again, it was 3 a.m. I'd written over seven thousand words, a piece of work that would normally have taken me at least a fortnight to complete. Nothing had ever flowed out of me like that before. It was by no means a finished draft – almost every word was fought over in the weeks that followed – but it formed the template of the script that Jack eventually recited on stage.

There was something extraordinarily rewarding, too, about seeing the play being brought to life. Just hearing a professional actor deliver a joke I'd written was extremely gratifying, particularly when that actor improved it in the telling, as Jack frequently did. In theory, the fact that the play was a collaborative effort should have diluted the amount of egotistical satisfaction I got every time I saw it performed. But, paradoxically, I think I derived more pleasure from it than I would have done if it had been all my own work. In this respect, putting on a play is like competing in a team sport: the fact that it's a collective enterprise, rather than an individual one, increases the amount of satisfaction you get from it; the pleasure is multiplied, rather than diluted.

Knowing that the play was going to be performed in front of an audience felt particularly good because, as a journalist, I was used to having my work completely ignored. I'd written cover stories for the *Spectator* – articles I'd laboured over for weeks – that hadn't produced a single comment. With the stage play, by contrast, it was almost as if I'd written a seven-thousand-word article that was then going to be read out loud by a professional actor in front of an audience of people who'd actually paid to be there. Not only that, but dozens of my colleagues would be obliged to write pieces of their own about my piece. Good or bad, this play would get a reaction, which was more than could be said about 99 per cent of my journalism.

At the end of the rehearsal process I felt as if I'd discovered a form of writing that, temperamentally at least, I was better suited to than any other. Playwrighting might not be as financially rewarding as screenwriting – or, indeed, journalism – but in terms of job satisfaction it knocked everything else into a cocked hat.

As the lights went down at the Soho Theatre, I had a terrible attack of first-night nerves. If I'd been in almost any other branch of journalism, I could have depended on a certain amount of fraternal feeling among my fellow hacks – but not drama criticism. On the contrary, the fact that this play was about one of their colleagues would, if anything, make them even more hostile. I couldn't help remembering the definition of satire given by George S. Kaufman, the famous American playwright: 'That which closes on Saturday night.'

For the first few minutes the audience watched in a kind of appalled silence, as if they couldn't quite believe that a mere hack had the gall to turn his life into a one-man show. Jack seemed to sense this and his trembling voice betrayed his fear. I turned to Tim who was sitting next to me and we looked at each other in horror: *Oh, God! What have we done?*

Then, the audience began to laugh. It was a slow trickle at first – a snigger here, a titter there – but as Jack began to grow in confidence it became louder and louder. About ten minutes in, Jack got his first *bona fide* roar, followed by a spontaneous round of applause, and, after that, he completely relaxed into the part. By the end, he only had to do a double-take to have the entire audience in hysterics.

I immediately thought of a passage in *Act One*, Moss Hart's autobiography, in which he recalls the feeling he had after the curtain went down on *Once In A Lifetime*, his first Broadway play: 'Is success in any other profession as dazzling, as deeply satisfying, as it is in the theatre? . . . There is an intensity, an extravagance, an abundant and unequivocal gratification to the vanity and the ego that can be satisfied more richly and more fully by success in the theatre than in any other calling . . . No success afterward surpasses it. It roars and thumps and thunders through the blood . . . '

Like Moss Hart, I could hardly wait to read the reviews in the following day's papers.

'The man is so totally shameless that he doesn't seem to mind in the least that, even when he is portrayed by actor Jack Davenport, he comes across as someone with the charm of a lizard and the IQ of a hamster,' wrote the *Guardian*.

I read and reread this review. Surely, there must be some mistake? The critic had given the play one star out of five. How could she be so scathing when the audience had been roaring with laughter? It was baffling.

I tossed the *Guardian* aside and opened the next paper in my pile.

'The show ultimately turns self-deprecation into an ego trip and will probably appeal only to anyone who is desperate to have a script optioned by Miramax,' wrote *The Times*. 'No wonder it's playing within staggering distance of the Groucho Club.'

I felt like Max Bialystock in the opening scene of *The Producers* when he opens the *New York Times*, reads a bad review of his latest Broadway play, and screams: 'Who do I have to fuck to get a break in this town?'

I flipped through the rest of the papers, but the verdict of the critics was more or less unanimous.

'This lame adaptation would have been better on Radio 4' – the *Daily Express*.

'The hour passes entertainingly enough, but there's nothing to it' – the *Financial Times*.

'More a book-reading with bells on than a show in its own right' – *Time Out*.

Needless to say, the worst review was Rhoda Koenig's in the *Independent*.

'I laughed twice, and at lines that were not intended to be funny,' she wrote. 'My second laugh was caused by Young's saying that "nothing had prepared me for the realisation that I wasn't one of life's winners". A cosseted life indeed, for a 39-year-old man of emotional immaturity, gross insensitivity, and repellent appearance.'

The only good review it got was in the *Stage*, the trade paper of the theatrical profession. ('The script sparkles, the dialogue is witty and fast-paced.') I showed it to Tim, expecting him to be delighted, but he was pretty underwhelmed.

'Haven't you heard the gag?' he said.

I gave him a blank look.

'What are the two most useless things in the world?'

'I give up.'

'The pope's balls and a rave in the *Stage*.'

18

THE PRAM IN THE HALL

When Caroline and I left Queen Charlotte's clutching our newborn baby we were given the hospital equivalent of a goodie bag. Thrown in among some quite useful items, such as a couple of disposable nappies, was a glossy magazine called *Dad*. This publication, paid for by the Government, was an attempt to make fatherhood look like an attractive lifestyle option – a bit like trading in your Mazda MX5 for a Mercedes E320 estate. Presumably, this was New Labour's way of trying to discourage men from abandoning their partners as soon as they gave birth – quite a common occurrence in Shepherd's Bush. In this particular edition, the likes of David Beckham shared space with features on the latest Sports Utility Prams, while doe-eyed toddlers were pictured kicking balls around with muscular young men in T-shirts. The message couldn't have been clearer: Babes were out and babies were in.

It soon became apparent just how misleading this was. The first time I cradled Sasha in my arms she did a projectile vomit all over my new Turnbull & Asser shirt. I was so shocked I almost dropped her on the floor. Indeed, it came out of her mouth in such a thick, powerful jet I half expected her head to start rotating as she recited passages from the Bible backwards. The situation wasn't helped when Caroline and her mother – who were both looking on – doubled up with laughter.

The notion that men can treat babies as glamorous style accessories, requiring no more adjustment to their self-image than a new car, is a complete falsehood. Take the baby sling, for instance. If a more emasculating item of clothing has ever been designed, I've yet to see it. My theory is that they're a way for wives to avenge themselves on their husbands for all the indignities they've had to suffer during pregnancy. They've spent the best part of a year waddling around with a baby hanging over their trousers, so we can jolly well see what it's like.

You might as well put a bumper sticker on your Mercedes E320 estate that says: 'Eunuch On Board.'

In my experience, the reaction of men to the new arrival in the household is one of general bemusement – particularly when it comes to the social rituals associated with the happy event. In the weeks following Sasha's birth, I simply couldn't understand why Caroline's friends insisted on coming round to 'see the baby'. Occasionally, their reluctant partners followed them through the door and they always had that bored, hangdog expression that you see on men standing outside women's changing rooms in clothes shops. You could tell that they would have preferred to be doing practically anything else. They'd only agreed to come because, for some inexplicable reason, their wives or girlfriends attached an almost religious significance to this ritual.

The only time men like to show off their babies is when it comes to emailing a picture to all their friends and that's because it involves (a) a digital camera; and (b) a computer.

The whole viewing ritual would have been a lot more interesting if I'd been allowed to teach Sasha some tricks to perform in front of our guests. Sean Langan and I became intensely competitive about whose baby was more intelligent and, since they weren't exactly the same age, this involved drawing up a chart to determine how many weeks it took each of them to hit various 'Developmental Milestones'.

Caroline knew nothing about this until Sean and Anabel came round to 'see the baby' and I tried to demonstrate just how much progress Sasha had made on the crawling front. Admittedly, this involved a certain amount of pushing and pulling while she was lying, face down, on the floor – but I thought she did pretty well considering she was only ten days old. Caroline, on the other hand, was horrified. She whisked Sasha up into her arms and made me promise not to give her any more crawling lessons for at least six months.

Of course, there are some aspects of the baby experience that men can enter into wholeheartedly. Buying a pram, for instance. I'm convinced the reason Maclaren is the market leader in the UK is because the company knows that this task is nearly always entrusted to men and, as a result, has gone to great lengths to make its pushchairs sound like motorised vehicles. There's the *Volo* and the *Quest*, for example, not to mention the *Rally Twin*. Just in case this is too subtle, there's even one called a *Triumph*, presumably in the hope that the poor, deluded fool standing in Mothercare with his wallet out can make believe he's buying a motorbike.

It worked for me.

Like most men, I'm sure I would have developed more of an interest in parenthood if shops like Mothercare had a gadget section. Why doesn't the R & D department of Tommy Tippee come up with a giant bottle that you can attach to the side of babies' cots so they can feed themselves like pet mice? I suggested rigging up just such a device when Sasha was four weeks old, but Caroline vetoed it on the grounds that Sasha wasn't old enough to manoeuvre herself into the feeding position. I pointed out that if you deposit a newborn on its mother's stomach it will instinctively wriggle its way towards her breasts. Couldn't we trick Sasha into thinking that Caroline was lying beside her in the cot? I suggested we get hold of a blow-up doll and attach the teat of the giant bottle to one of its nipples.

'*Darling*,' Caroline groaned. 'I don't want my baby sharing her cot with any of your old sex toys.'

This was an issue particularly close to my heart since I was responsible for Sasha's middle-of-the-night feed. At first, cradling her in my arms as she methodically worked her way through her bottle was rather moving. I experienced a distant echo of what Caroline must have felt when she fed her. However, after I'd been doing it for a month, I didn't find the experience quite so charming. For one thing, it took half an hour – and Sasha had to be *burped* afterwards, which meant throwing her over my shoulder and rubbing her back until she puked. Sometimes her baby sick would trickle down my shirt and find its way into my trousers.

My one consolation was that I was able to rig up the baby-feeding equivalent of a hands-free kit. I put Sasha on her side, stuck the bottle in her mouth, and then propped it up on a pile of cushions so it was at just the right angle. Provided she didn't make any sudden movements, I could sit beside her and read a book while she got on with draining the bottle. The essential thing was to remain completely silent since if I made any noise at all she was liable to jerk her head in my direction, bringing the whole Heath Robinson contraption down on top of her.

This arrangement worked quite well until I started reading *Yellow Dog,* Martin Amis's most recent novel. I managed to hold it down until I got to a scene set in a tabloid newspaper called the *Morning Lark.* Amis introduces us to a journalist called Clint Smoker who's labouring over a lurid description of a royal scandal involving a Chinese meal. Clint concentrates so hard on the task – producing over a hundred words involving one excruciating pun after another – that another character is prompted to ask him what he's writing. 'Photocaption,' he replies.

It was that word that did it. Involuntarily, I let out a loud guffaw of laughter and all hell broke loose. Sasha swivelled round to look at me, the bottle fell to the floor and milk ended up spilling all over everything.

Funnily enough, one of the characters in *Yellow Dog* has a baby daughter and the book ends with her taking her first, tentative steps. It's a pivotal moment in which the child's father becomes acutely aware of his responsibilities for the first time. Amis clearly believes that men can be redeemed by the experience of fatherhood – but just how quickly is it supposed to happen?

One of the reasons it *feels* emasculating to become a father is because, physiologically speaking, it is. According to a spate of recent scientific studies, fathers have lower levels of testosterone than single men. An American study in 2003 discovered that men in committed, romantic relationships have 21 per cent lower levels of testosterone than men not in relationships – and a 2005 study established that testosterone levels dip even further when men become fathers. In other words, having a child has an almost identical effect on the male sex drive as having a testicle removed.

From an evolutionary perspective, this makes perfect sense. For one thing, it means men are less likely to stray once their partners have given birth, thereby making it more probable that their offspring will survive. For another, it reduces the likelihood that fathers will kill their sons in a fit of sexual jealousy. High levels of testosterone are linked with aggression, assertiveness and the drive to seek out new sexual partners, all of which are serious impediments when it comes to being a responsible husband and father. Emasculation, it seems, is a necessary condition of a happy marriage.

None of which makes it any easier to accept. Someone once told me that if you put a penny in a piggy bank every time you have sex with your partner before marriage and then take a penny out every time you have sex afterwards, there will always be pennies left in the piggy bank no matter how long you stay together. I don't know whether this is true, but you're unlikely to be making many withdrawals in the six months following the birth of a child. Indeed, you probably won't even take the piggy bank down from the shelf. It'll just sit there staring at you, a cruel reminder of what being a man used to mean before one of your testicles was removed.

The drastic reduction in my own level of testosterone was

underlined by Caroline's insistence that I accompany her and Sasha on a seemingly endless round of shopping trips. I realised that the designer clothes she'd been talking about buying weren't intended for me when she dragged me into a shop called Bonpoint.

'Aren't these adorable?' she said, picking up a tiny pair of trousers and holding them against herself.

I was tempted to reply that she might have trouble squeezing into them, but thought better of it. Caroline was back to within a whisker of her pre-pregnancy weight, whereas I'd yet to lose the stone and a half I'd put on in the previous nine months. Why is it that young mothers are so anxious to spend money on their new-born babies? My theory is that they're making up for lost time. It's the post-natal equivalent of overeating during pregnancy: shopping for two.

During the first few months of her life, Sasha seemed to acquire a new designer outfit every week. The upshot was that she soon had a more expensive wardrobe than me. Given that she was bound to grow out of all these clothes almost immediately, I couldn't help feeling that they were a colossal waste of money – but experience quickly taught me not to say anything. Men have only two functions when their partners take them shopping with the baby: to produce their credit cards and carry the bags. On one trip to Old Bond Street I saw a man nervously fingering his Visa card as his wife enquired about the price of a Burberry nappy bag with black leather trim. Answer: £275.

In the most advanced cities in the West, fathers now occupy a similar role to that of women in the Islamic world – trailing along behind, never opening their mouths, occasionally exchanging sympathetic glances with fellow sufferers.

In one respect, though, I still occupied a traditional role in our household: that of breadwinner. Clearly, I was going to have to make a fortune if I was to keep my daughter in the style to which she was becoming accustomed. When Sasha turned three months, Caroline dragged me along to Bonpoint again and made me buy a little cashmere outfit with matching mitts and booties. *Kerching!* (A better name for the shop would be 'Cashpoint'.) If I was going to have to produce something as extravagant as that every time Sasha passed the three-month mark, what would I get her for her twenty-first? A GulfStream V?[1]

The best moneymaking scheme I could come up with was to start a chain of baby shops that appealed exclusively to men. Instead of designer nappy bags, they would sell camouflage Babygros and miniature paintball guns. There would be an assault course in the basement – for the dads, naturally – and a furnace into which we could pitch the leopard-skin papooses we'd been forced to wear. Yummy mummies would be allowed in, but only on the understanding that they'd have to perform lapdances on request. (Okay, okay, I was feeling *very* emasculated.)

My inability to incorporate fatherhood into my masculine self-image provoked some fairly inexcusable behaviour. The birth of your first child is meant to be one of those defining moments when you finally become a grown-up, but it seemed to have the opposite effect on me. Far from maturing, I started behaving like a fifteen-year-old boy.

For instance, three days after Sasha was born, I asked Caroline if she'd mind if I popped out for a round of golf. Admittedly, this was a pretty shoddy request, but I still wasn't prepared for her response.

'Don't you want to spend some time with your daughter?'

Jesus Christ, I thought. *Robert Louis Stevenson was right. Marriage is a battlefield and our baby has already been weaponised.*

So naturally I picked up my clubs and marched out the door.

Another example: less than a week after Sasha was born, I waited for her and Caroline to fall asleep and then tiptoed out of the house to go to a party at a nearby club. Admittedly, I only stayed for about

---

1 The cost of bringing up a child from birth to university was estimated at £164,000 by a research team working for Woolworths in 2004.

an hour, but it was long enough to bump into several of Caroline's friends, all of whom called her the next day to tell her how surprised they were to see me out on the town. When she confronted me about this, I did what any normal teenage boy would do under the circumstances: I stormed off, slamming the door behind me, and went and watched *Baywatch Hawaii* at my best mate's house.

The verdict of Caroline and her friends was that I was 'in denial'. According to these armchair psychologists, it wasn't unusual for men to start 'acting like idiots' after the baby arrived. It was just our way of 'dealing with the situation'. It was like an extended stag night, apparently. We needed to run around 'behaving like prats' before settling down. It was nothing to get 'stressed out' about. I'd be fully domesticated within a couple of weeks.

Naturally, I preferred a more respectable-sounding explanation. I began to read the health section of the daily paper, constantly on the lookout for some bit of psychobabble I could use to justify my behaviour.

I struck gold when I discovered that the National Health Service was setting up a helpline for men suffering from post-natal depression. Incredible as it might sound, the South Essex Partnership NHS Trust had begun to distribute a pamphlet to all new fathers in Basildon that included details of how to get in touch with the helpline. The booklet was called *Fathers Matter – In Tune With Dads*.

As soon as I read this I tried it out on Caroline.

'I'm sorry about all these sophomoric high jinks, darling, but I think I've discovered the explanation: I'm suffering from post-natal depression.'

'Don't be absurd,' she snapped as she busied herself with changing a nappy. 'Next you'll be telling me you've got your period.'

I debated whether to point out that my periods weren't due to resume until six weeks after the baby's birth, but thought better of it.

The following week there was an even more promising story in the paper. According to Dr Tim Cantopher, the medical director of the Priory Clinic in Walton-on-Thames, men who try to combine helping out around the home with a successful career at work are in danger of suffering from 'Atlas Syndrome', a new psychiatric condition named after the Greek god who supported the world on his shoulders. 'This syndrome affects men who are too good,' said Dr Cantopher. 'They are too strong, capable and caring.'

I liked the sound of that, so I ran it up the flagpole as Caroline was sterilising one of Sasha's bottles.

'I don't think that applies to freelance journalists,' she said, her voice dripping with sarcasm. 'In your case, taking an active role in childcare would mean watching slightly less daytime TV.'

I decided to soldier on.

'Listen to this,' I said, reading from the paper. '"It used to be mainly women who suffered from this as they felt compelled to be the perfect employee while having all the pressures of running the home and caring for the family. But in the last few years men have added new responsibilities to their traditional role of being aggressive and successful at work."'

I began to fantasise out loud about writing a bestselling book on the subject, the male equivalent of Shirley Conran's *Superwoman*. I'd call it *Superdad*.

'Great idea,' she said, picking up the remote and switching off the TV. 'I think you should get started straight away. We could use the money.'

After a few months, I finally worked out what lay at the root of all my problems: an irreversible shift in the balance of power between Caroline and me. Until Sasha appeared, I may not have 'worn the pants', but I was at least the most *responsible* member of our household. I paid the mortgage, I paid all the bills and if something went wrong with the plumbing I got down on my hands and knees and fixed it. (Okay, okay, I called the plumber.) But all these things paled into insignificance next to the monumental responsibility of keeping a child alive. Suddenly, Caroline had been catapulted into the stratosphere and I'd been reduced to an ever shrinking spec on the horizon.

This became apparent in all sorts of ways. Take the informal unit of barter and exchange, commonly referred to as 'the brownie point', that Caroline and I had always depended on to keep our relationship on an even keel. If I wanted to go and play golf on a Friday afternoon I could use up some of the brownie points I'd banked earlier in the week. Similarly, if she wanted me to go out to dinner with a couple of her married friends, she could use up a few of the points she'd stored away.

But Caroline had earned so many brownie points simply by virtue of giving birth she'd effectively broken the bank. What could I possibly do to catch up? The whole currency had been devalued.

In the run-up to Sasha's birth I'd steeled myself for a shift in my status in the household pecking order. But I wasn't prepared for just how radical this change turned out to be. To paraphrase Dean Acheson, I'd lost an empire and had yet to find a role.

Presumably, something like this went through the mind of Hugh Hefner in 1953, prompting him to start *Playboy*. When the first issue hit the news-stands, Hefner was married and living in cramped accommodation with his wife and baby daughter. The area of Chicago his apartment was in could even be described as the Shepherd's Bush of the Midwest.

Unfortunately, there the similarities end. Hefner was twenty-eight in 1953. By the time he was thirty-nine – my age when Sasha was born – the *Playboy* empire had an annual turnover of $48 million and he had his own private jet. The 'Big Bunny' was equipped with a disco, a cinema, a wet bar and sleeping quarters for sixteen people. Needless to say, Hef was usually the only male passenger on board.

19

'ZZZHHOOM. WHAT WAS THAT? THAT WAS YOUR LIFE, MATE.'

I think it's the closest I've ever come to dying.

It was past midnight and I was lost in one of the most remote parts of the British Isles. This wouldn't have been so serious if I wasn't caught in a snowstorm – and even that might not have mattered if I was dressed in the appropriate clothing.

Unfortunately, I wasn't wearing any trousers.

The reason I found myself in this predicament is that I'd decided to try and simulate the rigours of the infamous SAS Selection Course. Armed with a copy of *How to Pass the SAS Selection Course* by Chris McNab, I'd set off that morning on a fifteen-kilometre hike across the Brecon Beacons carrying a compass, a map and a 25-lb rucksack. The following day I was going to climb Pen Y Fan – the highest peak in the region – and then walk a further twenty kilometres, but in the meantime I was planning to spend the night under the stars.

One of the reasons the SAS holds its selection course in the Brecon Beacons, rather than its headquarters in Hereford, is because the weather is so changeable. Temperatures can fall to arctic levels in the middle of winter and more than one SAS hopeful has died of hypothermia. When I'd set out that morning it had been a clear, sunny day, but by the time I was ready to make camp it had begun to snow heavily and visibility was poor.

Luckily, my 'survival kit' included a thermal sleeping bag designed to withstand temperatures of −17 °C – a 'green maggot', in SAS-speak – so I didn't need to worry about the weather. At least, I wouldn't have needed to if I'd had the sense to stay in the bloody thing. But at around midnight I suddenly got an overwhelming urge to pee.

I gingerly wriggled out of my sleeping bag, being careful not to dislodge the stick that was holding up the roof of my 'bivi', and pulled on my boots. It was pitch black so I was going to have to walk a few yards to make sure I didn't pee on my Bergen, the army-style rucksack I was using to carry all my kit. I had on a Norwegian Army shirt, but I didn't bother to put my trousers on or take a torch. After answering nature's call I was hoping to be back in my 'green maggot' within a matter of seconds.

That's funny, I thought a few minutes later. *I could have sworn it was right here.*

I'd carefully retraced my footsteps but, bizarrely, my campsite was nowhere to be found.

Where had it gone?

Not surprisingly, this eventuality isn't covered in *How to Pass the SAS Selection Course*, so I was forced to improvise. I got down on all fours and started methodically searching the area with one of my arms extended in front of me like an ant.

Nothing.

After ten minutes of this, the seriousness of the situation began to dawn on me. Here I was in the middle of nowhere in sub-zero temperatures with no torch, no sleeping bag, and dressed in a pair of Y-fronts. This was less like a Boys Own adventure than *Mr Bean Goes Camping*.

Hereford, we have a problem.

*

My decision to embark on this lunatic adventure was prompted by the fact that I turned forty on 17 October 2003.

Throughout my thirties I spent a good deal of time fantasising about how I'd celebrate this momentous occasion. I imagined an incredibly decadent party at which I'd be surrounded by these scantily clad models. Instead of a cake, I was planning to have a couple of waiters come in at midnight bearing a huge, gilt-edged mirror with the number '40' written on it in cocaine. Theme: Growing Old Disgracefully. Dress: Age-Inappropriate.

In the event, my birthday wasn't quite as glamorous as I'd hoped.

'Ooh, look! Tommee Tippee!' said Caroline as we arrived at the Baby Show at Olympia. 'I hope you brought your wallet.'

Given the presence of a newborn baby in my life, I suppose it was inevitable that my birthday would be a fairly low-key affair. But I hadn't anticipated spending it at a baby show. A few days later, I decided I owed it to myself to mark the occasion with something a little more dramatic and persuaded Caroline to give me a forty-eight-hour furlough.

Why did I want to simulate the SAS Selection Course?

Partly, it was an opportunity to take stock. Was I serious about wanting to become a proper writer? If so, shouldn't I give up the day job? I'd recently been made the restaurant critic of *ES Magazine*, in addition to being the drama critic of the *Spectator*, and trying to fit in other work around my two weekly columns, particularly with a newborn in the house, was proving increasingly difficult.

Spending the weekend in Brecon was also a test of character. As Chris McNab writes in chapter four of *How to Pass the SAS Selection Course*: 'Defeatism, depression and a failure of determination are amongst the foremost reasons for failure. All those who attend Selection will reach the point of maximum exhaustion, but only those who have the grit and determination to push through the pain of fatigue and even injury will get through.'

But my main reason for doing it was that I'd become really, really fat.

George Orwell said that at fifty, everyone has the face they deserve, but what had I done to merit these three chins at the age of forty? As for my ever expanding girth, I'd given up buying suits. Why spend £500 on an outfit that's no longer going to fit you in three months' time? (Admittedly, Caroline didn't apply this logic when it came to buying clothes for Sasha.) I was on the point of investing in a pair of drawstring trousers and a kaftan top when it dawned on me that this would be tantamount to throwing in the towel. I had to make one last effort to lose weight. My weekend in Brecon was going to mark the beginning of a new fitness regime.

Before setting off, I decided it would be prudent to seek some advice so I dropped in on my next-door neighbour, Harry Meade-Briggs. In addition to being a wine merchant, Harry is a member of the Honourable Artillery Company, a unit of the Territorial Army, and he assured me he'd spent many a weekend 'yomping' in Brecon.

'We're special forces trained so I know a few of the boys in the Regiment,' he said, tapping his nose confidentially. (No one in the Armed Forces calls the SAS 'the SAS'. Rather, they refer to them either as 'the Regiment' or they drop the definite article and pronounce 'SAS' so it rhymes with lass.)

The first thing he did when I told him of my plans was subject my kit to a 'routine inspection'.

'What's this for?' he asked, pulling my tent out of my rucksack.

'To sleep in.'

He looked at me as if I'd just confessed to having a penchant for playing with dolls.

'No member of the Regiment would ever – and I mean *ever* – sleep in a tent,' he sniffed, tossing it to one side. 'That's civvy kit.'

Next up was my compass.

'That's what I'd call an emergency compass,' he remarked, holding it at arm's length as if it was a used condom. 'If you're behind enemy lines and your GPS unit has gone tits up that'll be about as useful as a two-legged dog.'

He went down to his basement and reappeared with a Silva

compass which he said was 'standard SAS-issue'. He then announced that he was going to teach me how to navigate using a compass and a map, a skill he described as essential if I was to survive 'on the hill'.

He told me how important it was to 'orientate' my map, explained the difference between 'Eastings' and 'Northings', and provided me with a handy way of remembering what order they came in: 'You go along the corridor and up the stairs.'

Needless to say, I couldn't make head or tail of it.

Finally, he presented me with some 'mental cunt cake'. This was SAS-speak for Kendal Mint Cake, so-called because 'they're all mental cunts'.

As I was leaving, he asked me if I knew what the 'three Ps' stood for. The Regiment swears by them, apparently.

I had to confess that I didn't.

'Preparation, preparation, preparation,' he said. 'You do realise you're completely fucking insane?'

It wasn't just turning forty that caused me to behave so erratically. I also had to contend with Sean Langan's skyrocketing career.

Shortly after Sasha was born, I sat down with Caroline to watch the first episode of *Travels of a Gringo*, Sean's South American odyssey. It had been made 'Pick of the Day' in the *Guardian*, *The Times*, the *Daily Telegraph* and the *Independent* – a 'clean sweep', as Sean put it.

The conversation between Caroline and me went something like this:

Me: He looks ridiculous with that stupid beard.

Caroline: You're just jealous.

Me: Don't be absurd! I couldn't be happier for him.

Caroline: Oh, yeah? In that case, why have you blacked out his teeth in all the pictures of him in today's papers?

Me: *All* the pictures? There were only three and one of them was the size of a postage stamp.

Caroline: Mee-ow!

Fortunately, not long afterwards I got a chance to claw back some of my self-respect. I was rung up by a PR woman who asked me if I'd be interested in finding out more about Remington's new range of electric shavers. I was about to hang up when she explained that it would involve a day at the Nigel Mansell Racing School at Brands Hatch.

Now *that* was an offer a man in the throes of a mid-life crisis couldn't refuse.

The PR lady asked if I could recommend any other journalists and I immediately suggested Sean. He may have beaten me in the game of life, I told myself, but here was a chance to show him that when it came to pure, unbridled testosterone I could still give him a run for his money.

When the day of reckoning came, Sean and I rendezvoused with some other hacks at Paddington Station and made our way to Brands Hatch. Following a mercifully short presentation about Remington's new product range, we were then given a briefing on what the day held in store by a man called Richard from the Racing School. First, we'd learn the basics by going round the track a few times with an instructor in an Audi TT; then, provided we weren't 'total muppets', we'd graduate to single-seater racing cars and compete against each other for ten laps.

'Don't go completely mental,' said Richard. 'We've had a real problem with journalists in the past. The only people worse than you lot are the police.'

Naturally, Sean and I decided to play it cool in the Audi TTs and after acquitting ourselves respectably we returned to the pits and climbed into the single-seaters.

The moment of truth had arrived.

There were only two cars separating us on the starting grid, but Sean screamed out of the gate so fast that by the time we'd completed the first lap he'd overtaken an additional four cars. *Jiminy Cricket,* I thought. *He'll lap me at this rate.* I shifted down into third, applied a little more pressure to the accelerator and immediately passed two cars, narrowing the gap to four. Eight laps later, I'd closed it completely.

Richard had told us that under no circumstances were we to pass anyone on the left. If the driver in front of us refused to give way, we'd just have to stay behind him for the duration of the race. I hung on Sean's exhaust pipe for another lap, but it was abundantly clear that he had no intention of letting me overtake. I didn't blame him. In his position, I wouldn't have let him overtake me, either. There was only one thing for it. As we approached the finish line, I yanked the car over to the left, changed up to fourth and floored it.

I just managed to pip him at the post.

When we arrived back in the pits, Sean was furious.

'You cheated!'

'Loser!'

'No. What you did was illegal. I won.'

We decided to ask Richard to adjudicate.

'If you'd been in an actual race situation, Toby would have won, no question,' he said. 'But since this wasn't a proper race, what he did was technically against the rules.'

'Surely,' I objected, 'if the person in front of you is going *really* slowly—'

'Doesn't matter,' he said.

'But what if you know he's a screaming homosexual?'

'Oh, well, in that case . . . '

In fairness, Sean won on a technicality. Still, for a few fleeting moments I felt like the king of the castle – even if he did have his own series on Channel 4.

Standing in the middle of the Brecon Beacons in my Y-fronts, gradually succumbing to hypothermia, I remembered one of the more surreal bits of advice Harry had given me.

'If everything goes tits up, try not to panic.'

'Absolutely,' I said. 'That could cost me my life, right?'

'No, I mean if you're going to die, die calm. There's nothing worse than dying in a panic.'

Aha. I see.

Funnily enough, when the possibility that I might get lost had come up, Harry had given me some quite sensible-sounding advice.

'Follow a stream to a river, the river to a bridge, the bridge to a road and then flag down a car.'

I'd made camp at the foot of a mountain called Corn Du and I *could* just about make out the sound of running water. But I decided against trying to find the source of the Nile. Knowing how changeable the weather could be in Brecon, I thought my best bet was to sit tight and hope that the sky would clear, enabling me to see my campsite in the moonlight. The Norwegian Army shirt I was wearing had been lent to me by the six-foot-four Harry – 'It's the bollocks' – and it was so big that by squatting down I could completely encircle myself in it. I reasoned that if the snowstorm cleared within the next hour or so I'd probably be okay.

Trouble was, it showed no signs of abating.

My first reaction when I realised I might actually die was anger. *How could I be so fucking stupid?* Not only that, but the whole world would know just how idiotic I'd been. You wouldn't need to be Sherlock Holmes to figure out how I'd met my end. The obituarists would have a field day. Christ, I'd probably be eligible for a Darwin Award, the gongs handed out to people who contribute to the human gene pool by removing themselves from it in really stupid ways. Poor Caroline would have to cope with a church full of mourners sniggering behind their programmes.

As soon as Caroline entered my thoughts, I was immediately consumed with guilt. *What on earth was I thinking of, embarking on such a reckless adventure when I had a twelve-week-old baby at home?* Caroline would now have to bring up Sasha on her own, a situation made worse by the fact that I didn't even have any life insurance.

And what of poor little Sasha? How would she fare in the world without a father to guide her? (Actually, given how galactically stupid her father was, probably a good deal better than if he were around.)

Some might think that the presence of a baby in my life would be a source of comfort as I stared death in the face. After all, even if I was to expire in the next hour, at least my DNA would live on. Having a child is a way of cheating death of its victory.

But to paraphrase Woody Allen, I didn't want to achieve immortality through my children. I wanted to achieve it by not dying.

Admittedly, I'd probably have felt a lot worse if I was still childless. But one measly kid wasn't much to show for four decades. I couldn't help comparing myself to Boris Johnson, an exact contemporary of mine at Oxford. Not only was he the editor of the *Spectator* and the Member of Parliament for Henley, he also had four children.

I was reminded of one of John Cleese's more memorable soliloquies in *Fawlty Towers*: '*Zzzhhoom*. What was that? That was your life, mate. Oh, that was quick. Do I get another? Sorry, mate, that's your lot.'

For the second time that year, I began to pray. *Please God. Don't let me die out here. I know I didn't keep my promise to be a better person last time, but this time I will. Honestly, I really, really will . . .*

Suddenly, the air was filled with the theme from *On Her Majesty's Secret Service*. Was it a sign?

No, it was my mobile phone ringing.

Unfortunately, it was in the bottom of my rucksack, so I couldn't actually see it – but at least I had something to orientate myself by. I ran in the general direction of the sound, terrified that it might stop at any moment. After a couple of stumbles, I managed to locate my rucksack and there, right beside it, was my sleeping bag.

I was safe.

I pulled the 'green maggot' up around me and tipped the rucksack upside down, spewing its contents all over my campsite. The phone tumbled out at my feet.

'Whoever this is, you just saved my life,' I said.

Beat.

'That's a bit melodramatic, isn't it?'

It was Caroline. She'd just finished giving Sasha her 11 p.m. feed and was calling to see how I was getting on. I told her the story and, before long, we were both in fits of hysterics. I've never loved her more than at that moment.

'Come home, bubby,' she said. 'I don't think you're special forces material.'

The following morning I decided to cut my losses and return to base.

20

YOU'LL NEVER SERVE LUNCH IN THIS TOWN AGAIN

Date: 3.11.03
To: Rob Long
From: Toby Young
Subject: Urgent Advice Requested

I need your advice about the film version of *How to Lose Friends & Alienate People*.

If you recall, my choice of which production company to sign up with last year – after an exhaustive round of meetings – was FilmFour. To my seasoned eye, they looked like the best outfit.

Six weeks later, they went belly up.

Since then, FilmFour has been resurrected, but on a much more modest scale. (Annual budget of $15.8 million, as opposed to $50 million.) I recently had a tête-à-tête with the company's new head – a woman called Tessa Ross – who told me that they still want to make *How to Lose Friends*, but given how meagre their resources are she and I are going to have to appoint an independent producer capable of raising the moolah. To that end, I've embarked on another series of meetings with all the same people I met with last year – and every encounter begins with them ripping the piss out of me for rejecting them in favour of a company that went bust six weeks later. (Great fun, as you can imagine.)

However, there are two new faces in the mix: Stephen Woolley and Elizabeth Karlsen. (They're married, so they come as a package.) I don't know if Woolley's name means anything to you, but in the world of independent British cinema he's a bit of a legend. Along with his then partner, Nik Powell, he produced some of the key British films of the eighties – *The Company of Wolves*, *Mona Lisa*, *Scandal* – and since then his credits have included *The Crying Game*, *Interview with the Vampire*, *Michael Collins* and *The End of the Affair*. He has a good relationship with Harvey Weinstein – which raises the possibility that *How to Lose Friends* might become a FilmFour-Miramax co-production – and his wife, Elizabeth, has a distinguished list of producing credits in her own right.

I had a meeting with them yesterday and came away completely mesmerised. It wasn't *their* credentials that impressed me, so much as their opinion of *mine*. Stephen said he wasn't surprised to hear I was writing a picture for Mr Hollywood – 'He's great at spotting talent' – and Elizabeth told me she thought *How to Lose Friends* was one of the landmark books of our generation.

'You should think very carefully about who you choose to produce this project,' she said. 'The temptation will be to just turn it into a conventional romantic comedy, but the source material is so strong there's an opportunity to do something really groundbreaking here.'

When my head stopped spinning, I realised they were probably just blowing smoke up my arse. What do you reckon? Are they the right people to produce the movie?

Date: 3.11.03
To: Toby Young
From: Rob Long
Subject: Re: Urgent Advice Requested

Of course they didn't mean it. *Duh!* Such shameless flattery is the *lingua franca* of the entertainment industry. Out here, if you begin a conversation *without* engaging in a bit of ass-kissing, the person you're talking to thinks you're insulting them.

But here's the thing: insincere flattery isn't completely worthless. After all, even if someone is lying through their teeth – as Woolley and Karlsen clearly were – the fact that they're bothering to flatter you is in itself quite flattering. In their eyes, you're someone worth schmoozing.

As I told you before, deal-making is a lot like dating – only this time you're the supermodel. Woolley and Karlsen may not have been on the level when they told you how smart they thought you were – I mean, of course they weren't – but there's no disputing their desire to get into bed with you.

My advice is the same as it always is: your job is to write a funny movie, not to produce one. So the sooner you appoint someone else to do that for you, the sooner you can do your job – which is to write the damn thing.

I have to confess, Woolley and Karlsen's names don't mean anything to me, but I checked them out on the IMDb and between them they've produced over forty movies. So I guess they know what they're doing.

Date: 12.11.03
To: Rob Long
From: Toby Young
Subject: The First Meeting

I took your advice and appointed Woolley and Karlsen. We had our first meeting about *How to Lose Friends* today and . . . well, it was very different from our last meeting.

The purpose of the get-together was to discuss the second draft of the treatment which, miraculously, I turned in last week. It was scheduled for 4.30 p.m. at their Soho offices, but Karlsen's secretary called about an hour beforehand and changed the location to Starbucks in Notting Hill Gate. Then she called back and said, actually, could we meet in Soho after all? Then she called for a third time – can you believe it? – and asked if they could reschedule for 4.45 p.m. By the time I got there, Woolley and Karlsen were in another meeting with Terry Gilliam and I sat in the corridor, cooling my heels, until Karlsen finally emerged at 5.15 p.m. *About fucking time*, I thought. But in fact she was just popping her head out to tell me that she had to be somewhere else at 6 p.m. and therefore we'd have to keep it short – whereupon she went back into the Gilliam meeting.

Eventually, at around 5.30 p.m., Karlsen came out and sat down beside me in the corridor – I didn't merit being invited into their office, apparently. Almost the first words out of her mouth were, 'I think we're going to have to bring in another writer. You've submitted two treatments now and the structure just isn't there.'

I was completely gobsmacked. When I pointed out that this would mean splitting my screenwriting fee with someone else, she said, 'Well, you want this film to get made, don't you?'

She then threw out a name: some guy who did 'additional dialogue' on *Absolute Beginners*, a legendary turkey that she and her husband co-produced in 1986.

I wandered the streets of Soho afterwards in a kind of stunned trance. I couldn't help remembering that old Hollywood adage about the first meeting always being the best. I mean, if this was what they were like at our first meeting, what the fuck were they going to be like at the second?

Okay, here's my plan. Since they're so keen for me to collaborate with someone – a 'veteran screenwriter', as Karlsen put it – why don't I put your name forward? I've been wanting to work with you on something for ten years and if somebody's going to get half my fee, I'd rather it was you than anyone else.

Do you have a sample script you can send me so I can pass it on to Woolley and Karlsen?

Date: 12.11.03
To: Toby Young
From: Rob Long
Subject: Re: The First Meeting

It's always nice to have someone trying to put money in my pocket, but I have a sort of business posture (which has earned me a tidy amount so far) of not actively soliciting jobs in the feature world unless I'm already somehow connected to the studio. It's supposed to keep my price and prestige up. So far, it has; but so far, I haven't taken a big spec out to the market, either – though that's changing in the fall, when I take two out. The idea here is for me to do two small pictures and one big spec sale before I start actively looking for assignments. Or so I'm told.

So it's a bit tricky for me to send any material to Woolley and Karlsen, though it's totally understandable why they'd want to see some of my work. I mean, of course they do.

The trouble you find yourself in, though, is that they already like the guy they want to sign you up with – there's some previous relationship, there was probably some kind of promise to him a few years ago – and so anyone you want to bring in is going to be viewed as 'your' person, when what they really want is 'their' person.

If you really want to push it, why not give them a copy of *Conversations With My Agent*, which is, after all, mostly in script form? That way, I let them make the move which preserves my street cred and doesn't veer from the careful plan I paid my agent about $300,000 to come up with.

But if you'll permit me: I think the real trouble for you here is that collaborating with someone is difficult – and it may end up watering down your final script, or at the very least, muddying it. If they're really intent on your working with this other guy, then you should insist that you be given the chance to deliver a first draft – call it a 'working draft' – before they attach anyone else. 'Give me a shot at it,' you should say. Forget fees and credits and all of that bullshit. Just ask for the chance to get a rough draft together in the basic shape that you like before they make you sit in a room with someone else. How long do you think that would take? If they balk at that (which they probably will), do it anyway. Just start writing it the way you want to – and delay and obfuscate the timetable for collaboration, until when you finally meet the guy and officially 'start' working on it, you've got a document that serves as a starting point.

The guy they want to attach is probably some simpering toady – which is why they like him – who is also, a fair bet, lazy to boot. So he'll like this plan a lot when he discovers it.

Miss Graydon yet?

P.S. I hate it when anyone uses the word 'structure'. People use it to mean so many different things, from making sure the script isn't boring to making sure it has a satisfying ending. I mean, I've done almost 100 episodes of *Cheers* and I've done rewrites on a few big movies, and so far I've yet to really understand what anyone means by 'structure.' Usually it means that they don't know what it means.

Date: 13.11.03
To: Rob Long
From: Toby Young
Subject: Re: Re: The First Meeting

I like your plan a lot and I intend to follow it to the letter. But before I sit down and start writing the screenplay could I ask you to take a look at my treatment? So far, I've had almost no feedback on it and I need to know if I'm thinking along the right lines. I know it's a lot to ask – I hate reading other people's work-in-progress – but it shouldn't take you more than half an hour. It would mean an enormous amount to me.

Date: 2.12.03
To: Toby Young
From: Rob Long
Subject: Your Treatment

Sorry it's taken me so long to get around to your treatment. It did take me a while to read – sorry – and then a few days to think about. Ultimately, I'm not sure that what I can say about it is going to be very helpful, really. So feel free to chuck this out and ignore it.

The trouble is, you've written a script about what you THINK your book is about, but, as everyone knows, the worst person to ask about a book is its author. What your book is REALLY about, in case anybody asks, is a fairly smart guy who for some reason is incredibly shallow and fame-obsessed, and who – despite hilarious and epic attempts – simply fails to attain his goal of becoming a Media Prince, fails to get into the 'in' crowd, fails to bed the supermodel – fails, as we realize, not because he's a loser or a failure (that's where the book parts company with reality) but because there's a part of him deep down that still knows it's all bullshit, it's all straw, that the movie stars and the Graydon Carters aren't worth either emulating or worshipping – or even noticing, really.

It's a story about a guy, in other words. Not a magazine. Or a career. But about a guy's character and how it changes for the better by having its ass kicked around New York.

Your treatment is a perfect example of why it's hard for smart people to write screenplays. It's too complicated and too detailed, and you've connected all of the dots – and some of the dots that aren't even really dots – and I know that you've read screenplay books (probably Syd Field, from the looks of it) because that's what smart people do. They look really hard at the trees, buy books about the trees, Google-search tree types, and, of course, miss the fucking forest.

Here's my advice: chuck the whole thing. Empty your mind. Go out and take a walk and have a nice lunch somewhere. Sit away from the computer and, with a notebook and a pencil, make a list of 15 or 20 scenes – real scenes, though, where funny things happen and people say funny things, like your first meeting with Graydon, or trying to get into the VF Oscar party, or meeting your wife for the first time – and then put them in some kind of natural order, which may or may not be the actual order in which they occurred. That's your movie.

Arrange the scenes so that each little subplot is evenly scattered throughout the story. Meet your wife early. Fall in love with her.

Then blow it with her. Then win her back. That's four or five scenes right there. Mix in a few calls from Alex de Silva[1] – that's four calls, so now we're up to nine scenes. Some stuff at VF is at least five scenes. So now we've got 14 scenes already, all intertwined to keep up the pace, and if each scene is, say, seven pages long, you've already got a script of roughly 98 pages and you haven't even broken a sweat. Or cracked the spine on Field – or taken a course by McKee – or any other of that nonsense.

Then make sure that the scene order makes sense from only ONE perspective: the movement the main character (you) makes from shallow blindness to wise husband. Make sure that five, say, of the early big scenes have some kind of rhyming scene later on, to balance them out. An example: I love the scene in which you meet Graydon for the first time and you're really impressed by him, but I think you need a scene later that reveals that he's just a slavish toady like everyone else – that, to use the metaphor of the book, there is no 'inner room.' Graydon certainly isn't in the seventh room – he's just a socially terrified striver like everyone else, everywhere. (I remember someone who worked for Reagan telling me how ultimately deflating it was to work in the White House and spend time in the Oval Office – the seat of world power, the most important 100 square feet on earth – when what you ended up worrying about was the Council of Rural Mayors, or how the one-term idiot Congressman from East Bumfuck was going to vote . . .)

I'm digressing. The point is, you worked way too hard on it. You followed the Syd Field plan – I noticed the Plot Point One and the Act Structure – but the truth is, that's all bullshit anyway. 15 or 20 scenes of funny, dramatic action about a character getting the shit kicked out of him – figuratively or literally – and then falling in love, learning a lesson, winning back the girl – that's a movie. It's all right

1 Alex is a successful screenwriter whose adventures I chronicled in *How to Lose Friends*.

there in front of you. So stop looking for it. Stop structuring it. String it together like lights on a Christmas tree, and the whole thing will hang together much better and be a terrific movie – funny, smart, fast-paced – and the irony is, it will eventually conform to all of that structure crap anyway. Because a good movie is a good movie.

My thoughts, anyway. Feel free to rail against me in person or in an email, if you like. There's a great script there. It should take you all of two weeks to weave it together . . .

Date: 4.12.03
To: Rob Long
From: Toby Young
Subject: Re: Your Treatment

Thank you very much for producing such a thoughtful response to my treatment.

Learning how to write screenplays strikes me as being a little like learning how to write journalism. First, you have to learn all the rules; then you have to unlearn them. But you don't end up back where you started – not quite. It's odd. You can't discover your own voice – which is really the voice you started out with – until you've been through this process.

As you can tell, I'm still very much at the learning-all-the-rules stage and I'm not confident enough to do what you're recommending which is to throw them all out.

But all of this is somewhat academic because I've now been 'let go' from the project. It turned out the 'additional dialogue' guy was working on a script of his own, so they approached a number of other writers to see if they'd be interested in collaborating with me and – surprise, surprise – none of them were. The list of those who turned down this opportunity is ridiculously long, but there was one name on it that sent me into a spiral of self-loathing and despair: Ben Elton. Do you know this guy? He started out as an 'alternative' comedian, railing against Thatcherism and the like, and now earns a fortune writing the librettos for truly awful West End musicals. I mean, his name has become a byword for shameless hackery. He's the biggest sell-out of his generation. And even he turned down this assignment. It's too humiliating to contemplate.

P.S. How do you feel about being a character in my next book? I'm planning to write a sequel to *How to Lose Friends* and it would be great to have a character that echoed the Alex de Silva character in the first book, a Hollywood writer who's a good person, rather than a bad person. Not that Alex is a particularly bad person, but you get the idea. Happy to change your name if you want me to – and muddy the waters to make you unidentifiable.

Date: 4.12.03
To: Toby Young
From: Rob Long
Subject: Re: Re: Your Treatment

Well, first of all, I have no doubt at all that you could whip out a very funny first draft of a script for your book without too much trouble – and if the producers have fired you, it's because they don't want you hanging around making trouble. The problem with all of those screenplay books isn't that they're wrong; it's that after you read them, you get all bollixed up and constipated and it's impossible to have the right amount of energetic recklessness it takes to get out a first draft. In my (admittedly limited and unhappy) experience with feature scripts, the mantra is always 'I'll fix it later.' It's the second and third drafts where you put in the structural touches. Easier said, I know. But it's silly to have you kicking yourself thinking it's harder or more complicated when in fact the opposite is true.

I'd be pleased to appear in your next book – especially as a sage. Though I hate to think that when it comes out, people will compare me to Alex and say, 'Hey, buddy, he fucked all of those supermodels. What's so cool about YOU?' Though it's a risk I'm willing to take for a few moments of notoriety. As far as making me unidentifiable, it's been my experience that being unidentifiable just sort of happens to me automatically, without any special effort.

I insist, however, that you begin work on the _____ _____ screenplay immediately just to prove to yourself that it's not such a painful ordeal.

P.S. I feel for you over the Ben Elton business. I know exactly who he is.

PART FIVE

A NEW WORLD DAWNS

21

LOS ANGELES WITHOUT A SAT-NAV

On 9 April 2004 I finally achieved one of my lifetime ambitions: I moved to Los Angeles.

Okay, it was only for three months, but still. My plan was initially to go for ninety days – the maximum amount of time a foreigner can stay in America as a tourist – and, provided everything worked out, apply for a five-year visa. In the meantime, I managed to persuade the *Spectator* and the *Evening Standard* to give me three-month sabbaticals so if everything went pear-shaped I'd be able to take up where I left off.

The ostensible reason for the trip was to do some research on a Hollywood novel I was planning to write, but my real objective was to try and establish myself as a screenwriter. Stephen Woolley and Elizabeth Karlsen may have dispensed with my services, but I still had one string left to my bow. I'd finally turned in a full-length screenplay to Mr Hollywood and moving to LA seemed like the best way of consolidating my relationship with him. When he rejected the script and asked me to have another crack at it, as he inevitably would, my plan was to take him up on the offer he'd made eighteen months earlier and get an office at the studio. Once I'd got my foot in *that* door, there'd be no stopping me.

Needless to say, selling the idea to Caroline was far from easy. 'You want to move *where*?!?'

At my insistence, we'd spent our honeymoon in Los Angeles and she didn't have particularly fond memories of the place. I'd booked us in to the Leo DiCaprio Suite at the Chateau Marmont, but thanks to my tardiness we missed the plane and ended up spending the first night of our honeymoon watching *Jurassic Park III* in a shopping centre a few miles west of Heathrow. By the time we arrived at the Chateau, the DiCaprio Suite had been given to someone else and we had to make do with a much smaller room directly beneath it (the Troy McClure Suite). The final straw was when my old friend Alex de Silva turned up to welcome us to LA. At one stage, he was briefly engaged to a supermodel and the first thing he did on entering our room was point to the sofa and announce that he'd shagged his ex-fiancée in that very spot.

'I won't forget that night in a hurry,' he chuckled.

'Thanks, Alex,' said Caroline. 'That's really added to the romantic atmosphere.'

Apart from her reservations about LA, Caroline was understandably nervous about moving to a foreign city. It was one thing being a full-time mum in London where she had friends and family around to keep her company and share the burden, but quite another to be stuck holding the baby in a place where she didn't know anyone. I knew from experience just how important this support network was. In the end, she only agreed to the move on the condition that we rent a house in a posh neighbourhood with a swimming pool and a spare bedroom so her parents could come and stay.

The upshot was that I had to borrow against my mortgage in order to finance the three-month trip.

Another of the reasons Caroline was reluctant to go is because travelling anywhere with a baby is a logistical nightmare. We had discovered this when we'd flown to Scotland a few months earlier.

We ended up taking so much stuff – a pram, a baby seat, a steriliser, an assortment of bottles, a changing mat – that in order to get to Heathrow I had to hire a taxi with one of those special pods on the roof that's usually reserved for ski equipment. I've known super-models with less luggage.

Once we got on the plane our real problems began – and it only takes ninety minutes to fly to Scotland. I don't think I've ever seen such a crestfallen expression as that worn by the man who had to get out of his seat so Caroline could squeeze past him clutching our daughter. If you're an aeroplane passenger, the sight of a mother car-rying a baby is only marginally less horrifying than an Arab carrying a ticking briefcase.

According to *What to Expect . . . the first year* – the sequel to *What to Expect . . . when you're expecting* – babies are supposed to be fed during take off and landing to help them adjust to the change in air pressure. But I challenge anyone to pull this off without pro-ducing a torrent of projectile vomit. (It gives new meaning to the term 'Jet Stream'.) By the time we landed in Aberdeen I don't think there was a single drop of milk in Sasha's stomach. Eight fluid ounces, on the other hand, were evenly distributed over every pas-senger within a twenty-foot radius.

'What did you just say?' asked Rob Long incredulously.

It was my second day in Los Angeles and I was sitting opposite him in Campanile, a show business restaurant on La Brea.

'I said that Mel Karmazin has just ankled Viacom.'

'That's what I thought you said. It's just that I've never heard anyone use the word "ankled" before.'

'But Variety *uses it all the time,' I said, reaching into my briefcase and pulling out a copy of that day's edition. 'Look, it says it right here on page one: "Mel Karmazin has ankled as president and chief operat-ing officer of Viacom."'*

'For Chrissake, put that away,' said Rob, frantically looking over his shoulder. 'Nobody reads the trades in public. Nobody.'

'But, surely, everyone in the Industry—'

'And no one uses the word "Industry", either,' he said, whipping my copy of Variety *off the table. 'It's "the Business", okay? "The Business." Jesus Christ, you've got a lot to learn.'*

He explained that it was a well-known piece of Los Angeles lore that you can always spot the out-of-towners because they're the ones reading Variety *and the* Hollywood Reporter *in public. Out-of-towners are under the impression that the trades carry all sorts of interesting information about show business – stock quotes, reviews, box office figures, etc. – when, in fact, the only reason people actually employed in the entertainment business read them is to find out how much their competitors are being paid.*

'That's why they read 'em in private,' Rob explained. 'Because discovering this information is nearly always accompanied by a string of expletives.'

'Does that mean I won't be needing this book?' I asked, fishing a copy of Variety's Slanguage Dictionary *out of my briefcase. This offered definitions of some of the more arcane bits of Hollywood slang, many of them coined by the paper.*

'Oh, my God,' said Rob, beginning to hyperventilate. 'If you don't put that away right this second I'm never going to have lunch with you again.'

Flying to Los Angeles proved no less painful than the trip to Scotland. Caroline and I simply couldn't get Sasha to stop crying, a fact that didn't exactly endear us to our fellow passengers. (If looks could kill, all the passengers in our immediate vicinity would have been arrested when the plane touched down at LAX.) When she eventually nodded off – about four hours into the flight – the chief steward appeared and asked Caroline if she'd like to put her head down in Club Class. He explained that his wife had just had a baby and he knew how important it was for 'Mum' to get her beauty sleep.

'I'm sure Dad won't mind looking after her for a bit,' he said, winking at me.

I was tempted to ask him if he could stick Sasha in Club instead. She was momentarily exhausted from the effort of screaming her head off for four hours, but I knew from experience that her voice box would be fully restored after less than five minutes' sleep. Unfortunately, Caroline leapt out of her seat and started powering down the aisle before I could open my mouth.

Everything was fine until Sasha woke up a couple of hours later and immediately launched into an impression of a pet shop being burnt to the ground. I could tell that her nappy needed changing – everyone within a hundred-yard radius could tell – but I didn't know what Caroline had done with the Pampers. I searched in her hand luggage, but couldn't find any. She'd obviously put them somewhere – but where? There was only one thing for it: I'd have to ask her. I undid my seatbelt and went in search of Caroline, leaving Sasha bawling in the seat next to me.

I made it as far as the galley separating World Traveller Plus from Club when I was met by an astonishing sight. There, looking for all the world as if he'd personally prepared the meals for 422 passengers, was the celebrity chef Gordon Ramsay. What was he doing in the galley? I glanced behind me, expecting to see a camera crew filming a reality show, but we were alone.

It was too good an opportunity to miss.

'Mr Ramsay,' I said, tapping him on the shoulder. 'I'm sorry to have to tell you this, but both the chicken and the beef were an absolute disgrace.'

I braced myself for a tirade of abuse, but, instead, he burst out laughing.

'That's quite funny,' he said.

I introduced myself, told him I was a restaurant critic and – rather miraculously – managed to strike up a conversation. It turned out he was flying to LA to negotiate a deal with Fox about doing a version of *Hell's Kitchen* in the US. He asked me if I'd like to join him in a glass of champagne and, naturally, I said yes. I was so starstruck, I'd forgotten all about the baby.

It wasn't until Caroline came padding into the galley from Club Class, all bleary-eyed, that I suddenly remembered what I was supposed to be doing.

'That's not Sasha I can hear crying, is it?' she asked.

'Ah, there you are, darling,' I said, glugging down the champagne. 'I've been looking for you everywhere.'

To Gordon's obvious amusement, she took me by the ear and dragged me back to steerage.

As Rob and I got stuck into our main courses at Campanile, he patiently took me through the Hollywood ritual known as 'the Business lunch'.

The first thing I had to master, apparently, was how to behave appropriately on entering a high-powered restaurant. According to Rob, table-hopping is generally frowned upon at lunchtime because everyone likes to maintain the illusion that they're actually doing some work. But not to acknowledge someone, even a very distant acquaintance, is considered bad manners. So in order to solve this problem a vast repertoire of hand gestures has evolved, with a different one for each person you salute, depending on their place in the Hollywood food chain.

For instance, if you glimpse your accountant or orthodontist somewhere in the back, the appropriate gesture is something called 'the Vegas fist', whereby you shake your fist and smile at the same time, as if to say, 'You devil, you.' If you see someone of equivalent professional standing, by contrast, a 'finger point' is more appropriate, while if you spot a superior, a 'wave' combines just the right amount of informality and respect. However, if you see someone really important – 'such as the president of a television network' – the suitable greeting is 'finger point, wave, finger point', a piece of kabuki that Rob discreetly demonstrated for me behind his menu. The only time any sort of physical contact takes place, apparently, is when an agent passes a client on his way to a high-visibility booth. The correct gesture here is for the agent to squeeze his client's shoulder as he breezes past, only stopping to whisper a juicy bit of gossip in his client's ear if he happens to be one of his top earners.

Gossip, not surprisingly, plays a big part in the typical Hollywood lunch. People usually begin with 'salad course stories', in which minor titbits about friends and colleagues are imparted, then progress to an exchange of 'fish course stories' – usually gossip involving major celebrities – and only when the 'decaf cappuccino portion' of the meal has been reached will they finally get down to any real business. In this way, Rob explained, the lunch can be claimed as a legitimate expense, even though it's essentially just an excuse to trade inside baseball.

'But before you tell any stories, you have to make sure you're not going to be overheard by anyone else in the Business,' he said. 'I usually make a trip to the men's room before I tell my first salad course story so I can see who's sitting at the next-door tables. After all, no one wants to get a reputation as a gossip. In this town, that's the kiss of death.'

Before Caroline and I arrived in Los Angeles we made the mistake of renting a car sight unseen from the LAX branch of Budget. We debated whether to get the obligatory red Mustang convertible, but decided against it. Caroline and I had rented one of these when we came to California on our honeymoon, imagining it was 'typically LA'. We quickly discovered our mistake. The only other people in red Mustang convertibles were out-of-towners like us. The low point was when we spotted two parked outside Fred Segal and they both turned out to belong to British honeymooning couples.

This time around, I simply followed the advice of the Budget rental agent I spoke to on the phone. She recommended a 'compact', something I took to be a particular make of American car, like a Pontiac, but which turned out to be a generic term for a small, inexpensive vehicle. The 'compact' in question was a Hyundai Accent. Unfortunately, by the time I discovered my mistake, it was too late to do anything about it. I'd taken advantage of a special offer and rented this vehicle for three months.

'It's all about what car you drive,' said Rob over the 'decaf cappuccino portion' of our lunch.

He explained that, like many people in 'the Business', he had two cars: one for everyday use and one that he just kept for show. Paradoxically, though, the 'show car' was a beaten-up old wreck, whereas the 'runabout' was an expensive German sedan.

'I keep the shit pile in my driveway so I can point to it whenever anyone comes over and say, "Yeah, I don't play that silly, money-obsessed game. I'm not about to surrender to a sick craving for status and misbegotten respect. I like to thumb my nose at the foolishness of the Hollywood machine." In fact, I've only ever driven that piece of crap to this restaurant once and when I handed my keys to the valet guy I said, "Be careful with my wife's car."'

I reached down and took a notebook out of my briefcase.

'What are you doing?' said Rob.

'I need to make some notes. This is great stuff.'

'I don't think that's a good idea. People might think I'm having lunch with a reporter.'

'But you are *having lunch with a reporter.'*

'Listen, in this town no one talks to reporters.'

'That can't possibly be true.'

He lowered his voice.

'I mean not in public. Never in public.'

After my lunch with Rob, I returned to LAX, tracked down the Budget rental agent who'd recommended my Hyundai Accent and demanded an upgrade. A heated argument then followed, only coming to an end when I agreed to hand over my credit card so she could make a suitable 'adjustment' to my original agreement. The upshot was that I drove away in a Mercury Mountaineer, a car that by no stretch of the imagination could be described as a 'compact'. On the contrary, it was an SUV. Not only that, but of the three types of SUV on offer at Budget – 'mid-size', 'standard' and 'full-size' – the Mountaineer fell into the latter category. After Mr Hollywood's Cadillac Escalade, it was the largest car I'd ever seen.

When I first got behind the wheel of this juggernaut I was almost paralysed with fear. Indeed, I was so nervous about hitting a pedestrian it took me forty-five minutes just to get it out of the car park. I'd had dinner the night before with Chris Ayres, *The Times*'s LA correspondent, and he told me that he'd been rear-ended at a Stop sign by a woman in an SUV. She was on her mobile at the time and even though she was travelling no faster than 5 mph she did $2000 worth of damage.

'Before being posted here I was embedded with the US Marines in Iraq,' said Chris, 'but that was nothing compared to driving in LA.'

Not surprisingly, it didn't take me long to acquire a taste for the Mercury Mountaineer. As I come careering towards a Stop sign, trying to wrestle this beast to a halt, all the smaller cars in front of me would scurry out of the way. Occasionally, Caroline and I would spot another British couple behind the wheel of a red Mustang convertible and the look of terror on their faces as they saw this battleship bearing down on them almost made up for the astronomical fuel costs.

Rob was right: It was all about the car.

22

THE CASINO

When I'd told Rob over lunch about my reasons for wanting to move to LA he was flabbergasted.

'Are you nuts?' he said. 'Once Mr Hollywood hears you've moved out here, you'll stop being this exotic, English writer he's trying to seduce and become just another Hollywood whore.'

'But there can't be that many English writers in LA. I'll still be quite exotic, surely?'

'*What*?!? You can't walk ten blocks in this town without bumping into a Brit. Hollywood is one of the few places in the world where you can make a ton of money without having to do much work. For some reason, that really appeals to you guys.'

I soon discovered just how right he was. The place was crawling with Brits hoping to become screenwriters. Some of them were graduates of the two big screenwriting courses offered by UCLA and USC, but most were just footloose young men who'd given up their day jobs to move to LA and pursue their dream. Needless to say, the vast majority had met with no success and after running through their savings had been reduced to taking low-paying jobs in the service industry. Indeed, of the various service personnel I came into contact with during my first week in LA – the valet guy, the pizza deliveryman, the cable guy, the babysitter, the pool boy – over half were aspiring British screenwriters.[1]

The reason they didn't pack it in and go home was that, very occasionally, one of their number struck gold. For instance, in 1994, a Cambridge graduate called Miles Millar sold a script about an orang-utan to New Line for $1,050,000. At the time, it was the equal highest amount ever paid for a screenplay by a first-time writer. (One embittered rival described it as '*Every Which Way But Loose* meets *Every Which Way But Loose.*') Miles had gone on to have a very successful Hollywood career, earning writing credits on *Lethal Weapon 4, Shanghai Noon* and *Spiderman 2*, among other pictures, and co-creating a hit television series called *Smallville*. The general attitude of the expats I came across was that if Miles could do it, so could they.

Even Rob Long had inspired a few of these hopefuls. An old university friend of mine called David Astaire had graduated from the UCLA screenwriting programme in 1994 and over the course of the next ten years had gone through the bulk of his inheritance as he failed to sell one script after another. This, in spite of winning a BAFTA Fellowship, a Samuel Goldwyn Award and a clutch of other prizes. When I caught up with him in 2004, he was down to his last £10,000, but rather than cut his losses and return to England, he was intending to blow it all on a heli-skiing trip to Alaska.

'It's Rob's leather jacket theory,' he explained. 'When Rob was almost out of money and thinking of going back to New York, he spotted a $500 leather jacket in a shop window on Rodeo Drive. His brother advised him to buy it on the grounds that you have to hit rock bottom in this town before you can make it. So he bought the jacket and when he got home there was a message from his agent telling him he'd landed a job as a staff writer on *Cheers*.'

---

1 And the other half were . . . aspiring French screenwriters, aspiring German screenwriters, aspiring Spanish screenwriters . . . etc. A few years ago, *Esquire* featured a chimp and a typewriter on its cover, accompanied by the words: 'Is anyone in America *not* writing a screenplay?'

I, too, had been inspired by someone else's good fortune. My friend Alex de Silva had abandoned a promising career on Fleet Street to move to LA in 1995 and had ended up selling a script before he'd even graduated from his screenwriting course. Since then he'd gone on to have a meteoric career, as documented in *How to Lose Friends & Alienate People.* Indeed, a screenplay of his had just been made into a $100 million picture by one of the biggest directors in town. Unfortunately, I couldn't call him for advice because he'd severed all contact with me after reading my book. He was one of the few friends I'd lost and alienated as a result of writing it.

'I've got a theory about this town,' I told Rob after I'd been in Los Angeles for a few weeks. 'It's essentially just a more respectable version of Las Vegas. Everyone is playing some version of roulette in which they're hoping against hope that their number will come up. They know the odds are stacked against them, but the reason they don't leave is that once in a blue moon one of the bleary-eyed gamblers huddled around the spinning wheel hits the jackpot.'

'Keep your voice down,' said Rob, looking over his shoulder. We were having lunch at Toscana, a 'Business' restaurant in Brentwood, and he had yet to make his usual sweep in order to check out who else was there. Only after he'd satisfied himself that he couldn't be overheard did he respond to my point.

'There's more than a grain of truth in what you say, but you can never – *never* – use that metaphor in public. The only people who describe the Business as a crapshoot are those who haven't made it. It's a way of making themselves feel better about the fact that they're still waiting tables. Those that have made it take a very different view, believe me. As far as they're concerned, it's because they're these hugely talented artists – the Rembrandts and Michelangelos of the entertainment business. Luck just doesn't enter into it. [Beat.] In fact, I've known writers who've started out espousing the crapshoot theory and then, as soon as they've sold a script, embraced the talent theory.'

'How long a period of time usually elapses before they switch from one theory to the other?'

Rob glanced over his shoulder again.

'About thirty seconds.'

Towards the end of my first month in Los Angeles, I struck up a conversation with a screenwriter as I was waiting for a friend at the Polo Lounge. He'd sold half a dozen screenplays, two of which had been made into multi-million dollar blockbusters, and he'd just made a deal with a studio to direct.

'I hope you don't mind me asking,' I said, 'but how old are you?'

'I'm thirty-one – which makes me forty-six in Hollywood years.'

I was tempted to ask him how old that made me in Hollywood years, but thought better of it. Instead, I asked him how he managed to stop such phenomenal success going to his head. He seemed pretty grounded, given how young he was. What was his secret?

'I pretend I'm an anthropologist,' he said. 'I tell myself I'm not a participant in this crazy, fucked-up business. I'm just a dispassionate observer. I spend my time making mental notes for this imaginary paper I'm going to write for a distinguished German periodical.'

'Does it work?'

Beat.

'Nah. I spent the afternoon yelling at my assistant because my Aston Martin DB9 still hasn't been delivered and the reason I'm talking to you is because my dumb-ass actress girlfriend is over an hour late. She's probably fucking her yoga teacher – *again*.'

Funnily enough, a real-life anthropologist called Hortense Powdermaker did spend some time studying 'the Business' in the 1940s. The upshot was a book called *Hollywood: The Dream Factory*, one of the most intelligent and insightful essays ever written about the movie colony. Many of her observations are as relevant today as they were sixty years ago. Take what she has to say about Hollywood's over-reliance on market research:

In parts of East Africa, the entrails of chickens are used for divining the future, while among the Karen of Burma it is the gall bladder of a pig; in Hollywood polls are used to determine the mysterious tastes of the audience. Will they like this or that title and this or that plot, with this or that star? The methods now used to determine, a year in advance, the tastes of potential audiences are not too different from trying to foretell the future by examining the spots on an animal's liver.

For the purposes of writing a chapter called 'The Scribes', Powdermaker interviewed ten different screenwriters and gave each of them a label in order to protect his or her identity: Mr Hopeful, Miss Sanguine, Mr Pretentious, Mr Modest, Mr Cynic, Mr Acquiesce, Mr Coincidence, Mr Literary, Mr Gifted and Mr Truly Interested. The most wretched of these is probably Mr Cynic because he's bitter about having sold out: 'Mr Cynic disparages his own work, jeers at his employers, but enjoys his comfortable home and a substantial bank account.' The most content, on the other hand, is Mr Truly Interested. Unlike Mr Cynic, he didn't start out wanting to write the Great American Novel; rather, he's always wanted to be a screenwriter. For him, moving to Hollywood wasn't a trade-off between his literary aspirations and his need to make a living: 'Mr Truly Interested passionately cares about movies and persists in trying to reach his goals through this medium.'

Back in the 1940s, Mr Truly Interested was an anomaly because it was fashionable to regard Hollywood movies as mindless escapism. The stereotypical screenwriter was someone who'd enjoyed a modicum of literary success on the East Coast and then been brought out West by a producer who'd got him a writing contract at one of the studios. Either he enjoyed no success at all, in which case his contract wasn't renewed and he told himself he simply wasn't enough of a 'hack' to make it in Hollywood, or else he began to inch his way up the ladder, in which case he despised himself for prostituting his talent.

Is this still true today? The answer, broadly speaking, is yes. In spite of the evangelical efforts of 'gurus' like Robert McKee, most of the screenwriters I came across in Los Angeles still believed that big-budget commercial pictures are, essentially, pabulum. Even if they started out as Mr Hopeful, they soon became Mr Cynic. According to Stephen Schiff, the New Yorker-journalist-turned-screenwriter: 'It's the *Story of O* scenario. The writer is the most wooed person in Hollywood – then, as soon as the story is extracted from him, he's lashed to a post and beaten senseless.'

The main complaint was that there was virtually no room for self-expression. Listening to McKee evangelise about the heroic role occupied by the screenwriter in contemporary Hollywood, I'd formed the impression that they were these two-fisted warrior poets in the same mould as Ernest Hemingway and Norman Mailer.[1] But I soon discovered that this was a hopelessly romantic view. The problem with thinking of the screenwriter as a John Wayne-like figure, moving to the beat of his own drum, is that it's completely at odds with the reality of what those who manage to make a living at it actually do. The process by which a screenplay emerges – at least in Hollywood – has a lot more in common with the Ford production line than a John Ford Western.

Take the script for *Alien³*. In 1986, cyberpunk author William Gibson (*Neuromancer*) was hired to write 'two drafts and a polish', only to be interrupted by the 1987 writers' strike, and, when that was over, Eric Red (*Near Dark*) was brought in to do a 'five-week job'. At this stage, Renny Harlin (*Die Hard 2*) was attached to direct, but when he read the script he handed in his notice. The next writer to come on board was David Twohy (*Buffy The Vampire Slayer*) and while everyone liked his version he'd neglected to write a part for Sigourney Weaver, the star of the franchise. So in 1991

---

1 'Every epoch has a dominant art form, and the dominant art form of the twenty-first century is the cinema,' McKee claimed at his Story Structure seminar. 'The people who create the stories of this art form will be recognised as the great storytellers of the twenty-first century.'

the producers hired Vincent Ward (*The Navigator*) and put him to work with Jon Fasano (*Another 48 Hours*). Fasano was replaced by Greg Pruss, but after 'five arduous drafts' Ward and Pruss quarrelled and Larry Ferguson (*The Hunt For Red October*) was called in to do a 'four-week emergency rewrite'. However, when Sigourney Weaver read this version she threatened to pull out, so producers Walter Hill and David Giler knocked out a draft of their own. The version that eventually reached the screen in 1992 was a combination of this and another script written by David Fincher, the film's twenty-seven-year-old first-time director. Of Gibson's original screenplay, only one detail survived. 'In my draft, this woman has a bar code on the back of her hand,' he told me during a newspaper interview. 'In the shooting script, one of the guys has a shaved head and a bar code on the back of his head. I'll always privately think that was my piece of *Alien³*.'

On this evidence, David Mamet's conception of the role of the writer in Hollywood is closer to the mark: 'Working as a screenwriter, I always thought that "Film is a collaborative business" only constituted half of the actual phrase. From a screenwriter's point of view, the correct rendering should be, "Film is a collaborative business: bend over."'

Even William Goldman, the closest thing there is to an *auteur* screenwriter, echoes this view. Soon after I arrived in Los Angeles, I came across the following quote that he'd given to the *Guardian*: 'Look, there's wonderful money in it compared to real writing. There's terrific travel. Sometimes you can make memories for people. But if you want your own sensibilities to be on display, forget it. You don't go into the film business thinking you're a poet.'

Given how little creative satisfaction most successful screenwriters derive from their work, why was I still trying to join this club? The answer, apart from the money, is because I saw myself as Mr Truly Interested. Unlike most of the writers I came across in Los Angeles, I'm a big fan of the local product. I'm not talking about the kind of films that get recognised by the Academy of Motion

Picture Arts and Sciences, either. The sort of movies I like are precisely those that people in the entertainment business dismiss as mindless escapism. Even in the brief period I'd been in LA I'd seen several films I liked. *Mean Girls*, for instance, struck me as a genuinely witty teen comedy.

Perhaps it's unrealistic to single out such an exceptional film. In other respects, 2004 was hardly a vintage year, giving us *King Arthur, Troy, Van Helsing, The Chronicles of Riddick, The Day After Tomorrow, I, Robot* and *Around the World in 80 Days*. In his autobiography, Ben Hecht quotes David Selznick's rule-of-thumb regarding the film industry's strike rate. 'A few good movies,' said Selznick, summing up his career as one of Hollywood's most celebrated producers. 'Thirty years – and one good movie in three years is the record. Ten out of ten thousand.'

If I did succeed in becoming a professional screenwriter, maybe I, too, would become disillusioned. My best work would probably never be produced and those scripts that were turned into movies would be bastardised beyond all recognition. Even in the extremely unlikely event of being hailed as a genre master – the highest compliment I could imagine – I'd probably go on to write a string of turkeys, thereby tarnishing my reputation. When Moss Hart handed Billy Wilder the Oscar for best screenwriter for *The Apartment* in 1961, he whispered: 'This is the time to stop, Billy.' 'And how right he was,' Wilder told his biographer fifteen years later, by which time he'd made *Avanti, Fedora* and *Buddy Buddy*.

Still, I had to give it a shot. Listening to the jaded screenwriters I encountered, I realised that no amount of horror stories could ever put me off. My love for Hollywood was unconditional. Even if I was just a faceless drudge on a production line, I wanted to work in the Dream Factory.

23

STALKING MR HOLLYWOOD

After six weeks had elapsed and I still hadn't heard anything from Mr Hollywood I decided to call him.

'Can I help you?'

It was Lauren, his second assistant.

'This is Toby Young calling. We met about eighteen months ago.'

'I'm sorry, who?'

'*Toby Young.* I've just written a screenplay for your boss. I was wondering if it might be possible to have a quick word with him?'

'We don't accept unsolicited manuscripts, I'm afraid.'

'No, you don't understand—'

'Can you hold?'

Before I could respond, I heard the unmistakable chorus of 'Loser', Beck's 1993 hit: *I'm a loser baby so why don't you kill me.*

After five minutes had elapsed and she still hadn't resurfaced, I decided to hang up and call her back.

'Can I help you?'

'Hi, Toby Young again. I wonder if you could get a message to _____ for me?'

'Can you hold?'

'Actually, I don't mean to be rude, but—'

I'm a loser baby . . .

Clearly, trying to reach Mr Hollywood by phone was hopeless. So I decided to send him a postcard at the studio instead: 'Well, I took your advice and moved to Los Angeles. Any chance of meeting up to discuss the screenplay? I'd love to buy you lunch some time. I'm still on the same mobile number, but in case you've lost it here it is again . . . '

I then waited another month – but, again, nothing. By this time I'd been in America for seventy-eight days, which was dangerously close to my ninety-day limit. Desperate measures were called for. I considered loitering outside the studio in the hope of intercepting him, but I didn't fancy standing in the flight path of his Cadillac Escalade. If he spotted some maniac standing in the middle of the road trying to flag him down he'd probably instruct his driver to run him down. What was I going to do?

Then I had a brainwave.

In the course of researching my Hollywood novel I'd befriended a cockney paparazzo called Danny Tuffin who spent his life tailing celebrities in a Jeep Cherokee with blacked-out windows. Indeed, on one occasion he was pursuing Britney Spears when she crashed into another car on the Santa Monica Freeway. He 'hosed her down' with his Nikon D1H SLR digital camera and sold the set for $10,000. 'Not bad for an afternoon's work,' he said.

I called him up and explained my problem. Would he be willing to lie in wait for Mr Hollywood outside the studio with me riding shotgun? The plan would be to follow him home and then drop me off so I could ring on his doorbell. If the mountain wouldn't come to Mohammed . . .

'Course I fucking would,' said Danny. 'Sounds like a right laugh.'

Such a plan may strike the uninitiated as a bit drastic, but Mr Hollywood's stories were full of plucky little characters who'd dressed up as mailmen and police officers in order to bluff their way past studio security. During our first tête-à-tête at the Hotel du Cap, he'd told me how Steven Spielberg had managed to sneak into the Universal lot at the tender age of seventeen by wearing a suit and carrying his father's briefcase. He found an office that wasn't being used, stuck some plastic letters on the door and put his name in the building directory: Steven Spielberg, Room 23C. It was months before this ruse was discovered, by which time he'd managed to make several important allies who were later to prove invaluable in launching his career.

Of course, for every Hollywood legend who's managed to sneak in the studio gates there are probably hundreds who've been arrested for trespass. As a rule, these kinds of stunts only pay off if you possess a smidgen of talent – and that was still an open question in my case. Maybe the reason Mr Hollywood hadn't been in touch was because he *had* read my screenplay, not because he *hadn't*. If that was the case, he probably wouldn't be very pleased to see me when I turned up, uninvited, on his doorstep in the middle of the night.

I'd modelled the screenplay on *Citizen Kane*, utilising what its writer, Herman J. Mankiewicz, called the 'prismatic method'. The first act opened with the record producer being taken to the emergency room, having been discovered unconscious in a Los Angeles flophouse. As he lies in his hospital bed, dead to the world, a young doctor goes through his stuff, trying to discover whether he has any health insurance. He comes across a batch of yellowing newspaper cuttings in the producer's wallet and realises that this patient, whom he'd taken to be a homeless person, is in fact a show business legend. So he starts calling his nearest and dearest, but soon discovers that no one – including the man's only son – is willing to foot his bill. The doctor becomes more and more curious, wondering how on earth this person managed to alienate so many people, and, bit by bit, the record producer's life story is revealed.

The second act begins the following day, when the doctor comes in and discovers his patient sitting up in bed, having made what appears to be a miraculous recovery. At first, the doctor is wary of this peculiar man – he's a monster, after all – but he gradually falls under his spell as the record producer regales him with tales of showbiz derring-do. His greatest ever triumph was in 1974 when he arranged a comeback tour for a burnt-out rock and roll band, masterminding a revival in their fortunes that saw them become the number one musical act in the world.

At the beginning of the third act, the producer has suffered a relapse and the doctor calls the band's current manager to see whether anyone in the group can be persuaded to pay his medical costs. The answer is no. It turns out the producer behaved appallingly as soon as the band hit the big time. He reneged on various agreements, double-crossed his partners and tried to cheat the band members out of their share of the profits. The film ends with the record producer's death and the doctor paying his hospital bill.

Re-reading the screenplay after I'd turned it in, I wasn't particularly happy with it. Its main shortcoming was that the producer's entire life story was told in a series of flashbacks, something that every screenwriting 'guru' maintains is a complete no-no. In other respects, it conformed to most of the rules – each act ended with a 'plot point', for instance – but it lacked anything that distinguished it as a piece of work by me, as opposed to anyone else. I'd failed to put my personal stamp on the material. I began to regret not going with my first idea, whereby I included myself as a character and drew a parallel between Mr Hollywood's hiring of me and an episode in the record producer's life in which he plucked some unknown band from obscurity. So what if it was too reminiscent of *Adaptation*? If the words 'It's been done before' were considered a good reason for not doing something in Hollywood the studios would have gone out of business a long time ago. As Dorothy Parker said, 'The only "ism" Hollywood believes in is plagiarism.'

'That's him,' I said, pointing at the black SUV nosing its way out of the studio gates. It was 7.15 p.m. – exactly the same time Mr Hollywood had left work two years earlier. Danny allowed a couple of cars to come between him and his prey, then gently eased his way into the flow of traffic.

We were in business.

After we'd been following the Escalade for ten minutes or so it suddenly made an illegal left turn and then took off like a rocket. I was terrified that we'd been spotted – all the paparazzi in LA drive 4×4s with blacked-out windows – but Danny didn't seem to mind.

'Wanna play games, eh?' he said, throwing the Jeep into the turn. 'Let's see what you've got.'

By now it was pretty clear that we'd been 'made'. The Escalade was switching lanes, dodging oncoming vehicles and generally behaving as if it was being driven by James Bond. But Danny had the bit between his teeth and wasn't about to give up. I held my breath and began to pray: *Please God, don't let Mr Hollywood crash into anyone.* If he did my plan was to leave the scene of the accident as fast as my little legs could carry me.

'Fuck me,' said Danny, after the Escalade made a right on Robertson. 'I think I know where he's going.'

Instead of following him, Danny drove straight on, then took a right, followed by another right. Seconds later, he pulled up opposite the Ivy, one of the most famous restaurants in LA. Sure enough, the black Escalade was sitting right outside, disgorging its passengers. First Mr Hollywood emerged, then a woman I recognised as his wife, followed by a second man and then, bringing up the rear, Halle Berry. *No wonder they'd been trying to outrun us!* Clearly, the four of them were having dinner together.

I was debating whether to ask Danny if he'd be willing to wait a couple of hours, when I noticed him reaching for his Nikon on the back seat.

'What are you doing?'

'What's it look like?' he said as he brought the camera up to his face and started adjusting the lens. 'I can get at least a thousand dollars for a set of Halle Berry.'

Suddenly, _____ spotted us.

With a thunderous expression on his face, he began striding across the road. He looked like Clint Eastwood about to face down a gang of *pistoleros*.

I scrambled over my seat and tried to hide in the back.

'For Christ's sake, Danny, let's get out of here.'

'What you doing?' said Danny, laughing. 'He can't see you through these windows.'

Just before Mr Hollywood reached the car, Danny activated the central locking system.

'GET OUT HERE, YOU CHICKENSHIT MOTHER-FUCKER,' said _____, tugging wildly on the drivers' side door. 'I'M GONNA SHOVE THAT CAMERA UP YOUR ASS.'

'I'm begging you, Danny,' I whimpered. 'This'll be the end of my Hollywood career.'

Danny leaned over his seat and took a photograph of me cowering in the footwell.

'I thought you wanted to 'ave a word with him?' he said. 'Well, now's yer chance.'

'Please. I'm begging you.'

Mr Hollywood was now tugging on one of the rear doors.

'YOU'RE FUCKING DEAD. DO YOU HEAR ME? DEAD.'

'Look out,' said Danny, nodding towards the Ivy. 'Here comes the cavalry.'

I peeped out of the window and spotted a pair of the Ivy's security guards heading towards us. One of them was swinging a tyre iron.

'For fuck's sake, Danny, they're going to pry the doors open. We really have to go. RIGHT NOW.'

'All right, mate, calm down.'

Danny shoved the Jeep into gear and we squealed away, leaving a couple of black streaks on the asphalt.

I looked through the rear windscreen and saw Mr Hollywood standing in the middle of the road flanked by the two security guards. It was the last time I'd ever see him.

24

NOT AGAIN!

With less than a week to go before the ninety days were up, I awoke with a jolt at 5.30 a.m. to see Caroline standing at the foot of the bed. In the half-light I could just make out that she was holding some sort of flat stick.

'Not again!' I croaked.

''Fraid so.'

How the fuck had that happened?!?

Well, I knew how it had happened, obviously, but it wasn't supposed to have happened. *Sasha was only ten months old, for Christ's sake.* We'd had unprotected sex exactly once a few weeks earlier and Caroline had assured me there was absolutely no possibility she could get pregnant. So much for the rhythm method.

Any hopes I had of persuading Caroline to stay in Los Angeles were now completely dashed. I tried to argue that we'd be doing the child a favour if it was born in LA because it would then be entitled to US citizenship, but she wasn't buying it. Caroline had three loyal sisters, a protective brother and two doting parents, all of whom lived in London, and if she was going to have another baby she didn't want to be more than half an hour's drive from any of them.

At first, this struck me as grossly unfair. Why should her happiness come before my career? If she was making a contribution to the household income – and her job required her to be in London – that would be one thing. But hadn't she sacrificed the right to make decisions of this magnitude when she'd elected to become a full-time mum? Given that I was the sole provider, shouldn't I be able to dictate where we lived if it affected my career? It seemed to me that Caroline wanted to have her cake and eat it. She wanted all the benefits of being an equal partner in our marriage, yet she wasn't willing to share the burden when it came to paying the bills. Like many women of her generation, she'd embraced those aspects of feminism that suited her and ignored the rest.

'I don't think you've fully grasped the feminist case,' Caroline said when I put this argument to her. 'Equality for women was never supposed to be conditional on their joining the labour force. Women should no more have to earn their right to equal treatment than men.'

'I'm not arguing that housewives shouldn't have the vote,' I said. 'But if a woman chooses to enter into a traditional marriage, isn't she obliged to defer to her husband when it comes to certain decisions? If I think staying in LA would be good for my career, it's not unreasonable to expect you to support that decision, given that I'm the sole breadwinner.'

'What makes you think I *chose to enter into a traditional marriage*? Men may have made all the decisions for five millennia, but that doesn't mean it should continue to work that way for ever. Thanks to feminism, the marriage contract has been renegotiated. If I thought becoming your wife would involve delegating all my decision-making power to you, I never would have married you in the first place.'

'When exactly was it renegotiated?' I protested. 'I don't remember you setting out your terms before we got married – and if you had I'm not sure I would have agreed to them. We've gone from being *dinkies* to *sitcoms* in less than nineteen months.'

'What's a dinky?'

'Double Income No Kids.'

'And a sitcom?'

'Single Income Two Kids Overextended Mortgage.'

Beat.

'Fine. Let's get divorced. I'll take Sasha and go back to London and you can get a Thai mail-order bride.'

I knew Caroline was right. If I ignored her wishes our relationship would never survive. The state of Sean Langan's marriage was testimony to that.

Sean and Anabel had had another child at this point, but Sean showed few signs of slowing down. For the majority of Anabel's second pregnancy, he was making a documentary in Iraq about the aftermath of the war, a film that he proudly described as the riskiest he'd ever made. He'd dodged bullets in the Sunni Triangle, gone on patrol with the 82nd Airborne and obtained secret footage of a suicide bomber preparing to blow himself up. At one point, he even had to be rescued from an angry mob by the local militia.

From a career point of view, Sean's efforts had undoubtedly paid off. He hadn't yet finished editing the film – it was due to be shown on the BBC in the autumn of 2004 – but he'd managed to get an interview with one of the leaders of the Iraqi insurgency, a coup that no other Western journalist had pulled off at this stage. That alone would ensure his promotion to the premier league of foreign correspondents.

His marriage, on the other hand, wasn't faring so well. He came home a week before Anabel gave birth to their second child – only to take off again two weeks later. By the time he returned to London in the spring of 2004, Anabel was no longer prepared to live under the same roof as him. After sleeping on friends' floors for six weeks, he managed to negotiate a temporary reprieve by agreeing to write a weekly column for the *Daily Mail* – only to give it up a month later. Anabel had hoped he might switch to a more sedentary form

of journalism, but his pride was too great for that. It didn't help that
the column involved taking television presenters and soap stars out
to lunch and trying to get them to talk about their sex lives. 'If I have
to interview another D-list celebrity I'll go mental,' he said. Twenty-
four hours after resigning from the *Mail*, he was setting up another
documentary at the BBC, this time involving a nine-month stay in
Afghanistan. Before long, he was back to sleeping on friends' floors.

As I prepared to resume my freelance career in London – a career
that quite often involved interviewing D-list celebrities about their
sex lives – I couldn't help envying Sean his single-mindedness.
Admittedly, he wasn't exactly facing up to his responsibilities as a
husband and father, but Anabel had left him – he hadn't left her.
'She knew what I did for a living when she married me,' he said.
Her mistake had been in thinking he would change in response to
their new circumstances; that he would put his family first. In a
sense, Sean was making the same bargain Achilles had made: he was
choosing immortality over domestic happiness, even though it
might very well lead to an early death.

Was I wrong to have made the opposite choice?

I told myself that the reason I didn't behave more like Sean was
because I had a more developed sense of responsibility – my con-
science wouldn't allow it. But suppose my career as a screenwriter
had really taken off. What if Mr Hollywood had been so impressed
by my script about the record producer he'd hired me to write his
next sci-fi action blockbuster? That was the level of success Sean was
currently enjoying. If Mr Hollywood had insisted I stay in LA as a
condition of giving me that job, and Caroline was just as adamant
about returning to London, would I have behaved any better than
Sean? I expect that I, too, would have stayed away from home for
nine months.

Even if I *had* done the right thing, it wouldn't necessarily have
been out of a sense of duty. For all my whinging about being a 'sur-
rendered husband', I'd rather taken to family life. Indeed, I
generally preferred spending an evening at home with Caroline and

Sasha than going out – and this was *after* I'd already spent all day with them. On the very few occasions I'd been apart from them for more than twenty-four hours, I'd begun to miss them terribly. For purely selfish reasons, I couldn't bear to be separated from my family for six days, let alone six months. I felt incomplete without them – only half there. No doubt this was partly due to my falling testosterone level, but it made it much easier for me to put my family first.

Nevertheless, I did find the prospect of a second child somewhat daunting. When Caroline and I talked about the adjustments we'd have to make, she made it clear that I'd be expected to do my fair share of the childcare – which would mean even less time for my writing. I tried to put forward a variation of the argument I'd made before: why should I have to do anything around the house when I was the sole provider? If she decided to get a job and ended up contributing 25 per cent of the household income, I'd happily do 25 per cent of the domestic labour. But as things stood, why should I do 50 per cent when she earned nothing?

'I'm not asking you to do 50 per cent,' she said. 'Obviously, when you're working, I'll probably end up doing everything just like I do at the moment. But during the evenings and weekends I don't think it's unreasonable to expect you to do the same amount as me.'

'But what if I want to work at evenings and weekends? During office hours, all my time is taken up with freelance journalism – with earning the money that pays the mortgage and puts food on the table. Unless I'm allowed to work outside office hours, I'll never be able to progress as a writer. I'll just be a hack for the rest of my life.'

Caroline looked upset.

'Don't you want to spend time with your family?'

'Of course I do, but why does it have to be either/or? Why do women like you and Anabel force your husbands to choose between their families and their careers? It's almost as if we're in the same position our mothers were fifty years ago: either we get married and have children or we have satisfying careers – but we can't do both. I was worried that if you gave up work you'd experience the same regrets my mother did. In fact, I'm the one who's in danger of turning into my mother.'

Caroline thought for a moment.

'Are you sure this isn't just an excuse? Next you'll be telling me that the reason you haven't managed to establish yourself as a screenwriter is because you're too busy changing nappies. The truth is, writing your columns takes up no more than a few hours a week and you've had ample opportunity to write at least a dozen screenplays, but you've spent your time faffing about instead. If you actually did some work during office hours, instead of just twiddling your thumbs, you'd have plenty of time to spend with your family.'

I debated whether to draw her attention to the passage in *Screenplay* where Syd Field talks about 'resistance', but thought better of it. In the past, whenever Caroline had complained about how little work I did, I pointed out that all writers indulge in 'displacement activity' and maintained that it was an essential part of the creative process. *While it might look as though we aren't doing anything, our unconscious minds are hard at work, devising the plots of our soon-to-be-written novels.* Unfortunately, now that there was going to be a fourth mouth to feed, I knew that if I so much as used the phrase 'creative procrastination' a soiled nappy would come flying through the air at 60 mph.

It was ironic that I was trying to negotiate longer office hours because since we'd arrived in LA Caroline had been urging me to spend *more* time at my desk, not less.

She would wake me at 8 a.m. each morning and if I wasn't in my little office above the garage by 9 a.m. she'd start looking at her watch and making throat-clearing noises. To begin with, I had no excuse. There was no daily newspaper to read, no Radio 4 to listen to – I couldn't even work out how to connect to the

Internet. So for the first week or so I had no choice but to drag myself away from the breakfast table and sit down in front of my computer. Not that I actually wrote anything, of course. I did what most writers do in this situation – I stared at the screen until I thought a respectable amount of time had passed and then poked my head round the kitchen door and asked what we were having for lunch.

Fortunately, at the beginning of the second week I hit upon a perfect time-wasting device. At around 9.45 a.m., by which time Caroline's throat-clearing was beginning to sound like someone trying to start a tractor on a cold morning in Reykjavik, I dropped down on all fours and started making googly noises at Sasha on her play mat. On every previous occasion when I'd tried to 'communicate' with our daughter she hadn't paid me the slightest bit of notice, but this time she actually responded – sort of. For about a nanosecond, she turned her attention away from the yellow-and-orange striped giraffe hanging a couple of inches above her head, looked vaguely in my direction and said, 'Goo.'

Now, that may not sound like much, but to the parents of a young baby every sign of cognitive development is regarded as a major breakthrough. In my eyes, it was as if Sasha had suddenly sprung to her feet and performed a tap dance while singing 'Yankee Doodle Dandy'.

'Did you see that?' I asked Caroline. 'Did you see *that*?!?'

As luck would have it, Caroline *had* witnessed this miracle and as a result she was happy for me to remain on all fours, repeating the word 'Goo', for the next ninety minutes. Needless to say, Sasha's eyes didn't stray from her giraffe once, but it didn't matter. I had the excuse I'd been looking for.

The following day, when Caroline whipped away my just-finished bowl of Cheerios, I announced that it was time for Sasha's 'story'. I took her into the sitting room, propped her up on the sofa, and began reading aloud from *Service with a Smile* by P. G. Wodehouse.

'Wait a minute,' said Caroline, standing in the doorway. 'Couldn't you at least find a fairy story to read to her? Why does it have to be the book you just happen to be halfway through?'

She had a point, but luckily Sasha gave every indication that she was actually enjoying herself. 'Goo,' she said when I told her about Lord Emsworth's prize-winning pig. Clearly, my ten-month-old daughter was an excellent judge of literary merit. For a second, I began to fantasise that Sasha might grow up to be a writer, just like her old dad. Who knows, in forty years' time she, too, might be reading P. G. Wodehouse to her baby as an excuse not to start work.

25

SURRENDERING TO A HIGHER POWER

Returning to London was a bitter disappointment. Ever since I'd received that phone call from Mr Hollywood, I'd dreamt about moving to Los Angeles and becoming a full-time screenwriter. Now I'd been brought back to reality with a bump (and it was inside my wife's stomach). Back in Hollywood's golden age, a writer's first contract with a studio typically lasted six months and if it wasn't renewed – and he had to go back home – that was considered a humiliating failure. What was I supposed to think, having lasted half that long?

I was tempted to blame Caroline. After all, if it wasn't for her insistence that we move back to London I could have stayed in LA indefinitely, even if that involved remortgaging the house for a second time. I might not have made any headway – either with Mr Hollywood or anyone else – but at least I'd be able to tell myself I'd given it a shot. Now, I'd be in the unhappy position of not knowing whether I could have made it or not. In twenty-five years' time, when I was still interviewing D-list celebrities about their sex lives, I'd look back and think, 'What if?'

However, something happened towards the end of 2004 that led me to reassess the impact of my marriage on my career: I started drinking again.

I'd sworn off alcohol in 1999 and, even though I fell off the wagon two years later, I rarely drank more than a couple of glasses of wine. In the autumn of 2004, though, all that changed. I started polishing off the best part of a bottle of Scotch every night. It felt good, too, like being reintroduced to an old friend. As the twelve-year-old Macallan slid down the back of my throat, I felt a surge of exhilaration. The self-mastery I'd painstakingly acquired over the past five years, and which had become a source of pride, suddenly seemed like an encumbrance. I'd forgotten just how pleasurable it was to be out of control.

Unlikely as it may sound, the cause of this relapse was that I briefly became a professional actor. After the commercial success of the stage adaptation of *How to Lose Friends* at the Soho Theatre, I joined forces with a twenty-two-year-old producer called Ian Osborne and we spent eighteen months trying to mount a production in the West End. All our efforts came to naught and we were about to give up when a last-minute cancellation suddenly meant a six-week slot opened up at the Arts Theatre. Initially, we hoped Jack Davenport would agree to reprise the role, but at the eleventh hour he was offered a part in *Pirates of the Caribbean 2* and, not surprisingly, he decided to do that instead. After a frantic search for a replacement, Ian reluctantly turned to me and I unthinkingly said yes.

Needless to say, I soon realised how foolhardy this was. Appearing in a one-man show in the West End is a nerve-racking prospect for an experienced actor, but for someone who's last gig had been playing a spear-carrier in a student production twenty-one years earlier it was terrifying. Even the normally unflappable Caroline was filled with anxiety on my behalf. During the rehearsal period she forbade me to mention the play after 8 p.m., claiming it had the same effect on her as drinking a strong cup of coffee. Once she started thinking about it, she couldn't get to sleep.

She was right to be worried. On the night of my theatrical debut, about ten minutes into the performance, I completely forgot what my next line was.

The director, Owen Lewis, had warned me what to do if this happened.

'The important thing is not to panic,' he said. 'Take a deep breath, start walking round the stage in a circle and, hopefully, by the time you're back where you started you'll be able to remember your next line.'

I decided to follow his advice. As long I stayed calm and relaxed maybe no one would notice anything was wrong. I just had to keep my cool.

Unfortunately, by the time I'd completed my walk round the stage I still couldn't remember my next line. So I just skipped to the next bit I could remember. This succeeded in digging me out of the hole I was in, but it was only a temporary solution because I had no idea how many lines I'd left out. As I was rattling through the rest of it, a little voice in the back of my head was saying, 'What if you've jumped to five minutes before the end? People will be walking out, looking at their watches, thinking, Ten minutes? That was a bit short.'

As it turned out, I'd only omitted a couple of lines and I got through the rest of the show relatively unscathed. But it was a nerve-shredding experience.

If that was the only thing that had gone wrong I might have been able to hold out. But combined with the events of the press night three days later it was enough to plunge me into an alcoholic spiral.

I was dreading having to perform the play in front of my fellow drama critics – and, sure enough, the wheels fell off the bus about ten minutes into my performance. I'd reached exactly that point in the play where it had all gone wrong on the first night when a woman in the front row suddenly cupped her hands to her mouth and shouted 'PULP FICTION'. I managed to recover and stammer out the next line, but after about thirty seconds she did it again: 'PULP FICTION.'

By now, I was in danger of losing the audience. Everyone was craning their necks, trying to get a glimpse of the heckler. I could hear people whispering: *Who is she? Does she have an axe to grind? Why is she shouting out 'Pulp Fiction'?*

I stumbled on, but my confidence was shattered. For the next fifteen minutes, I kept stealing nervous glances at the heckler, wondering if she was going to do it again. Instead, she did something even more discombobulating: she fell asleep. Owen Lewis, the director, had warned me about 'sleepers', too, telling me not to pay them any mind. But it was difficult to ignore this woman after she'd made such a spectacle of herself. It was as if she'd waved her arms around, saying, 'Hey, you up on stage, look at me,' and then, as soon as she'd got my attention, fallen asleep. She remained unconscious until ten minutes before the end, when she was woken by her mobile phone going off. Needless to say, it continued to ring for several minutes as she dug around in her bag, trying to find it.

Afterwards, Ian Osborne intercepted me on my way to the press night party. He'd invited various journalists to come along and the only thing they were interested in was the heckler. Who was she?

I told him I had no idea.

He thought for a moment.

'Okay, if anyone asks, this is what you say: a disgruntled actress out for revenge after you gave her a bad review in the *Spectator*. It'll make a great diary story.'

'But—'

'Toby,' he said, laying a hand on my shoulder, 'this show needs all the help it can get.'

Five minutes later, I was standing at the bar of the party, being interviewed by a gossip columnist from the *Daily Mail*.

'So who was the heckler?' she asked.

'Apparently, she was a disgruntled actress out for revenge after I gave her a bad review in the *Spectator*.'

She began writing this down, when, out of nowhere, Sean Langan appeared.

'No, no, Tobe, I'll tell you who it was. It was Charlotte from Sky Television. She hates you ever since you went round telling everyone you could get a blow job off her for a line of coke.'

So that's who it was!

At this point the journalist stopped writing, looked at Sean and me, then crossed out everything she'd written so far and started scribbling away again with renewed vigour.

The reviews were just about good enough – and the ticket sales just about robust enough – for Ian to extend the run to twelve weeks in total, but after these two incidents my nerves were completely shattered. As I came off stage each night, I had an overwhelming urge to get drunk. It didn't help that I knew Caroline wouldn't be waiting up for me. Heavily pregnant, and with a demanding one-year-old to look after, she was usually asleep by 9.30 p.m. She was a heavy sleeper, too, so she wouldn't know what time it was when I slipped between the sheets. In effect, for the first time in my married life, I had a pink ticket.

The Arts Theatre was in the heart of the West End and as I emerged from the stage door at 10 p.m., I was faced with a cornucopia of restaurants, bars and clubs. First stop was usually the Ivy – a two-minute walk – followed by the Soho House, then an after-hours club I'd discovered beneath the Phoenix Theatre on Charing Cross Road. My drinking companion was usually Sean Langan, who at this stage was back living with his mum in Archway. It was almost like being a bachelor again.

After twelve weeks of this, however, the novelty began to wear off. I could feel myself sinking back into the pit I'd managed to haul myself out of in 1999. That in itself was bad enough, but the stakes were much higher now because I was shortly to be a father of two. (The impending escalation in my parental responsibilities may have had something to do with my behaviour.) I only had to look at Sean to see what fate awaited me if I didn't pull myself together. I'd probably end up sleeping in the other spare room at his mum's house.

It was this plunge back into my old life that made me reassess the relationship between my marriage and my career. I often complained to Sean about the tight rein Caroline kept me on, but it dawned on me that without her presence in my life I would have succumbed to alcoholism long ago. Indeed, it became clear that, far from holding me back, everything I'd achieved in the previous five years – writing a book, buying a house, appearing on stage in the West End – was entirely due to her. I flattered myself that, unlike Sean, I'd put my family before my career and that's why my marriage had survived and his hadn't. But without Caroline I wouldn't have had a career. She'd given me the stability – as well as the discipline – that had enabled me to write. If I hadn't produced anything of much worth, that wasn't because Caroline and Sasha were taking up precious hours that would otherwise have been spent at my writing desk. On the contrary, it would have been spent hanging out with Sean, getting shit-faced. Now that I thought about it, the very idea that my family was somehow an impediment to my career was laughable. The only thing Caroline was an impediment to was rack and ruin.

In a sense, my three-month drinking binge had a sobering effect. I achieved one of the fundamental aims of a twelve-step programme: I accepted my humility in the face of a Higher Power – and Her name was Caroline.

Yet if this episode brought home to me where my priorities lay, it was nothing compared to the drama surrounding the birth of my son.

The first indication that something was wrong came on 13 March 2005 – forty-eight hours after Ludo was born. Caroline awoke after a mid-afternoon nap to discover she was covered in spots. She first noticed some small, pink blemishes on her torso three days before she gave birth, but since there were only two of them at that point she didn't really think anything of it. Now they'd multiplied – and I mean *really* multiplied.

The likeliest diagnosis was chickenpox so, that evening, I looked it up on the Internet. After noodling around for a few minutes on a medical site I saw a link that said 'Infant Complications of Chickenpox in Late Pregnancy'. I clicked on it and this is what I read:

> If a woman presents symptoms of varicella-zoster virus in a seven-day period stretching from five days before to two days after delivery her newborn is at risk of acquiring a life-threatening infection. Left untreated, the mortality rate in such cases exceeds 30%.

At first, I couldn't take this in. What was varicella-zoster virus? I looked this up and discovered it's the medical term for chickenpox. But surely chickenpox isn't 'life-threatening'? I'd had it myself as a child and the spots came and went in less than a fortnight.

How could the mortality rate possibly exceed 30 per cent?

I immediately typed the words 'chickenpox', 'pregnancy' and 'newborn' into Google and started trawling through hundreds of websites. I discovered that the reason varicella is so dangerous in the last week of pregnancy is because the mother won't have had time to develop any of the antibodies and pass them on to her baby in the womb. Newborns are 'immunocompromised' – their immune systems haven't started working yet – and, consequently, if my son had caught 'neonatal varicella' (newborn chickenpox), he'd be completely defenceless against it.

Luckily, it was treatable. According to my research, Ludo had to be given a shot of something called 'Varicella Zoster Immunoglobulin', or VZIG for short. This is a blood product containing chickenpox antibodies. A Scandinavian study involving a sample of a hundred newborns exposed to the virus had established that 50 per cent of those that received VZIG remained free of infection – and of those that went on to develop the disease only a low percentage got it severely. The mortality rate among the infected babies that weren't treated, by contrast, was 31 per cent.

There was a catch, though. The VZIG is only effective if it's administered within seventy-two hours of the baby's first exposure to the virus. It was probable that Ludo's first exposure had been when he was born sixty hours earlier so I had just twelve hours in which to get him the shot.

I immediately started working my way through the Yellow Pages, trying to find a paediatric accident and emergency department willing to treat Ludo. Unfortunately, all the doctors I spoke to said they wouldn't be prepared to give Ludo the VZIG unless Caroline *definitely* had chickenpox and they wouldn't know that until she'd been subjected to various tests. The problem was, they wouldn't get the results back from those tests for at least two days, by which time it would be too late. I tried to argue that Ludo should be given a shot anyway – after all, there were no harmful side effects – but to no avail. They all assumed – correctly, I suppose – that I was just another over-anxious parent with a broadband connection.

Eventually, persistence paid off: I found a paediatric nurse at Chelsea and Westminster who grasped the seriousness of the situation and told me to bring Caroline and Ludo in straight away. By now it was past midnight and they'd gone back to bed, but the *ticking clock* (suddenly I was in a movie!) meant I had to wake them up and drive them to hospital. I'm a complete hypochondriac and often imagine I'm suffering from various diseases after reading about them on the Internet, so I was worried Caroline would think I was being my usual, hysterical self. In fact, she was very understanding and agreed that, when it came to our newborn son, it was better to be safe than sorry.

It turned out that Caroline *did* have chickenpox, but, luckily, Ludo received a shot of VZIG within seventy-two hours of exposure. The virologist who treated Ludo advised us that if he ended up getting neonatal varicella nevertheless, there was a 14 per cent chance he'd develop life-threatening complications. These included pneumonitis, when the virus spreads to the lungs, and encephalitis, when the lining of the brain becomes infected. The first of these is more likely to be fatal, but the second can lead to what the virologist described as 'permanent neurological damage'. Those are three words guaranteed to strike terror into the heart of any parent. All we could do now was wait and see. The virologist told us that if Ludo still hadn't presented any symptoms after twelve days he'd be out of the woods.

Exactly thirteen days later, and with Ludo still showing no signs of chickenpox, Caroline and I breathed a huge sigh of relief. *It was over!* We decided to celebrate by taking him and Sasha out to lunch at Frankie's Italian Bar and Grill in Knightsbridge. It was the first time we'd been out together as a family since Ludo had been born – the first *normal* thing we'd done. I had a glass of Prosecco and, almost immediately, got quite tipsy. All the tension seeped out of me like some noxious gas and I couldn't remember when I'd felt so happy.

'During the entire ordeal, I never once turned to God,' I said to Caroline, feeling quite pleased with myself. 'There may be no atheists in foxholes, but there was at least one in the paediatric ward of Chelsea and Westminster.'

The following day, Ludo got chickenpox.

He was readmitted to Chelsea and Westminster and given a course of an anti-viral drug called acyclovir. We were told that this would ameliorate the effects of the illness and make it less probable that he'd develop any secondary infections.

We soon discovered that one of the advantages of your baby having an infectious disease on a paediatric ward is that you're given a room to yourself. Admittedly, there was a big yellow sign on the door saying 'DANGER OF INFECTION', but still.

Our delusions of grandeur were shattered when a consultant appeared wearing what looked like a nuclear, biological, chemical suit. (Welcome to the leper colony!) After examining Ludo's spots, he told us he wanted to put a 'line' into his neck. He explained that the acyclovir is much more effective if it's delivered intravenously and, given that Ludo was going to continue receiving it until the neonatal varicella had cleared up, the most practical thing to do was to get a 'central line' in to one of his carotid arteries.

'Of course,' he said, 'he'll have to be given a general anaesthetic.'

That put the wind up us, an anxiety that the assistant anaesthetist did nothing to allay when he asked us if we'd like to kiss Ludo before he wheeled him into theatre. To my ears, it sounded awfully like he was asking us if we wanted to kiss our son goodbye just in case this turned out to be 'the anaesthetic from which none came round'.[1]

We both declined.

Needless to say, it all went like clockwork and Ludo was fine. (Well, as fine as a two-week-old baby can be with a whacking great tube sticking out of his neck.) He received his first dose of acyclovir that afternoon. All we could do now was take it in turns to sit with him as he remained in a 'cubicle' – a perspex box – at Chelsea and Westminster. At least if he did develop any secondary infections, he could be treated immediately. The 'central line' could just as easily be used to deliver penicillin as it could acyclovir.

That evening, as we both watched Ludo sleeping in hospital, I did my best to reassure Caroline that everything would be okay. I reminded her that since Ludo had received the VZIG within seventy-two hours of being exposed to the virus, there was an 86 per cent chance that he'd be completely okay. Those were pretty good odds.

'What you're saying is, he'd have to be terribly unlucky?'

'Yes.'

'Well, hasn't he been unlucky so far? What makes you think that's going to change?'

---

1 This is one of the ways Larkin describes death in *Aubade*, his famously morbid poem.

She was right, up to a point. Ludo *had* been unlucky so far. To begin with, it was unlucky that Caroline had never had chickenpox before – 95 per cent of the UK population have. Then it was *extremely* unlucky that Caroline got it at just the time she did: only one expectant mother in 34,000 develops chickenpox in the last week of pregnancy. Finally, it was unlucky that Ludo had become infected in spite of the fact that he'd received the VZIG: 50 per cent of babies in Ludo's situation don't.

However, you didn't need to be a Las Vegas casino operator to know that a run of bad luck doesn't affect a person's ongoing chances one way or another. The probability of Ludo developing a life-threatening infection was still only 14:100, regardless of how unlucky he'd been so far. To think otherwise was to give in to fatalism.

Even so, while I was saying this I couldn't help feeling a little bit fatalistic myself. I began to discern a tragic pattern in events, with Ludo seemingly at the mercy of unknowable forces. It was almost as if the worst-case scenario had been preordained by some malignant being.

Ludo remained in hospital, receiving regular doses of acyclovir, while Caroline and I took it in turns to keep the bedside vigil. The low point came on the night of the sixth day – a night I happened to be on duty. A nurse came in to take his temperature at 10.45 p.m., something that happened every evening since his body temperature was the most reliable indicator of whether the infection had spread anywhere else. On every previous occasion Ludo's temperature had been normal, but I could tell from the expression on her face that something was wrong.

'What's the matter?'

'It's quite elevated,' she said.

She then measured his heart rate – and that, too, was high.

'I'm going to get a doctor to come and take a look at him,' she said.

After a few minutes, a very junior house officer appeared and drew some of Ludo's blood. She was going to send it to the lab so they could check his protein level. If that, too, was elevated, the next step would be a lumbar puncture in order to analyse his spinal fluid. I asked her if that would involve a general anaesthetic and she said it would.

'What d'you think it is?' I asked.

She gave me a slightly irritated look: clearly, she didn't want to speculate at this stage.

'Well, there's a possibility it could be encephalitis,' she said.

That was it – the final straw. The words 'permanent neurological damage' came flashing back into my brain. As I was waiting for the results of the blood test, I took Ludo in my arms, looked up towards heaven and started praying. I promised God that I'd try and be a better person. I'd help old ladies across the street. I'd do voluntary work with the disabled. I'd set up a lobby group to campaign for expectant mothers to be vaccinated against chickenpox. I'd do whatever He wanted only, please, please, don't let any harm come to my son.

As I was praying, the back of my head started tingling and I could feel goose bumps on my arms and legs. I looked down at Ludo and noticed that he was wide awake, staring up at me through unblinking eyes. The tears started rolling down my cheeks.

What a cretin I'd been to brag about not having turned to God earlier. There are no atheists in paediatric wards.

The house officer didn't reappear until 8 a.m., by which time she had the results of the blood test. Ludo's protein level *was* elevated, but it wasn't so high that they needed to do a lumbar puncture. They'd just keep a close eye on him.

By the afternoon of the seventh day, his temperature was back to normal.

We were allowed to take Ludo home the following day. At this stage, all his spots had crusted over, indicating that the neonatal varicella had run its course. The consultant told us Ludo would need to be treated with acyclovir for a further ten days, but he could be given it orally, rather than intravenously, and that was something Caroline and I could do at home. All that remained was for the 'line' to be taken out – and no, the consultant said, that wouldn't involve a general anaesthetic.

I asked him whether it was possible that Ludo could have suffered any complications that we'd only become aware of in time.

'Like what?'

'I don't know. Brain damage?'

He smiled and put his hand on my shoulder: 'Your son is going to be fine.'

It took a while for the good news to sink in. At first, I was a bit sceptical: how did he know Ludo was going to be 'fine'? Shouldn't he continue to receive the acyclovir intravenously until his spots had completely disappeared? Was the consultant just anxious to free up the 'cubicle' in order to meet his firm's performance targets?

It wasn't until I was giving Ludo a bottle after the consultant had left that I began to wind down. As I cradled his head in my lap, I noticed that his hair, which until now had been black and oily, was turning blond. Indeed, the sides of his head were almost completely blond. God knows why, but I took this as a sign that he was going to be okay and started crying – weeping with relief.

When I got home that night, I gave Sasha and Ludo a bath together for the first time and, seeing them looking up at me, I realised that my family was now at the absolute heart of my life. This wasn't a change that had come about as a result of having lived through this ordeal. Rather, it had been true for some time and I just hadn't been aware of it until now.

How could I have been such a shallow, narcissistic fool? Up until this point, I'd looked on the hours I'd had to spend with my family as a bit of a chore, a distraction from the really important thing in life which was to make a name for myself as a writer. But now it was clear to me that Caroline and Sasha and Ludo were at the centre of my existence. They were the priority and everything else, including my personal ambition, was secondary.

It occurred to me that, in this respect, my life was like that of millions of other men. I'd made most of the running during the courtship stage, choosing a mate and then doggedly pursuing her until she'd agreed to marry me. After that, the tables had been turned. She'd effectively taken charge, popping out children whether I wanted them or not and, in the process, changing my life irrevocably.

And – again, like millions of other men – it was only after this new state of affairs had come about, a state of affairs that I never would have chosen voluntarily, that I discovered just how happy it made me. This, it turned out, was where true satisfaction lay – not in winning an Oscar or a Pulitzer Prize, but *this*.

I remembered some lines from a poem by Philip Larkin called 'Love':

> *The difficult part of love*
> *Is being selfish enough,*
> *Is having the blind persistence*
> *To upset an existence*
> *Just for your own sake.*
> *What cheek it must take.*

It had been cheeky of me to upset Caroline's existence by insisting that she marry me and then stubbornly refusing to take no for an answer. But she had paid me back in spades – and I was so glad she had.

It was the afternoon of 24 August 2005 and, for once, Rob Long called me.

'Congratulations.'

'Thanks. But you do realise my son is almost six months old?'

'I'm not calling about your son, you idiot. I mean, that's great and everything, but I'd never actually call you about something like that. I'm a comedy writer, remember?'

'So what are you calling about?'

'According to this morning's *New York Times* you've got a big stage hit on your hands. Is that true?'

He was referring to *Who's The Daddy?*, a play I'd co-authored with Lloyd Evans, my colleague at the *Spectator*, whom I was now sharing the theatre beat with. It was being performed in a tiny, 110-seat venue in the back of a pub in north London, but it had got some nice reviews and the six-week run had already sold out. It was, by some margin, the most fulfilling writing experience of my life, even more satisfying than writing *How to Lose Friends & Alienate People* or adapting it for the stage. After struggling for twenty years, I'd finally found a form in which I appeared to have some natural ability: the lowbrow British sex farce. Lloyd and I hoped *Who's The Daddy?* would be the first of many such collaborations.

'So, did you ever hear back from Mr Hollywood?' he asked.

'No.'

'What, nothing?'

'Nada.'

'Did you at least get paid?'

'Yes. The only sign that he'd actually received the screenplay was a cheque from the studio.'

'How about the movie of your book? What's happening with that?'

'I got paid for writing that screenplay, too.'

'But I thought you never got beyond the treatment stage?'

'That's true, but Stephen Woolley and Elizabeth Karlsen arranged for me to be paid what I would have been paid by FilmFour if I'd written the script. I think it was their way of apologising for kicking me off the project. So now I feel really warmly towards them and all is forgiven.'

'Wait a minute. Let me get this straight. You got paid for a screenplay you didn't actually write?'

'Yes.'

Beat.

'From now on I'm calling you for writing advice.'

'They've also made me an associate producer.'

'Ah, well, I wouldn't get too excited about *that*. You know Billy Wilder's definition of an associate producer?'

'No?'

'The only person on the set willing to associate with the producer.'

I laughed.

'By the way,' said Rob, 'I saw a terrific documentary in San Francisco last weekend about the aftermath of the war in Iraq. *Mission Accomplished*. It was originally made for television by this British journalist, but it's so good it's been given a theatrical release over here. I was completely blown away. I mean, the risks this guy took! *Unbefuckinglievable*. He's like the James Bond of foreign correspondents. I wouldn't be surprised if it's nominated for a Best

Documentary Oscar. Hey, maybe you know him? I think his name is Sean Langan?'

Beat.

'Rob, I have to go. My son is crying and my daughter is standing in front of me clutching a big box of Play-Doh.'

Click. Dial-tone.

ACKNOWLEDGEMENTS

Although *How to Lose Friends & Alienate People* has attracted a considerable range of reviews since its British publication in 2001 and its American publication the following year, it has received one out-and-out rave – namely, for the first few sentences of the acknowledgements section. In January 2006, in *The Times*, Chris Ayres declared it the best disclaimer he'd ever read in a memoir. Since that disclaimer was so warmly received, and since it applies here as well, let me quote the first paragraph:

I was thinking of beginning the acknowledgements with one of those postmodernist disclaimers that call into question the whole notion of objective truth, but nearly everything that takes place in this book happened exactly the way I've described it. I say 'nearly everything' because I've occasionally given things a slight comic twist, but you'd be surprised how little exaggeration and embellishment there is. When I flick through the book's pages and read about all the humiliating things that happened to me I wish I had invented most of this stuff. Unfortunately, it's a pretty accurate account of what occurred.

In *The Sound of No Hands Clapping*, as in *How to Lose Friends*, I've muddied the waters from time to time in order to disguise people who would prefer to remain anonymous – and whom I would prefer not to antagonise, given how powerful they are. In the case of Mr Hollywood, I've tried to protect myself from his wrath by altering enough of the facts to render him unidentifiable. However, I didn't need to change anything to make him appear sympathetic – I genuinely liked him and I'm grateful for the amazing opportunity he gave me, as well as the insight he provided into 'the Business'.

As for the rest of the book, some latitude is generally granted to authors of comic memoirs and I've taken advantage of this licence once or twice. For instance, Rob Long isn't nearly as witty and intelligent as I've portrayed him as being. All those funny one-liners and smart observations about Hollywood – they're all mine.

That's bullshit, obviously. Virtually every one of those lines came out of Rob's mouth. I really couldn't have hoped for a better guide to Hollywood. For anyone trying to navigate those perilous waters, Rob is the ultimate pilot.

Other people I'd like to thank are Lloyd Evans, Cosmo Landesman, Sean Langan, Sean Macaulay, Christopher Silvester and Grub Smith, all of whom read and commented on earlier drafts, as well as my British and American editors – Richard Beswick and John Radziewicz – and my agent, Emma Parry. A few of the anecdotes in this book have appeared elsewhere and, in light of that, I owe a debt of thanks to those editors who unwittingly allowed me to road-test the material in their pages, including Roger Alton, Liz Anderson, Christena Appleyard, Guy Eaton, Geordie Greig, Boris Johnson, Dylan Jones, Ian Katz, Catherine Ostler, Sasha Slater, Peter Stevenson, George Thwaites, Veronica Wadley and Jacob Weisberg. It goes without saying that all the mistakes are my own. If you spot any – or just want to tell me what you think of the book – please email me at Howtolose@hotmail.com.

I'm much more grateful to Stephen Woolley and Elizabeth Karlsen than you'd think from reading these pages – I would have fired me, too – and I'd like to take this opportunity to thank them, along with Tessa Ross, the head of FilmFour, and Peter Straughan, the screenwriter they eventually hired and who's done a great job of adapting *How to Lose Friends* for the screen.

Above all, my heartfelt thanks go out to Caroline. Not many writers' wives would consent to being included in their husbands' books – particularly not as crude comic caricatures. But Caroline has always been incredibly good-humoured and relaxed about this – and for that, and a million other things, I'm extremely grateful. I don't deserve her and I live in a state of constant terror that she'll one day wake up to this fact.